The Reason for Life

The Reason for Life

*What They Believed:
Albert Einstein,
Sigmund Freud,
Fyodor Dostoevsky, and
Leo Tolstoy*

Waltenegus Dargie

Λάμψη

Berlin   New York   London   Sydney   Toronto

This edition first published in 2016
Copyright © 2016 by Waltenegus Dargie
Lamsi Publishing

All rights reserved. No part of this publication may be reproduced, stored in a retrieval system, or transmitted in any form or by any means, electronic, mechanical, photocopying, recording, or otherwise, without the prior permission of the author.

Library of Congress Cataloging-in-Publication Data
Dargie, Waltenegus
    The Reason for Life: What They Believed: Albert Einstein, Sigmund Freud, Fyodor Dostoevsky, Leo Tolstoy/Waltenegus Dargie
    p.cm
    Includes bibliographical references
    ISBN-13: 978-1541263031, ISBN-10: 1541263030
Biography & Autobiography / Philosophers
LCCN 2016921343   **2016**

Manufactured in the United States of America by CreateSpace Independent Publishing Platform
4900 Lacross Road, North Charleston, SC 29406

Acknowledgement

The author would like to thank Samantha Yeoh for her encouragement, excellent editorial work, and repeated and careful proof-reading.

What was to be the value of the long looked forward to,
Long hoped for calm, the autumnal serenity
And the wisdom of age? Had they deceived us
Or deceived themselves, the quiet-voiced elders,
Bequeathing us merely a receipt for deceit?
The serenity only a deliberate hebetude,
The wisdom only the knowledge of dead secrets
Useless in the darkness into which they peered
Or from which they turned their eyes. There is, it seems to us,
At best, only a limited value
In the knowledge derived from experience.
The knowledge imposes a pattern, and falsifies,
For the pattern is new in every moment
And every moment is a new and shocking
Valuation of all we have been. We are only undeceived
Of that which, deceiving, could no longer harm.

T.S. Eliot, *Four Quartets*

Table of Contents

Introduction 11
Part I: The Significance of God 21
    Freud 24
    Einstein 43
    Dostoevsky 60
    Tolstoy 76
Part II: The Purpose of Human Life 97
    Freud 100
    Einstein 117
    Dostoevsky 133
    Tolstoy 153
Part III: The Significance of the Bible 179
    Freud 182
    Dostoevsky 201
    Einstein 216
    Tolstoy 231
Summary 255
    The Significance of God 255
    The Purpose of Human Life 260
    The Significance of the Bible 263
Biographical Reference 269
Content Reference 269
Index 273

Introduction

Very few twenty-century scientists made as lasting an influence on modern society as Albert Einstein and Sigmund Freud. Physicists routinely use the theories Einstein developed a century ago to analyse and comprehend cosmological and quantum phenomena. The ripples in the fabric of spacetime physicists observed on September 14, 2015 at the Laser Interferometer Gravitational-Wave Observatory (LIGO) confirmed for the first time the existence of gravitational waves, which Einstein, using his Theory of General Relativity, predicted a hundred years ago. Similarly, some of the vital models contemporary psychologists routinely apply in order to explain psychosexual developments and human psyches are credited to Freud. We also owe to Freud most of the psychoanalytical expressions we ubiquitously apply to convey the psychological states of mind, such as neurosis, phobia, repression, fixation, projection, Oedipal complex, compulsion, transference, death instinct, erogenous zones, Freudian slip, disavowal, displacement, identification, libido, narcissism, and paranoia.

Perhaps less known to the general public is the magnitude of influence Dostoevsky and Tolstoy had on both Einstein and Freud. Einstein once declared: "Dostoevsky gives me more than any scientist, more than Gauss." To appreciate the weight of this declaration it suffices to remark that without the prior foundation laid by Gauss and his students (most notably Riemann), perhaps it would have been impossible for Einstein to develop his General Relativity Theory. Freud too ranked Dostoevsky's *The Brothers Karamazov* alongside the works of Sophocles and Shakespeare in terms of literary significance. Tolstoy had likewise influenced Einstein. The pacifist and anarchistic philosophy to which Einstein subscribed for nearly three decades before the advent of the Second World War and his lifetime mistrust of the military establishment were, for the most part, due to the influence of Tolstoy.

Two of the subjects, in which they held a common interest with comparable magnitude, were God and the purpose of human life. All of them, without exception, had passionately been occupied by and written and talked extensively about these subjects. Indeed, almost all of Dostoevsky's books contain frequent references to God and intense dialogues about the meaning of life and many of his literary characters are well versed in the Bible. Tolstoy became overtly occupied with religion shortly after the publication of *Anna Karenina* when he was turning fifty and for the next twenty-five years it became his primary occupation. Besides, in his autobiography he succinctly describes how he had been searching for the meaning and purpose of life for a long time and how he eventually believed in God and in moral principles, and argued why he considered the teaching of Jesus to be timeless and universal in its application. But he also unequivocally rejected the deity and supernatural conception of Jesus, the existence of miracles and prophecies, and the sacredness of the Bible. Furthermore, Tolstoy attempted to reconstruct the "original" narration of the New Testament by editing and "harmonising" the four Gospels. His book, *The Kingdom of God is Within You* is a culmination of thirty years of careful diagnosis of the faults and ills of modern societies and a passionate but rational entreaty to the prescription of *The Sermon on the Mount* in order to correct the faults and to heal the ills.

Freud investigated the origin of religion for more than forty years. In *Totem and Taboo* he investigates the anthropological and psychological roots of religion. In *Moses and Monotheism* he applies psychoanalysis to determine the emergence of Judaism and Christianity, and offers an alternative account as to how the Israelites "actually" made their exodus out of Egypt. In *The*

Future of an Illusion, he makes an in-depth study of the multifaceted relationships between religion and neurosis. In *Civilisation and Its Discontents*, Freud links the sense of guilt and the emergence of conscience in humanity to a secret wish for punishment, which in turn is linked to an original crime committed by humanity, the murder of the primordial father. Freud considered his study on religion as a well-connected and consistent development.

Even though the intensity of his interest in religion varied throughout his life, for Einstein it was a matter of great interest. Whilst living in Europe, he often shared his views among a few close friends and acquaintances, but during the latter part of his life, after he took residence in the United States following his persecution by the Nazis, he became publicly assertive and published a number of articles on religion and its relevance to modern societies. Einstein took his belief in God seriously and considered that all his scientific discoveries were consistent with his belief. Indeed one can justifiably argue that the main reason for Einstein to reject (or regard as incomplete) the claims of quantum physics is due to his religious outlook.

Notably my subjects represent diverse religious views. Dostoevsky and Tolstoy were born into Russian Orthodox Christian families; Dostoevsky never departed from his childhood religion whilst Tolstoy rejected his, becoming an atheist for two decades, then rejecting atheism, and eventually finding his own religion. Freud and Einstein were born into Jewish families. Freud rejected his childhood faith when he was still a youth and went on to become an outspoken atheist. Einstein never seriously adhered to Judaism but never entirely renounced it either. Instead, he accepted the existence of an impersonal God who has created a perfect and beautiful universe, but who does not interfere with his creation. The combined published works of this quartet on the matter of religion is a century old, an indisputable and uninterrupted chain of intellectual thinking on the existence of God and the purpose of human life.

The oldest among them, Dostoevsky, was born on 11 November 1821 in Moscow whilst the youngest of them, Einstein, was born on 14 March 1879 in Ulm, the Kingdom of Württemberg in the German Empire. In between these dates come Tolstoy and Freud, respectively, the former born on 9 September 1828 in Yasnaya Polyana, Russia, and the latter on 6 May 1856 in the Moravia town of Příbor, within the Austrian Empire.

These men possessed extraordinary intellectual independence and originality. Dostoevsky studied engineering at a well-known military academy in St. Petersburg and started off with a promising job in the same city as a lieutenant. But a year later, at the age of twenty-two, he resigned from the army in order to become a full time writer. Within a few years he won accolades from some of the most prominent literary critics of his time in St. Petersburg and was admitted into their inner circles. But he also became a subject of much ridicule and criticism within those same circles on account of his Christian faith and steadfast opposition to socialism. His position on these two subjects remained essentially unchanged throughout his life. Dostoevsky believed that even if it were humanly possible to attain the ideals of socialism on earth, the implementation of such ideals would rob individuals of their freedom to choose and to take responsibility for their own life. Dostoevsky strongly maintained his position that individual freedom is to be valued above the individual as well as the collective wellbeing.[i]

There was every indication that Tolstoy would conform to the patterns of the society into which he was born, for he was born a count to a rich family. Even though he grew up an orphan, his upbringing was by and large similar to other aristocratic minorities. As a young man, he enjoyed his privilege fully (he

had his own servant since childhood, who was condemned to serve his master even when he was in a university prison), frequented fancy and expensive high society balls, and gambled and caroused. He joined the University of Kazan at the age of sixteen but withdrew from it after a short stay. His professors labelled him as "unable" and "unwilling" to study. At the age of twenty-three and after having pursued a variety of avenues in search of happiness, losing a large sum of money in gambling, and burying himself deeply in debt, he suffered intense mental anguish and a sense of worthlessness. At this time it occurred to him that something in his life was fundamentally wrong, outright false, and superficial. He craved a fresh and authentic life and decided to leave everything behind him and lead a simple and hardworking life in the Caucasus. It was there in Caucasus that he tried to write seriously. The beauty of the open fields and the majesty of the mountains, the simplicity of life, the honesty of the people, brought out the best in him. Now away from the bustle and hassle of city life, he was able to recognise the illness of the society with which he had hitherto proudly identified himself. Aylmer Maude, Tolstoy's biographer, lists some of these ills: lies were easily told; etiquette demanded the adoption of French (albeit a borrowed language and imperfectly spoken); governmental positions were obtained through relationships and connections; young and old, men and women alike were infected by a viral and insatiable appetite for gossip at all levels of society; all sectors of society from the youth to the elderly were afflicted by a spirit of lasciviousness; people in his social circles wore fake and inconsequential religious masks; no authentic work was done in any governmental establishments; and everyone strove to get rich without risking investment and as quickly as possible.
In Caucasus Tolstoy joined the army as a non-commissioned officer and went to Crimea to fight against the allied forces of France, England, the Ottoman Empire, and the Kingdom of

Sardinia. He fought for two years bravely but Russia lost the war. Three months later he resigned from the army and for the next six years spent much of the time writing books and traveling in Europe. At the age of thirty-three he returned to his ancestral estate and settled there for the rest of his life, leading a reclusive life devoted to farming and literature.

Tolstoy's intellectual independence asserts itself in many ways. His stories about the Crimean war give candid accounts of the grimness of war as experienced on both sides (unlike the popular literary culture which romanticised battles and heroic death). His mature novels consistently lament the banality, shallowness, and moral deprivation of the Russian aristocracy. Later in life Tolstoy would pointedly attack the Russian Orthodox Church for having been an instrument of oppression and for having markedly departed from her initial purpose of existence. His criticism was consistent with his chosen lifestyle and his endeavour to change the lives of ordinary people. He abdicated virtually all forms of material ownership, refused to be served by anyone, not even by house servants and maids; he earned his own living, not only by writing, but also through hard labour in the field. As he grew old, his criticism of the established way of life became harsher and sharper. This is how he describes his feeling in his autobiography: "The life of our class, of the wealthy and the learned, was not only repulsive to me but had lost all meaning. The sum of our action and thinking, of our science and art, all of it struck me as the overindulgences of a spoiled child. I realized that meaning was not to be sought here. The actions of the labouring people, of those who create life, began to appear to me as the one true way. I realized that the meaning provided by this life was truth, and I embraced it."[1]

---

[1] LTCON p. 68.

An appreciation of the intellectual independence of Freud may be gained by considering the vast amount of controversy surrounding his theories and philosophy on human psychosexual development, the instincts of life and death, the Oedipal complex, the interpretation of dreams, and women's sexuality, to mention some of them. He studied medicine at the University of Vienna and embarked on a scientific carrier as a neurologist with a research focus on dysfunctions of microscopic regions in the human brain's nervous system. The apparent difficulty of explaining some nervous disorders physiologically persuaded Freud to gradually transfer his research focus away from neurology and towards the study of the psychological origins of these disorders. Freud thus immersed himself for the rest of his life deep into the study of human psychology, proposing several models and theories to comprehend, explain, synthesise, and govern the human psyche.[ii]

It would be presumptuous to write about the intellectual independence of Einstein in a brief introduction but it suffices to state that he was 26 years old when he questioned the fundamental premises of classical physics. Besides, he made some fundamental discoveries, including the existence of photons; and proved the existence of atoms and molecules. He demonstrated the inadequacy of Newtonian physics to explain the behaviour of objects travelling at a speed approaching the speed of light or those interacting inside a high gravitational field. He was not an established scientist at the time; neither did he hold a doctoral degree which would qualify him for a proper research career. Many years later Einstein once again asserted his independence by rejecting quantum mechanics as an incomplete science, even though he was unable to disprove Heisenberg's *Uncertainty Principle*.

The exceptional intelligence and literary insight of my subjects was well known to and recognised amongst themselves. In reviewing *Anna Karenina*, Dostoyevsky once wrote:

> Anna Karenina as an artistic production is perfection. It appears most opportunely as a thing to which European literature of our epoch offers no equal. Moreover, its idea is something of our own—native to us, distinguishing us from the whole European world—it is our national "new world" or at least its beginning, a word such as one does not hear in Europe, yet which, for all her pride, she greatly needs.[2]

In turn Tolstoy, in a letter he wrote to the philosopher Strakhov on 26 September 1880, expresses the following:

> Just recently I was feeling unwell and read *House of the Dead*. I had forgotten a good bit, read it over again, and I do not know a better book in all our new literature, including Pushkin. It is not the ton, but the wonderful point of view—genuine, natural, and Christian. A splendid, instructive book. I enjoyed myself the whole day, as I have not done for a long time. If you see Dostoevsky, tell him that I love him.[3]

During his brief correspondence with Freud, Einstein acknowledged in a letter he wrote on 26 April 1931 the solid contributions of Freud to the study of human psychology:

> I greatly admire your passion to ascertain the truth—a passion that has come to dominate all else in your thinking. You have shown with irresistible lucidity how inseparably the aggressive and destructive instincts are bound up in the

---

[2] AM pp. 399.
[3] JF p. 846.

human psyche with those of love and the lust for life. At the same time, your convincing arguments make manifest your deep devotion to the great goal of the internal and external liberation of man from the evils of war.[4]

Whereas the scientific community has closely examined the scientific works of Einstein and Freud, their philosophical works on the meaning and purpose of human life and what they believed about God are not as closely examined. The same can be said of the philosophy of Dostoevsky and Tolstoy on these subjects, even though their novels are widely read and their literary merits are well acknowledged. The purpose of this book is to survey the beliefs of the quartet as exhaustively but also as comprehensibly as possible by relying primarily on the body of works they published about their belief over a span of many years.

The book consists of three parts. The first part deals with God as the origin of life and his significance as regards human existence. Except Freud, who as an atheist believed that life is an accidental phenomenon, all the others believed that God is the origin of life. This part surveys the different views of my subjects about God and the justifications for their views. The second part deals with the philosophies of my subjects about the meaning and purpose of human life. The third part deals with the significance of the Bible for modern life. As they developed their philosophies, all of them, without exception, considered it indispensable to examine the Bible and its claims. Indeed, Tolstoy and Freud went to the extent of rewriting parts of the Bible in order to "re-establish" accounts which they believed were deliberately removed, distorted, modified, or added to by biblical writers and editors. The final chapter provides a compact and comprehensible summary of the book.

---

[4] NNEIN pp. 186-203.

---

[i] Freud defends Dostoevsky's position in *Civilisation and Its Discontents* where he writes: "It does not seem as though any influence can induce human beings to change their nature and become like termites; they will probably always defend their claim to individual freedom against the will of the mass. Much of mankind's struggle is taken up with the task of finding a suitable, that is to say, a happy accommodation, between the claims of the individual and the mass claims of civilisation. One of the problems affecting the fate of mankind is whether such an accommodation can be achieved through a particular moulding of civilisation or whether the conflict is irreconcilable (SFCIV p. 33)."

[ii] Stefan Zweig, the famous Austrian writer, once expressed his view about Freud as follows: "I believe that the revolution you have called forth in the psychological and philosophical and the whole moral structure of our world greatly outweighs the merely therapeutic part of your discoveries. For today all the people who know nothing about you, every human being of 1930, even the one who has never heard the name of psychoanalyst, is already indirectly dyed through and through by your transformation of souls (PG p. 457)."

Part I
The Significance of God

In this part I shall examine the significance of *God* to human existence. Except for Freud, who believed that God is a creation stemming from human existential anxiety, all the others accepted the existence of God and attribute to him the creation of the universe, including human life. Dostoevsky and Tolstoy believed in a personal God for whom human actions and behaviours (choices) are important, whilst Einstein rejected the notion of a personal God and claimed that human actions and behaviours are determined by infinite causes and effects in the same way the motion and rest of corporal objects are causally determined. Therefore, human beings are not responsible for their actions and behaviours. In other words, Einstein rejected the assertion that human beings possess freewill.

The analysis on Freud highlights (1) the different theories Freud proposed to explain the origin of God (God as a result of the externalisation of psychic realities) and (2) his attempt to interpret religion as the psychological conditions of *neurosis* and *mass delusion*. Freud explained God as the projection of human fatherhood into two ways. In his first explanation, he alleged that the sons of the first family which achieved self-consciousness murdered their primal father on account of their contention with him for the women he exclusively possessed and jealously and violently guarded. The murder experience induced in them deeply-felt regret and an insatiable desire to atone for the wrongs they committed as well as a fear of the spirit of the dead father who, they believed, would avenge himself. These emotions perpetuated the memory of the primal father and eventually elevated him to the status of a god. In his second explanation, Freud viewed God as the exalted father who was once regarded by the child as an omnipotent authority.

The analysis on Einstein highlights Einstein's recognition of (1) design in the configuration of the universe and the higher mathematics required to comprehend a very small portion of it and (2) the "apparent absence of evidence" comprehensible to the rational mind to suggest divine intervention. It also examines the relationship between Spinoza's causal determinism and Einstein's scientific discoveries, most importantly, his General Theory of Relativity. Einstein agreed with Freud that the biblical depiction of God is essentially anthropomorphic, for the biblical writers supposedly ascribed to God their own emotions and wishes, but rejected Freud's claim that God is the creation of human fantasy and existential anxiety. Instead, Einstein ascribed human beings' deepest craving for experiencing and worshipping God to an innate cosmic religious feeling. This same feeling, according to Einstein, is the primary motivation for scientific inquiry and discovery. He maintained that God not only instils in human beings the desire and capacity to seek and experience him, but also made his universe and the laws governing it accessible to human scrutiny, so that they can pursue the knowledge of God and love God. Einstein identified such persons as Democritus, Moses, Jesus, Francis of Assisi, Copernicus, Newton, and Baruch de Spinoza as people in whom the cosmic religious feeling was well developed.

The analysis on Dostoevsky's belief in God highlights (1) Dostoevsky's admiration of good stories and his recognition of good stories in the Bible, (2) his identification with the suffering of biblical characters and appreciation of the authenticity with which their suffering is related, and (3) the experimentation in his great books with ideas and actions which are contrary to biblical values and their detrimental impact on personal and social life. Dostoevsky emphasised that disappointment with God is often a result of acutely perceived divine indifference and the absence of reason for the suffering in creation. In addition, he argued that love and freewill (that is, human freedom) would have been impossible without admitting suffering into creation. Interestingly, the rebellious characters in Dostoevsky's books who reject God on account of divine indifference and the absence of justice in the world order he established end up rejecting justice altogether and become themselves indifferent to life.

The analysis on Tolstoy highlights his lifelong pursuit of perfection in all aspects of his life (physical, mental, and professional) and his discovery of perfection in Jesus Christ and in his *Sermon on the Mount*. Tolstoy, like Dostoevsky, maintained that the pursuit of perfection necessarily entails pain.

Freud

For more than forty years Freud explored the origins of God, demons, spirits, hell, and the afterlife, and how human beings first developed the consciousness of sin and guilt. He applied psychoanalysis techniques on children, paranoids, neurotics, and "primitive tribes" in order to establish the relationship between the processes of *psychic externalisation* and religion, maintaining that the claims of religion are essentially the product of psychic externalisation. Freud identifies three essential components of religion, namely, the capacity in human beings to experience religion, the substance of religion, and the process by which the substance of religion is developed. According to Freud, human beings have affinity for religion because either they are fearful of life or yearn to be unified with the world. The fearful regard the world as hostile to them whilst those who yearn to be unified with the world are acutely aware of their individuality and regard themselves as isolated from the world. We can demonstrate the relationship between the three components of religion with an example: A belief in *afterlife*. Freud identifies two interconnected primary causes for it. Accordingly, the ancients believed that the spirit of the dead desperately wished to return to his original dwelling, the body of the dead, and always remained in the vicinity of the body. At the same time, they believed that the spirit envied the living for enjoying life without him and wished to punish and draw the living after him. The living, fearful of revenge and never feeling safe, buried the dead far away from their immediate surroundings, in a location, as it were, beyond a river which marked the boundary between one's dwelling place and the wild, or on an island. So, for the ancients, the spirits of the dead were thought to live literally beyond the river; and the expression "here" and "beyond" originated in this way. Freud maintains that civilised races unconsciously and gradually abstracted the distance separating the two physical locations and in this way, heaven is considered an extension of the "beyond".

Freud likewise claims that the origin of the strong yearning and the capacity for religion in human beings are the emergence of self-awareness and the feeling of incompleteness it gives rise to in human psyche. According to Freud, normally "we are sure of nothing so much as a sense of self, of our own ego. This ego appears to us as autonomous, uniform, and clearly set off against everything else." In reality, however, this is a delusion, for "the ego extends inwards, with no clear boundary, into an unconscious psychical entity that we call the id, and for which it serves, so to speak, as a façade... yet externally at least the ego seems to be clearly and sharply delineated."[1]

Freud maintains that this clear and sharp external distinction the ego perceives of itself is not an inborn awareness; it is rather a gradual acquisition of reality which comes through experience and pain. Initially, an infant's ego does not distinguish any frontier between itself and the world. Indeed, not only the infant does initially feel its unity with the world, but also considers the world as belonging to it entirely. Its realisation of the distinction between self and the world it lives in begins to emerge partly as a result of pain. "It must make the strongest impression on him that some sources of stimulation, which he later recognises as his own physical organ, can convey sensations to him at any time, while other things—including what he most craves, his mother's breast—are temporarily removed from him and can be summoned back only by a cry for help. In this way the ego is for the first time confronted with an 'object', something that exists 'out there' and can be forced to manifest itself only through a particular action."[2]

---

[1] SFCIV p. 3-4.

Thus the infant begins to realise its distinctness and to separate off the external world from itself. But the initial sense of unity, the strong feeling of "an indissoluble bond, of being one with the external world as a whole"[3] remains inside, side by side with the newly acquired knowledge, even as the latter solidifies and becomes dominant as the child matures. Neither is the boundary between the ego and the external world indestructible, Freud warns, and indicates both normal and pathological conditions which can dissolve the frontier, the normal condition being the state of love:

> At the height of erotic passion the borderline between the ego and object is in danger of becoming blurred. Against all the evidence of the senses, the person in love asserts 'I' and 'you' are one, and is ready to behave as if these were so. What can be temporarily interrupted by a psychological [i.e., normal] function must of course be capable of being disturbed by morbid processes also. Pathology acquaints us with a great many conditions in which the boundary between the ego and the external world becomes uncertain or the borderlines are actually wrongly drawn. There are cases in which parts of a person's own body, indeed parts of his mental life—perceptions, thoughts, feelings—seems alien, divorced from the ego, and others which he attributes to the external world what has clearly arisen in the ego and ought to be recognised by it. Hence, even the sense of self is subject to be disturbances, and the limits of the self are not constants.[4]

When abnormal conditions obliterate the ego's boundary, they tend to isolate and shrink it rather than enlarge and unify it with the external world, in which case, the ego is susceptible to be

---

[2] Ibid. P. 5.
[3] Ibid. P. 5.
[4] Ibid. 5.

desirous of religion through which it yearns and strives to attain unity with the external world. In which case, according to Freud, psychic externalisation, a process by which an individual attributes an internal (psychic) reality to an external object or being, becomes the root source of the substance of religion. It typically occurs when the individual is simultaneously confronted with strong but opposing thoughts, one of them being the cause of intense mental anguish. Freud particularly identifies two primary types of externalisation mechanisms which give rise to religion, namely, projection and displacement.

During projection, the individual attributes ownership of his or her own thought to an external object. Freud lists several instances of this behaviour in human beings; one of them being the reaction of a person when another person she at once loves (admires) and hates dies. She grieves because that person is no longer alive but she also feels relieved because a secret death wish is now fulfilled. Such ambivalence creates anxiety and distress and a sense of guilt and leads the living person into believing that the departed person envies and hates her because she still enjoys life, and now wishes to punish her (to kill her) for being fortunate. Thus, the living dreads and perpetuates the existence of the departed in the psychic world and invents mechanisms (*taboos*) to protect herself from him.

The double feeling—tenderness and hostility—against the deceased, which we consider well founded, endeavours to assert itself at the time of bereavement as mourning and satisfaction. A conflict must ensue between these contrary feelings, and as one of them, namely, the hostility, is altogether or for the greater part unconscious, the conflict cannot result in a conscious difference in the form of hostility or tenderness as, for instance, when we forgive an injury inflicted upon us by someone we love. The process usually adjusts itself through a special psychic mechanism, which is designated in psychoanalysis as projection. This unknown hostility, of which we are ignorant and of which we do not wish to know, is projected from our inner perception into the outer world and is thereby detached from our own person and attributed to the other. Not we, the survivors, rejoice because we are rid of the deceased, on the contrary, we mourn for him; but now, curiously enough, he has become an evil demon who would rejoice in our misfortune and who seeks our death. The survivors must now defend themselves against this evil enemy; they are freed from inner oppression, but they have only succeeded in exchanging it for an affliction from without.[5]

Displacement is similar to projection, but here the individual seeks or finds a third object to which they can transfer psychic reality, such as fear or hatred or libidinal impulses. Freud observes that displacement is a ubiquitous attribute of normal as well as psychopathological conditions and its formation may be simple or very complex. For example, a child may hate and fear a tiger it has never seen in real life (but of which it has heard a lot or which it has seen on a paper) because it unconsciously associates the tiger's strength and autonomy with the strength and autonomy of the father it fears and admires at the same time. Thus the child transfers its feelings of ambivalence towards its father to the tiger and experiences the same intensity of ambivalence (anxiety and admiration in their mixed state) whenever it encounters a representation of a tiger. Freud shares another instance of displacement he once experienced during a therapy session in Vienna:

> My patient demanded that a utensil which her husband had purchased and brought home should be removed lest it make the place where she lives impossible. For she has

---

[5] SFTOT p. 48-49.

heard that this object was bought in a store which is situated, let us say, in Stag Street. But as the word 'stag' is the name of a friend now in a distant city, whom she has known in her youth under her maiden name and whom she now finds 'impossible'... the object bought in Vienna [becomes] just as taboo as this friend with whom she does not want to come into contact.[6]

In its positive sense, the formation or manifestation of displacement may not be apparent. Human beings may unconsciously or consciously transfer their affection to someone or something with which they associate some attribute of a person or an object they love. For example, a man may fall in love with a woman who reminds him of his mother, towards whom, according to Freud, he is (unconsciously) sexually attracted.

Freud maintains that externalisation is not limited to thoughts and feelings. In fact, the most elementary externalisation process begins with sexual impulses in childhood. These impulses exist from the very beginning but first they are dissociated from one another and are not directed towards any particular object. Instead, gratification is sought within one's own body, mainly through the experience of sensation. Then the child enters into a second phase in which the sexual impulses become more united but still object selection does not take place. Instead, the Ego becomes the object of gratification and the child acts as if it were in love with itself. With maturity, externalisation and with it object selection takes place. Even in its matured stage, however, the state of falling in love, Freud observes, contains an instance of a psychic displacement, for one is bestowing to an object the love that initially and essentially belongs to the ego:

---

[6] Ibid. p. 27.

> To a certain extent man remains narcissistic, even after he had found outer subjects for his libido, and the objects on which he bestows it represent, as it were, emanations of the libido which remain with his ego and which can be withdrawn into it. The state of being in love, so remarkable psychologically, and the normal prototype of the psychoses, corresponds to the highest stage of these emanations, in contrast to the state of self-love.[7]

Similar externalisation processes, Freud claims, must have led to the emergence of religion and everything that belongs to it. Ever since human beings became conscious of their existence and the existence of a mostly hostile and trying universe surrounding them, they have tried to harmonise internal realities with external realities. In the beginning, they overestimated their power and believed that harmonisation could be attained through strong wishful thinking, but gradually they began to grasp their true place (namely, their insufficiency compared to the vastness of the universe and the overpowering forces of nature) and, with the evolution of their perception, their ability to harmonise with nature changed, undergoing complex psychological transformations and adaptations. In the process, according to Freud, human beings unconsciously gave expression to their fleeting but precious feelings by personifying them in order to rediscover them outside of themselves. According to Freud the traces of these developments can be detected in primitive people, neurotics, and children.

> ...spirits and demons were nothing but the projection of primitive man's emotional impulses; he personified the things he endowed with affects, populated the world with them and then rediscovered his inner psychic processes outside himself, quite like the ingenious paranoiac

---

[7] Ibid. p. 64.

Schreber[i], who found the fixations and detachments of his libido reflected in the fates of the 'God-rays' which he invented.[8]

A neurotic person, Freud explains, believes that contact between real objects can be established in the same way it can be established between psychic realities. Because he can bring together thoughts and wishes which are temporary and spatially far removed from each other in a single act of fantasy, he mistakes an ideal connection (i.e., existing only in thought) for a real one and imagines that the control he has, or thinks he has, over his thoughts also enables him to wield corresponding control over real objects. For example, a neurotic person considers himself as a real murderer because he nurses a death wish towards someone, and firmly believes that the death wish will lead to actual death. Consequently, he suffers from a strong guilty feeling that is comparably equal in intensity to the guilt of a true murderer. Likewise, Freud supposes, in the beginning man must have externalised intense internal realities (wishes) towards external beings and seriously believed in his own fantasy.

Based on these essential premises, Freud proposes different theories to explain the emergence of religion as a consequence of externalised psychic realities. One of these theories is based on a child's early experience with the parents it idealises. The child realises that its parents gave life to it ("created it") and from its birth on supplied everything it needs to develop as a human being. As the child grows, its perception of the world progressively matures, but with this maturity so does its awareness of the vastness of, and the danger in, the world, and of the limitation of its parents as its providers and protectors, increase as well. So through an act of wishful thinking, it psychologically transfers the role of the parent to a more

---

[8] Ibid. p. 66.

powerful and more loving being whom it can, through an act of fantasy, access always and everywhere. Within this scheme, however, God as the creator, provider, and protector is nothing more than a projection of the parents, particularly, of the father.

The limitation of this theory is that in his theory of displacement, Freud identifies a third target entity, which is a real object or person, to which an internal ambivalence is transferred or attributed. In this theory, however, Freud implicitly rejects the existence of a third entity, God, (who, according to Freud, is rather a product of the child's imagination). So, the theory makes sense if only the child first creates God and then projects (attributes) the role of the parent to him. But in none of the cases of neurosis he investigated did Freud encounter patients who first created a non-existent object and then attributed or transferred psychic reality to it. If a man falls in love with a woman who reminds him of his mother, the woman is a real person; if a wife transferred her hostility of her maidenhood friend to a utensil, the utensil in question is a real rather than an imagined object; if a child transfers his ambivalence of his father to a paper tiger, the picture is a representation of a real tiger the strength of which is associated with the father.

Freud's second theory is based on the relentless striving of human beings to conquer and subdue the forces of nature and to make them useful for their own advantage. In the early stages of civilisation, Freud maintains, human beings perceived these forces (thunder, storm, earth quake, flood) as an expression of a strong emotion, rage. Since only living beings can produce and express rage, primitive people believed that the rage must have come from living beings who were invisible and much stronger than they, yet who were more or less like themselves. In the same way human beings invented physical tools to subdue and tame nature and increase their productivity;

they created psychological tools, namely, worship and sacrifice, to pacify these beings and to use them for their own advantages. In this respect, religion is simply an historical and psychological means of production.

The third theory, which is perhaps Freud's most profound endeavour to explain the essence of religion, is based on an existential tragedy that concerns the primal father. According to Freud, right in the beginning of human civilisation, the *system of Totem* took the place of all religion and social institutions. Even at the time he wrote *Totem and Taboo* (around 1913), he alleged that this was the case among several primitive tribes of the world which organised themselves into small clans, each clan taking the name of its totem.

A *totem* can be an animal, a plant or a force of nature, but most often an animal. A totem, according to Freud, is a projection of the tribal ancestor of a clan and its tutelary spirit and its protector. Freud identifies five prevailing *taboos* concerned with *Totemism*, and psychoanalyses their significance to uncover the underlying psychic realities they represent. Accordingly, first of all, members belonging to the same totem pledge allegiance to support each other in times of need. Secondly, marriage or any form of sexual relationship between members of the same totem is prohibited. Violation of this prohibition is punishable by death or by lifetime banishment from the clan. Thirdly, the totem animal shall not be killed except as a sacrifice during a solemn ritual or festival. However, on this occasion, all members shall come together, kill the totem, and partake in the sacrificial meal, eating the entire meat and leaving no part of it. Fourth, children inherit their maternal totem instead of their paternal totem.

Taboos, Freud explains, express themselves in prohibitions, renunciations, and restrictions against strong inclinations in the unconscious mind, for what is not desired to be done need not be forbidden. This characteristic is particularly apparent in compulsive neurotics, paranoids, and hysterics who impose upon themselves taboos in their attempt to displace unconscious desires and wishes. Freud claims that two compelling and innate wishes are encoded in the taboos of the totem animal. These wishes are the desire to commit incest and to murder those who are nearest and dearest. These wishes are by no means specific to primitive tribes, Freud underlines, rather they are inherent in all human beings, even though they may not be apparent or remain latent throughout a lifetime, never manifesting themselves to the consciousness mind. The more unconscious they remain, however, the less accessible they are for correction and, therefore, the stronger and the more active they function, influencing and shaping overt actions and behaviours. These two desires are intimately interrelated. A child's first 'sexual' relationship, Freud asserts, is with its mother through the act of touching or attachment. Since touching is the beginning of every act of possession, the child, psychologically speaking, starts to consider the mother as its exclusive love object. But the mother also belongs to the father, a fact the child quickly and painfully recognises and in consequence of which develops hostility towards its father and wishes him death, for the father has by now become a rival. At the same time, however, the father is also the child's protector and its provider. In this manner and at quite an early age the child learns to accommodate opposing and distressful feelings (Freud labels this condition as Oedipal complex). Through time, the child discovers other channels by which it can defuse erotic tensions thereby reconciling with the feeling of ambivalence and attaining psychic equilibrium. Freud maintains that the failure to discover alternative erotic channels is the prime cause of neurosis.

The same cannot be said of primitive men, Freud presumes. The primal horde father, who was jealous, possessive, and violent, not only took away the mother (emotionally speaking) from the child, but also literally took all the females for himself and drove away all of his grown up sons from his place and fiercely protected the women. Freud builds his theory on a hypothesis proposed by Thomas M. Savage who, in an article he published in the Boston Journal of Natural History (Vol. 5, pp. 1845-47), makes the following observation:

> We may indeed conclude from what we know of the jealousy of all male quadrupeds, armed, as many of them are, with special weapons for battling with their rivals, that promiscuous intercourse in a state of nature is extremely improbable... If we therefore look back far enough into the stream of time and judging from the social habits of man as he now exists, the most probable view is that he originally lived in small communities, each with a single wife, or if powerful with several, whom he jealously defended against all other men. Or he may not have been a social animal and yet have lived with several wives, like the gorilla; for all the natives agree that only the adult male is seen in a band; when the young male grows up a contest takes place for mastery, and the strongest, by killing and driving out the others, establishes himself as the head of the community. The younger males being thus driven out and wandering about would also, when at last successful in finding a partner, prevent too close breeding within the limits of the same family.

According to Freud, right at the beginning, soon after the first primal father and his household became self-conscious, the sons the primal father drove out joined forces, came back, fought with their father, and defeated him. Then the brothers slew and ate the father and thus put an end to his dominion.

Together they dared and accomplished what would have remained impossible for them singly. Perhaps some advance in culture, like the use of a new weapon, had given them the feeling of superiority. Of course these cannibalistic savages ate their victim. This violent primal father had surely been the envied and feared model for each of the brothers. Now they accomplished their identification with him by devouring him and each acquired a part of his strength. The totem feast, which is perhaps mankind's first celebration, would be the repetition and commemoration of this memorable, criminal act with which so many things began, social organization, moral restrictions and religion.[9]

After the event, Freud explains, the brothers experienced a series of fluctuating emotions; now a sense of exalted liberation, now a sense of consuming guilt; now a festive joy, now mourning; now a sense of satisfied triumph, now remorse; now relief, now an extraordinary longing for the father and a desire to atone for the horrible crime they committed. "They hated the father who stood so powerfully in the way of their sexual demands and their desire for power, but they also loved and admired him."[10] After all, that same violent and oppressive figure was their chief protector. Thus the brothers began to accommodate opposing psychic forces, which gave rise to strong ambivalence, and sought an external object towards which the ambivalence can be displaced. Which is how the totem animal came to existence, Freud concludes:

> They undid their deed by declaring that the killing of the father substitute, the totem, was not allowed, and renounced the fruits of their deed by denying themselves the liberated women. Thus they created the two fundamental taboos of totemism out of the sense of guilt of the son, and for this very reason these had to correspond with the two repressed wishes of the Oedipus

---

[9] Ibid. p. 97.
[10] Ibid. p. 98.

complex. Whoever disobeyed became guilty of the only two crimes which troubled primitive society.[11]

By treating the totem animal with respect the brothers expressed their respect to the father. But, by that same action, they were also declaring that had the father treated them the way they treated the totem animal, they would not have killed him. The slaughter of the animal and the partaking of the sacrificial meal were reminders to the brothers of what had actually taken place, and that each had contributed to the deed and should therefore overtly acknowledge his responsibility. Since the root cause of the problem was considered to be the ownership of all the females by a single male, the brothers agreed to remain monogamous and the prohibition of incest and the introduction of monogamy were thus introduced into the totem *taboo*.

Furthermore, unless they renewed their pledge with one another by means of a repeated ritual of sacrifice and communal meal, Freud asserts, the brothers knew that their pledge would eventually become weak and ineffective and that the bond that tied them together would break, endangering the existence of the tribe. That is how the totem ritual established itself and was passed over to subsequent generations. In the long run, according to Freud, the murdered father was exalted to the position of a protective spirit and then to a god.

Freud took his theory very seriously. He published *Totem and Taboo* in 1913 and took it as his primary reference for all the subsequent books and articles he was to write on religion. The last book he published was *Moses and Monotheism* in 1939, a few months before his death. In an article he wrote in 1928 about Fyodor Dostoevsky[12] he pointed out that it is not by accident that the central themes of three of the greatest works of

---

[11] Ibid.
[12] SFDOS

literature are parricide and incest. He was referring to Sophocles' *Oedipus the King*, Shakespeare's *Hamlet* and Dostoevsky's *The Brothers Karamazov*. In *Oedipus the King*, both parent and son try their best to avoid a fateful oracle, but in the end Oedipus kills his father and marries his own mother. In *Hamlet* the king father is murdered by his brother who marries the queen and claims the throne. In *The Brothers Karamazov*, a wicked father is brutally murdered by his illegitimate son but all the legitimate sons contribute to the murder, consciously or unconsciously. Here as well, women are portrayed as the prime motive for the murder. Father and son (Dmitri) bitterly compete to win the heart of a young woman and Ivan Karamazov is in love with his brother's fiancée.

If one removes poetic moderation from the stories, Freud explains, all three works deal with one and the same theme, which is the inextricable connection between parricide and incest. In *Oedipus*, poetical moderation displaces the child's wish to murder the father and commit incest with his mother to fate. In *Hamlet*, the displacement is made towards the uncle, but Hamlet's procrastination in killing him may be seen as an involuntary admission of his identification with the murderer. In *The Brothers Karamazov*, the wish to murder the father is made explicit whereas the desire to commit incest is implicit.

Freud sees a great externalisation at work in Dostoevsky's novel. Whilst murder plays a significant role in all Dostoevsky's mature books, it plays a particular role in *The Brothers Karamazov*, his last and most significant literary achievement, in which also Freud identifies a personal confession. In this book the real murderer of the patriarch figure is an epileptic just like Dostoyevsky himself. By identifying himself in this way with the murderer, Dostoevsky was neurotically admitting his own contribution to the murder of his father, Freud claims. The contribution was, of course, in the form of a death wish, which he had developed as a child and had subsequently suppressed to the extent of barely being conscious of it, until the actual death of his father came to pass when he was eighteen years old. Freud referred to two biographical incidents in Dostoevsky's life to defend his assertion. As a boy Dostoevsky suffered from the terror of death and used to leave a message when he went to bed, beseeching his family not to rush to bury him if he failed to wake up in the morning. Then in his adult years, Dostoevsky became epileptic and remained so for the rest of his life. Freud supposes that the epilepsy must have started when first Dostoyevsky heard the murder of his father and characterises the epilepsy as *affective* as opposed to a physical ailment of the brain. (Dostoevsky had a difficult and exacting father who suffered from nervous disorder).

These two incidents, Freud alleges, indicate the coexistence of a strong death wish and an equally strong ambivalence manifested by a sense of guilt and hysteria. As a boy, Dostoevsky dealt with the death wishes by taking the place of his father and wishing the death upon himself, which produced in him a terror of dying. Similarly, when he first heard of the death of his father, Dostoyevsky's impulsive reaction must have been to rejoice, Freud alleges, but soon a strong sense of guilt took its grip and produced a strong desire for punishment. The epilepsy was the punishment Dostoevsky inflicted upon himself.[ii]

To Freud, the greatness of the three literary achievements lies not merely in the greatness of the theme they admirably treat (Oedipal complex) but also in their capacity to reveal at once the three principal dimensions of aesthetic experience: the psychology of the protagonist, the psychology of the author, and the psychology of the audience, both implicating and illuminating one another. Thus, *Hamlet* the book discloses at once (1) the unresolved Oedipus complex by which its Prince is haunted and (2) serves as an oblique testimony to the Oedipal drama of its author and to the unfinished emotional business with which he is still wrestling. (3) The readers, in being deeply moved by the story, betray a clue to their discovery in the tragedy of the prince of their own secrete history.[13]

Freud maintains that the origin and significance of the two great monotheistic religions, Judaism and Christianity, can be explained by the theory of the murdered primal father. In both cases Freud recognises God as a powerful and harsh father and as the undistorted projection of the image of the murdered father. According to Freud, the murder story and the wish to atone for the guilt it generated are made explicit in Judaism and in its concept of atonement for sin while Christianity at once projects and replaces the primal picture. With the sacrificial death of the Son, Christianity unreservedly acknowledges the offence committed against the primal father and thereby satisfies human beings' deepest wish to atone for it. It also serves as reconciliation with the father, for Christianity "renounces" women for whose sake the sons rebelled against their father. In making the ultimate sacrifice, however, "the son also attains the goal of his wishes against the father. He becomes a god himself beside or rather in place of his father. The religion of the son succeeds the religion of the father."[14]

Freud considers Christianity as a deception, for he depicts Jesus the Son as one who has stolen the glory of the primal father.

Freud was not the first to claim that the externalisation of psychic realities was responsible for the creation of God and religion. Half a century previously Ludwig Feuerbach in his *The Essence of Christianity*[15] had already taken a radical position by claiming that instead of God having created man in his image, exactly the opposite was true. Feuerbach defines religion as man's (man as a collective rational being rather than as an individual entity) attempt to reflect to himself his most

---

[13] PG p. 318.
[14] SFTOT p. 104.
[15] LFESS

treasured and most sacred inner values and ideals, and for this purpose he devised a mirror. This mirror is God. Feuerbach regards religion as a sort of consciousness, only in a mistaken form. According to Feuerbach, the primary reason for the existence of God is man's misunderstanding of three psychic realities.

a) Firstly, man mistakes his deepest wish for perfection and completion for perfection and completion existing outside of him.
b) Secondly, man mistakes his ability to pursue and synthesise knowledge for knowledge existing independently of him.
c) Thirdly, man mistakes his ability to abstract and generalise ideas for an intelligent being that is divine and transcendental, existing outside and independent of him.

Thus, God, as an infinite and transcendent being, comes into existence. Feuerbach asserts that, in reality, God is nothing more than an expression of man's wish to become complete, purified and infinite and to transcend the individual mind and existence, in order to achieve collective consciousness and unity. Similarly, Feuerbach sees the afterlife as the consummation of human perfection and Christ as the fulfilment of the greatest human desire, which is, to overcome death and become (like) God. Man satisfies his longing for immortality through the resurrection of Christ.

The essential difference between Feuerbach and Freud lies in that, whereas Feuerbach ascribes man's innate positive nature to the creation of God whom he endows with good qualities (love, sacrifice, wisdom), Freud ascribes this to man's worst instincts, his selfishness, inadequacy, helplessness, viciousness, and anxiety.

If one were to accept Freud's *theory of externalisation*, one would be compelled to draw the following conclusions. First of all, the root cause of religion is a serious crime committed at the beginning of man's existence as a conscious being. Secondly, this crime was committed against a father or an authority figure. Thirdly, the guilt feeling, which was eventually pushed into the unconscious, was seminally transmittable (that is, inherited from the primeval sons only) to all subsequent generations. Fourthly, even though the females were the cause of the offence (albeit indirectly), the males were the prime culprits. Fifthly, the oldest religion is monotheism (the exaltation of the primal father) and that religion requires monogamy. This, of course, is the essential essence of both Judaism and Christianity, except that these religions claim that the disobedience of Adam was directed against God, who nevertheless, is regarded as the father of all. Even so all the descendants of Adam inherited the sinfulness of Adam the primal son, who rebelled against God, his father.

Einstein

"The most beautiful experience we can have is the mysterious. It is the fundamental emotion which stands at the cradle of true art and true science. Whoever does not know it and can no longer wonder, no longer marvel, is as good as dead, and his eyes are dimmed. It was the experience of mystery—even if mixed with fear—that engendered religion. Knowledge of the existence of something we cannot penetrate, our perceptions of the profoundest reason and the most radiant beauty, which only in their most primitive forms are accessible to our minds —it is this knowledge and this emotion that constitute true religiosity; in this sense, and in this alone, I am a deeply religious man."[16]

Indeed, Einstein believed in God, but he describes him in his writings as an impersonal God who possesses infinite intelligence and creative power. This God has created everything that exists, and governs it with a set of deterministic, timeless, harmonious, and potentially comprehensible natural laws. These laws are perfect (in that they are complete); therefore, there is no need for God to interfere in his creation. According to Einstein, the notion that God interferes in his creation makes God weak, irrational, and haphazard.

Einstein's idea of an impersonal God attempts to reconcile two existential paradoxes. On the one hand, there is an apparent and highly complex intelligence manifested in the construction and operation of the universe; but, on the other, there is no scientific evidence lending itself to rational scrutiny to suggest God's interference in his creation, in violation of the natural laws.

Einstein did not accept the assertion that the universe is an accidental phenomenon. He referred to the high standard of

---

[16] AEIDE p. 11.

mathematics required to comprehend even a very small fraction of the universe. To him all existing scientific observations suggest that things are put together with care and are conditioned by each other in a precise and deterministic order. Besides, although the universe may be subjected to scientific scrutiny, the task, nevertheless, requires painstaking discipline, singular devotion, and great mental strain, all of which exclude the possibility of accidental qualities in nature.

Einstein believed that it is possible to establish a concept of God through science as well as spiritual revelation, albeit an inherently incomplete one. Even an incomplete concept cannot be the achievement of an individual or a group of individuals, or even of a particular people or generation. Rather it is a result of a collective and gradual effort. However, some individuals may get a glimpse of the divine mind through exceptional endowment and devotion. (Among these, according to Einstein, are Democritus, Francis of Assisi, Spinoza, Kepler, and Newton). Einstein calls the scientific longing to unravel the mystery of creation and thereby experience God, a cosmic religious feeling, "without which pioneer work in theoretical science cannot be achieved."[17] The characteristic feature of this feeling is a deep conviction about the rationality of the universe and a belief that the only way to approach it is by rational examination. Persons who are induced by a cosmic religious feeling seek God dispassionately, with no wish for a reward or gain. A God who rewards and punishes human actions is inconceivable to them, because they consider that humans are not responsible for their actions or inaction any more than an inanimate object is responsible for the motion it undergoes.

Einstein maintained that the primary reason for a religion based on a personal God (who more or less resembles human beings and possesses desires and emotions similar to human desires

---

[17] Ibid. p. 39.

and passions) is existential fear. When primitive man, whose grasp of causal relations in the objective world was poorly developed, was confronted by hunger, wild beasts, sickness, and death, he imagined illusory beings (gods) more or less resembling himself, to whom he assigned the cause and control of the objects of his fears. As his cultural and social awareness developed, Einstein explains, man found additional functions for the gods; he realised that fathers, leaders, and elders could not always provide protection and comfort as well as a sense of continuity and permanence to their community. It was only natural to transfer these responsibilities to immutable, immortal, omnipresent and invincible gods (or God) to whom every member could turn in times of need. But the new role required a reciprocal commitment. On their part, the believers committed to serve and worship the gods and to refrain from displeasing them or provoking them to anger. In this way the concept of religion emerged. No matter how advanced and exalted the idea of a personal God may appear, Einstein maintains, such a religion is conceived by man to satisfy deeply felt human needs and to assuage pain.

On several occasions, over a period spanning more than three decades, Einstein declared that he believed in the God of Spinoza. Even though different philosophers had influenced Einstein in his lifetime (Kant, Hume, Schopenhauer, and Mach, among others), Spinoza's influence on Einstein, both in his personal and professional life, was profound and lasting. His commitment to a deterministic universe, his imitation of the philosopher's unpretentious life style, his lengthy and tireless odyssey in search of a single mathematical expression to unify gravitational and electromagnetic forces, his profound fascination with the subject of ethics, and his rejection of quantum physics as an incomplete science, may all be attributed to his belief in the God of Spinoza.

Spinoza asserts that since God's existence is not self-evident, it must be inferred from ideas that are incontrovertibly true. These ideas must be singular (atomic), comprehensible to common sense, and definite, so that no conceivable postulate should be found to refute them.

In order to explain the essence of God, Spinoza began in his *Ethics*[18] by categorising everything that exists into two fundamental classes: *substance* and *modes*. Since existence is a reality, substance is what necessarily exists, uncreated. It is the primary cause of everything else. Spinoza refers to substance as "God" or "Nature". God may be conceived of as having infinite intelligence and infinite attributes. Without such attributes, he maintains, it is impossible to establish any idea about God. God's attributes in turn manifest themselves through the modes they bring into existence (the word *mode* etymologically descends from the Latin word *modus*, which may mean *measure*, *extent*, or *quantity*. The word *modification* is conceptually linked to mode. Hence, in Spinoza's concept of modes, the nature of created things mirrors the nature of God, however imperfectly, due to the infinity of God's attributes). Spinoza further classifies modes into *infinite modes* and *finite modes*. Infinite modes directly originate from God's attributes, whereas finite modes are causally brought to existence by infinite modes or other finite modes. In other words, a contact with finite modes does not necessarily bring one into contact with God. The most important infinite modes are the natural laws, which determine the course of finite modes.

In Spinoza's universe, substance and modes are intimately woven into infinite and deterministic chains of causes and effects. None of them can exist independently. There are two causal chains emanating from God and extending to modes. These are the *chain of Thought* (ideas) and the *chain of Extension*

---

[18] BSCOM pp. 213-382.

(physical objects extending in time and space). It is these chains and their eternal arrangement which determine how things should act or acted upon. Nothing and no one is free to determine its own course.

The two chains do not cross each other, but they are both the manifestations of one and the same thing. For each conception of an idea in the realm of *Thought*, there is a corresponding physical manifestation in the realm of *Extension*. Likewise, for each action taking place in the realm of *Thought*, there is a corresponding action taking place in the realm of *Extension*, happening at the same time. Accordingly, it is erroneous to presume that a thought may precede a physical event or vice versa or that ideas and physical objects are linked with one another. From this essential assumption of independence, Spinoza concludes that the human mind cannot be absolutely destroyed with the body; something of it exists indefinitely: "In God there is necessarily a conception, or idea, which expresses the essence of the human body and which therefore is necessarily something that pertains to the essence of the human mind. But we assign to the human mind the kind of duration that can be defined by time only insofar as the mind expresses the actual existence of the body, an existence that is explicated through duration and can be defined by time. That is, we do not assign duration to the mind except while the body endures. However, since that which is conceived by a certain eternal necessity through God's essence is nevertheless a something, this something, which pertains to the essence of mind, will necessarily be eternal (*Ethics*, proof of Proposition 23).[19]"
Einstein, on the contrary, believes that the tenure of the human mind is limited by the life of the body. When the body perishes, so does the mind associated with it perish forever: "Neither can

---

[19] Ibid. p. 396.

I nor would I want to conceive of an individual that survives his physical death[20]".

Spinoza also rules out the existence of God outside of his creation. Neither does he accord him freewill. Subsequently, God exists necessarily, and, out of this necessity he causes the world and everything in it to exist. God could have created the world in no other manner or in no other order. Everything that should exist exists out of necessity and God left nothing uncreated that should have existed. Since creation and its relationship with God are complete, there is no reason for God to interfere in nature. Hence, God does not and cannot displace, replace, or modify natural causes or effects. Spinoza (and Einstein, too) also asserts that God does not have a particular purpose for the world he created. The desire to ascribe personal qualities to God, he alleges, arose from man's erroneous concept of cause and effect.

Human beings find in their surroundings certain things readily available for their use and certain things requiring their design and craftsmanship. From the experience of producing tools for their own use human beings erroneously conclude that someone must have designed the things they found readily available—including the entire universe—for their exclusive use. Because they create tools on purpose, they likewise think that God must have created the universe for some purpose. Similarly, Spinoza maintains that human beings do not possess freewill, for their actions and behaviour are determined by the chain of events surrounding their life, which, in turn, are determined by other causes and effects, *ad infinitum*. Therefore, he concludes that nothing exists or occurs by chance. It is only that humans ascribe to chance or miracles the causes of events they are unable to locate in the infinite chain:

---

[20] AEIDE p. 11.

> ...whatever the Jews did not understand, being at that time ignorant of its natural causes, was referred to God. Thus a storm was called the chiding of God, thunder and lightning were called the arrows of God; for they thought that God kept the winds shut up in caves, which they called the treasuries of God. In this belief they differed from the Gentiles, in that they believed the ruler of the winds to be God, not Aeolus. For the same reason miracles are called the works of God, that is, wonderful works. For surely all natural phenomena are the works of God, existing and acting through the divine power alone. So in this sense the Psalmist calls the Egyptian miracles 'the powers of God', because, to the surprise of the Hebrews, they opened the way to salvation in the midst of perils, thus evoking their extreme wonder (*Theological-Political Treatise*).[21]

While Einstein agreed with Spinoza's essential concept of an impersonal God, he, nevertheless, seems to have differed from Spinoza on two points. Firstly, Spinoza was optimistic about knowing God adequately through rational analysis, whereas Einstein believed that God, as well as the universe, is ultimately beyond human comprehension. Secondly, Einstein seems to have accepted the separation between God and his creation. His reply to the question as to whether he was a Pantheist was equivocal:

> I am not an Atheist. I do not know if I can define myself as a Pantheist. The problem involved is too vast for our limited minds. May I not reply with a parable? The human mind, no matter how highly trained, cannot grasp the universe. We are in the position of a little child, entering a huge library whose walls are covered to the ceiling with books in many different tongues. The child

---

[21] BSCOM p. 422.

knows that someone must have written those books. It does not know who or how. It does not understand the languages in which they are written. The child notes a definite plan in the arrangement of the books, a mysterious order, which it does not comprehend, but only dimly suspects. That, it seems to me, is the attitude of the human mind, even the greatest and most cultured, toward God. We see a universe marvellously arranged, obeying certain laws, but we understand the laws only dimly. Our limited minds cannot grasp the mysterious force that sways the constellations. I am fascinated by Spinoza's Pantheism. I admire even more his contributions to modern thought.[22]

On the singular issue of causal determinism, however, Einstein agreed wholeheartedly and consistently with Spinoza. Einstein's commitment to causal determinism was not a matter of mere ideological consent; instead he made causal determinism the whole foundation of his scientific enquiry.

In his *Ethics* Spinoza declares:

Nature is always the same, and its virtue and power of acting are everywhere one and the same, that means, the laws and rules of nature, according to which all things happen, and change from one form to another, are always and everywhere the same. So the way of understanding the nature of anything, of whatever kind, must also be the same, namely, through the universal laws and rules of nature.[23]

Some of the fundamental assumptions made by Einstein in his *Special and General Relativity* theories are due to his earnest commitment to causal determinism and belief in the universal applicability of the laws of nature. One of these is the *equivalence*

---

[22] GSV pp. 372-373.
[23] BSCOM p. 278.

principle, which asserts that objects in a gravitational field (for example, on earth) behave exactly in the same way as objects in an accelerated field (in space). This simple observation enabled Einstein to establish how the geometry of the entire universe influences the motion of massive bodies and how these massive bodies, in return, influence the geometry of the universe.

The significance of a scientific theory is often judged by three criteria, namely, by its prediction, explanation, and testability features.[24] Between 1915 and 1919, Einstein's General Relativity (*GR*) fulfilled the first two conditions, but there was no empirical data at the time to substantiate whether it fulfilled the third criterion. In May 1919, however, during the total eclipse of the sun, an opportunity presented itself for the acquisition of empirical data by which the claims of *GR* could be tested.

For more than two centuries prior to the introduction of *GR*, scientists had been trying to determine why, and by what magnitude, light was deflected (or bent) when propagating near a massive body (such as the sun). Newton made a plausible but tentative observation in 1704 but does not seem to have ever seriously dealt with the issue other than remarking that light consists of tiny particles and, therefore, like any other ordinary particles, should be subject to gravity. A century later (in 1801), the German astronomer Johann Georg von Soldner provided the first model to calculate the angle of deflection by taking light as a bundle of tiny particles moving at a very fast speed and by applying Newton's laws of motion and gravity. Within his calculation, a light that barely touches the surface of the sun would be deflected by an angle of 0.9 seconds of arcs. A century after Soldner's calculation, Einstein applied his newly developed theory to estimate the angle of deflection, and his calculation produced a value double that of the one calculated

---

[24] Refer to SHTIM pp. 5-6.

by Soldner. Einstein could not confirm the accuracy of his result for the lack of empirical data required in order to draw comparison with his theoretical prediction. In May 1919, however, two British expeditions were organised independently to take a picture of the region of the sky centred on the sun during a total eclipse, and to determine the deflection of light around the sun. The photographs were taken and analysed, and the outcomes of the empirical observation proved consistent with Einstein's prediction. Since then measurements obtained with the help of advanced cameras and powerful lenses have made it possible to make repeated observations, both within and outside of the solar systems, and all the observations confirm the accuracy of Einstein's model.

When Einstein was first informed of the outcome of the investigation by the British expeditions, he was not surprised. His faith in causal determinism had already convinced him that the natural laws that apply to everyday objects here on earth apply also to other things everywhere in the universe, producing predictable outcomes.

Yet hardly a decade passed before Einstein's causal determinism was put to a tough test. During the time span within which he developed the special and general relativity theories, the research field of quantum mechanics was also emerging, attracting some of the brightest minds of that time. The primary concern of this field is the determination of the fundamental particles that make up an atom and their properties and how they are related to, and conditioned by, one another. From the very outset, some of the experimental observations and the mathematical models proposed to explain the observations were unconventional, and, in some instances, even contradicted the laws of classical physics.

Ironically, it was Einstein himself who discovered photons (one of the fundamental atomic particles) and accurately determined their properties. These particles are massless, exhibiting properties that can only be attributed to *waves* (interference and the property of being at multiple places at one time), and yet, they produce effects that can be produced by massive particles. Traditionally a wave is understood as a disturbance of some medium (air and water, for example) and the magnitude of the disturbance at any given point in time and space can be accurately described by a *wave equation*. If photons were to be taken as a wave, then what medium would this *wave* disturb and propagate through? If, on the other hand, photons were to be taken as particles, how could a single photon be in multiple places at the same time and how could multiple photons interfere with one another without displacing or deforming one another? Einstein called this phenomenon *wave-particle duality*. Since then quantum physicists have gone so far as to assert that indeed reality is nothing but a series of fields. When these fields are given sufficient energy they vibrate, and from this vibration different sorts of massive particles come into existence. When, on the other hand, the particles give up their energy, they virtually disappear and become fields once again.

The physicists Louis-Victor de Broglie and Ervin Schrödinger were foremost among their contemporaries seeking to establish the scientific foundation of quantum field theory. The former claimed, and experimentally proved, that an electron, which has a definite mass, also acts as a wave (in other words, the wave-particle duality is not an exclusive property of photons). In fact, according to de Broglie, all corporal objects act as waves; we do not experience them as waves in real life only because they have very small wavelengths. By accepting de Broglie's w*ave* claim, Ervin Schrödinger proposed a field equation by which the state and energy of an electron in an atom can be predicted. The equation is perhaps one of the most consequential developments in the field of quantum mechanics, but it also belongs to a group of equations in quantum mechanics which are counter-intuitive. By definition, a wave or a *field* equation should express (in a deterministic sense) the magnitude and position of a wave as a function of time and space, but Schrödinger's equation suggests that it is not possible to precisely locate an electron around the nucleus of an atom; one can only build a probable sense of its whereabouts.

This admission of uncertainty is further underpinned by Werner Heisenberg, who discovered an unsettling inequality in a vital equation relating the momentum of an electron to its velocity. This inequality led to his famous *uncertainty principle*. Simply put, it states that under no condition can one determine both the position and momentum of an electron with arbitrary precision. The more accurately one of them can be determined, the more uncertain one becomes of the other, regardless of the quality of the measurement apparatus one employs. Indeed the margin of error has nothing to do with the measurement apparatus; it is mathematically impossible to reduce the margin of error below a set limit. Since then scientists have discovered several pairs of properties of subatomic particles which cannot be determined simultaneously with arbitrary accuracy.

One of the earliest phenomena supporting the quantum field theory is the creation of W+ bosons inside the sun as a result of the conversion of protons into neutrons. A single proton is made up of two fundamental particles, two up quarks and one down quark. Similarly, a neutron is made up of two down quarks and an up quark. In a process called beta decay or radioactive decay, a single proton can be transformed into a neutron; in the process, another fundamental particles, which is called a W+ boson, which is 80 times heavier than its parent proton, is created! The heavy boson, however, does not survive for more than a fraction of a second before it degenerates into two other fundamental particles, namely, a positron and an electron neutrino. Two questions, as regards this process have been challenging physicists ever since:

1. How can so many fundamental particles emerge from a single conversion process when they were not a part of the proton in the first place? (It is not that a proton is smashed to pieces and its fundamental building blocks are disintegrated.)
2. How can a proton produce a neutron (having a comparatively an equal amount of weight) and a boson in addition, which is 80 times heavier than proton?

Theoretical physicists refer to Heisenberg's *uncertainty principle* to explain this phenomenon. The equation that relates the error in the position and the error in the momentum of a particle to a constant number (Planck's constant) can also be expressed in terms of the error in the energy and the error in the lifetime of a particle. In plain terms this means that a particle with a large amount of energy (or mass) can be created out of nothing, provided that the particle exists only for a short time.

Heisenberg's uncertainty principle seriously challenges the assumption that the universe is a self-sustaining, predictable system, which is governed by a set of deterministic rules. It also suggests that the universe requires a fresh and perpetual supply of external energy to hold everything together. Max Planck,[iii] the father of quantum mechanics, in a speech he delivered to a group of scientists in Florence in 1944, suggests the existence of an intelligent force outside of the universe, which sets the universe in a perpetual motion:

> There is no matter as such. All matter comes into being and persists only by the virtue of a force that vibrates the particles of an atom and holds them together in the tiniest solar system. Since in the entire universe there is neither an intelligent force nor an infinite force—man is so far unable to invent the desperately longed for mechanism that sets things into perpetual motion—, so we have to assume the existence of a conscious intelligent

spirit behind this force. This spirit is the origin of all matter.[25]

Einstein, however, did not accept this assertion and rejected quantum mechanics as incomplete science, adhering to causal determinism to the end of his life. Einstein's uneasiness with quantum mechanics is not merely due to its potential contradiction with Spinoza's causal determinism but also due to its fundamental clash with human intuition. In classical physics, the motion of an object (or more generally, any change the object undergoes) is a result of a cause. This essential property is called causality. The object remains in its initial state indefinitely if nothing causes it to change its state. Newton's laws of motion essentially describe this simple fact. The imparting of energy to the object, which changes its state as a result, manifests a cause. The sum total of energy of the cause and the object before and after their interaction remains preserved. The same is true to the sum total of momentum. The laws of conservation of energy and momentum govern the preservation of energy and momentum. Causality upholds predictability or deterministic behaviour. For example, if the initial position and velocity of an object of specific mass is known, and a known amount of energy is imparted to the object, then it is possible to precisely determine its position, velocity, acceleration, and energy at any given time, regardless of where in the universe this object is found. This is essentially the mechanism by which scientists determine the position, velocity, and mass of planets and stars that are millions of light-years away from the earth.

Often, however, the complexity of real-world systems makes it difficult to determine their behaviour precisely, not because they are indeterminate by nature, but because determining all the interactions between their constituting elements and their

---

[25] MPWES

surroundings is difficult. A typical example is determining the weather of a particular location, which is a result of several forces acting upon each other. Towards the end of the nineteen-century, Professor Ludwig Boltzmann introduced the concept of statistical mechanics to describe the properties of and interaction between complex systems and to make their behaviour predictable in a probabilistic sense. However, in classical physics, the term probability is simply associated with the difficulty of accounting all forces acting upon a deterministic system. Hence, classical physics essentially complies with Spinoza's causal determinism. In quantum mechanics, however, the subatomic particles, which have the most basic structure and the action and reaction of which should be the simplest both to condition and determine, nevertheless, exhibit properties which are inherently indeterminate and do not subject themselves to the principle of causality or conservation of energy.

Since the time of Newton, mathematicians and physicists have developed models and equations by which the laws of physics (such as the laws of motion, the laws of thermodynamics, and the laws of electrodynamics) can be expressed. The essence of these models is that they are logical and intuitive. Similarly, the early quantum physicists, notably Heisenberg and Dirac, developed the mathematical models and expressions by which quantum reality can be explained. These models, however, are phenomenological, in that they yield results which agree well with experimental results but are not easily supported by theory; they are also neither intuitive nor rationally explainable.

Let us consider once again the problem of beta decay, which I briefly raised above. During beta decay, one of the up-quarks inside a proton (recall that a proton is made up of two up-quarks and a down-quark) gives up its energy and thereby transforms the proton into a neutron (which is made up of two down-quarks and an up-quark). The energy, which is radiated from the transformed proton, in turn, creates an electron and a W+ boson, but after a short while, the W+ boson itself decays into a photon and a positron.

One of the interesting aspects of this process is that the electron and the positron are said to be in an entangled state. The two particles are essentially the same but exhibit opposite properties—the electron is a negatively charged particle whereas the positron is a positively charged particle; if the electron spins in a clockwise direction, the positron spins in an anticlockwise direction. After the pair is created, the positron and the electron may part in any two arbitrary directions at a speed of light. Suppose, the two take opposite directions to be infinitely away from each other. As it were, any modification we make to one of them will necessarily affect the other, regardless of the distance of separation between them. If we make the electron spin in an anticlockwise direction, for instance, the positron will necessarily change its direction and spins in a clockwise direction. This is why the two particles are said to be in a state of quantum entanglement.

The existence of this property has been time and again experimentally confirmed and seems to be a consistent property of sub-atomic particles. It applies not only to the spin of particles but also to their position, momentum, and polarisation.

One aspect which deeply puzzles quantum physicists since the time of Einstein is how the two particles exchange information, so as to reposition or reconfigure themselves whenever one of them undergoes a change in its quantum state. There can only be two possibilities, Einstein, argues in a paper he published with two of his colleagues at Princeton University in 1935[26]:

    1. The two particles must exchange instant messages to tell each other the moment they undergo a change. Or,

---

[26] EPR

2. They knew a priori what possible states each of them will undergo in future and make use of this knowledge to adjust their own future state (in other words, the two particles are already predetermined to act in all possible complementary ways in future, a position Einstein considered as plausible, since this would be consistent with Spinoza's causal determinism).

The first possibility contradicts one of Einstein's seminal discoveries, the Theory of Special Relativity; because it leaves the possibility open for a message to travel between the two particles at a speed faster than the speed of light. According to special relativity theory, the maximum speed that can be attained in our universe is the speed of light. The second possibility is equally implausible because it assumes that the two particles have a memory faculty, which enables them to remember. Experiment results seem to exclude the second possibility but they have so far not been able to positively confirm the first possibility either. Another serious implication of quantum entanglement is that it seems to suggest that the way we regard the physical world essentially modifies its configuration or state.

Einstein called quantum entanglement spooky, and attributed it to the inadequacy (or, more precisely, the incompleteness) of the mathematical models or representations, which are used to describe quantum realities.

Dostoevsky

"I know not how it is with the others, and I feel that I cannot do as others. Everybody thinks and then at once thinks of something else. I can't think of something else. I think all my life of one thing. God has tormented me all my life," confesses one of Dostoevsky's characters, Kirillov, in *The Devils*.[27] Kirillov, like Dostoevsky, is an engineer by training and at the threshold of becoming an epileptic. His confession reflects to a certain extent Dostoevsky's own state of mind. His intense preoccupation with God is visibly manifested in all of his books. Indeed, because of his extraordinary preoccupation, many scholars (Freud[28] and Joseph Frank[29], his biographer, among them) have asserted that Dostoevsky must have suffered from frequent vacillation between belief in God and doubt. However, evidence is not very strong to substantiate this claim. Whilst it is true that some of his characters are tormented by doubt, they are either in transition towards belief in God (for example, Raskolnikov in *Crime and Punishment* and Dmitri Karamazov in *The Brothers Karamazov*), or are incapable of faith at all (Fyodor Pavlovich Karamazov in *The Brothers Karamazov*). The believers in Dostoevsky's books (Prince Myshkin in *The Idiot*, Alexei Karamazov and Father Zossima in *The Brothers Karamazov*) are firmly established in their faith in God and remain believers, never seriously questioning their faith. This is not to say that they are unchallenged by such questions as the problem of being, the problem of pain, or divine justice.

Dostoevsky understood very well the complexity of faith and the intellectual difficulties accompanying a belief in an

---

[27] FDDEV p. 127.
[28] SFDOS p. 177.
[29] JF pp. 407-412.

omnipotent and loving God who, nevertheless, permits suffering into his creation. At the same time, Dostoevsky could not subscribe to a concept of life that excludes God. "I can't understand how an atheist could know that there is no God and not kill himself on the spot," wonders the same Kirillov.[30] Dostoevsky himself once declared that "if someone proved to me that Christ is outside the truth and that in reality the truth is outside of Christ, then I should prefer to remain with Christ rather than with the truth."[31]

In *The Brothers Karamazov*, Father Zossima admits that much on earth is hidden from human comprehension, but he also adds that, in order to compensate for that, God has given human beings "a precious mystic sense of a living bond with the higher heavenly world."[32] According to Zossima, the origin of our thoughts and feelings are not here, but in other worlds, for "God took seeds from different worlds and sowed them on this earth, and his garden grew up and everything came up that could come up, but what grows lives and is alive only through the feeling of its contact with other mysterious worlds. If that feeling grows weak or is destroyed in you, the heavenly growth will die away in you. Then you will be indifferent to life and even grow to hate it."[33]

This statement is not a casual reflection or one of the many wisdoms of a dying monk. It essentially summarises what Dostoevsky strove to convey all his life with his novels. It is such characters as Raskolnikov in *Crime and Punishment*, Nicholas Stavrogin in *The Devils*, the faceless man of *Notes from Underground*, and Smerdyakov in *The Brothers Karamazov* in whom this feeling vanishes altogether leading them to a belief that they can kick up their heels against life.

---

[30] FDDEV p. 614.
[31] JF p. 408 (see also the reference therein.)
[32] FDBRO p. 293.
[33] Ibid. p. 293.

Certainly, Dostoevsky's faith was the sum total of many influences: spiritual, mental, emotional, and social. His parents and grandparents were devout Christians and he was instructed in the Christian religion from childhood. Nevertheless to Dostoevsky the writer and the literary critic, his faith appeared to have been influenced by the Bible in different ways.

First of all, Dostoevsky was deeply fascinated by the stories of the Bible and the unique beauty and profound truth he discovered in them. As a writer and respected literary critic, Dostoevsky was acutely aware of the difficulty of writing good stories and creating authentic characters. He was highly critical of and sometimes dissatisfied with his own characters even though some of them (such as Foma Fomich) had already been household names in his own time.[34] In contrast, Dostoevsky had repeatedly expressed his childhood and lifelong fascination with the quality and authenticity of the stories and characters in the Bible. In *The Brothers Karamazov*, Ivan Karamazov's Grand Inquisitor confesses the unlikelihood of the human mind to have conceived the three temptations of the devil in the wilderness and Christ's corresponding responses:

> And yet if there has ever been on earth a real stupendous miracle, it took place on that day, on the day of the three temptations. The statement of those three questions was itself the miracle. If it were possible to imagine simply for the sake of argument that those three questions of the dread spirit had perished utterly from the books, and that we had to restore them and to invent them anew, and to do so had gathered together all the wise men of the earth—rulers, chief priests, learned men, philosophers, poets—and had set them the task to invent three questions, such as would not only fit the occasion, but express in three words, three human phrases, the whole

---

[34] JF p. 265.

future history of the world and of humanity—dost Thou believe that all the wisdom of the earth united could have invented anything in depth and force equal to the three questions which were actually put to Thee then by the wise and mighty spirit in the wilderness? From those questions alone, from the miracle of their statement, we can see that we have here to do not with the fleeting human intelligence, but with the absolute and eternal. For in those three questions the whole subsequent history of mankind is, as it were, brought together into one whole, and foretold, and in them are united all the unsolved historical contradictions of human nature. At the time it could not be so clear, since the future was unknown; but now that fifteen hundred years have passed, we see that everything in those three questions was so justly divined and foretold, and has been so truly fulfilled, that nothing can be added to them or taken from them.[35]

When he was writing *The Idiot*, Dostoevsky was tormented by a fear of failure and admitted his misgivings in a letter to his sister-in-law:

The main idea of the novel is to portray a positively beautiful man. There is nothing more difficult in the world, and this is especially true today. All writers, not only ours but Europeans as well, who have ever attempted to portray the positively beautiful have always given up. Because the task is an infinite one. The beautiful is an ideal, and this ideal, whether it is ours or that of civilised Europe, is still far from having been worked out. There is only one positively beautiful figure in the world...[36]

---

[35] FDBRO p. 228.
[36] JF p. 563.

The figure he refers to here is Christ. Dostoevsky recognised Cervantes' *Don Quixote* and Dickens' *Pickwick* as beautiful characters, but also pointed out that this is particularly because they are capable of inducing human sympathy, for they are "depicted" as "ridiculous characters". His effort, on the other hand, if one can judge from *The Idiot*, was to create a character that can be taken as an ideal who fulfils "the most important law of nature"[37], which is to freely love one's neighbour as oneself. Dostoevsky regarded love and human freedom as unique existential gifts and hell as a state of being in which the mind has irrevocably lost these gifts. One of his reasons for having been an obstinate objector of socialism was his conviction that it encroaches upon individual freedom and, therefore, would rescind the capacity to love in human beings. This was despite his acute realisation that almost all forms of existing social ideologies of his time had invariably failed to enable all members of the society to live with dignity and without the crippling worry of everyday life. During his visits to the United Kingdom and continental Europe, Dostoevsky had personally witnessed the extreme wealth imbalance and vicious social divide that had been created as a consequence of the absence of social consciousness and social justice amongst the rich and the privileged minority which guarded its advantages from the working class majority in the name of freedom of ownership. The church, too, which had in its inception demonstrated the practical implementation of "love your neighbour as yourself", had fallen short of its vision in nineteen-century Europe and been frequently criticised by the intelligentsia for being an instrument of oppression. Still, Dostoevsky believed that socialism admits confinement and conformity in exchange for safe and secure existence and refused to endorse it:

---

[37] Ibid. pp. 407-408.

Naturally there is something very tempting about living, if not fraternally, then at least on a purely rational basis, i.e., it is fine when all protect you and require of you only work and agreement. But here a mystery arises: it seems that man is completely protected, promised food, drink, and work, and for all this he is asked only a small drop of his personal freedom for the good of all, the tiniest, tiniest drop. But, no, man does not like to live by such conditions; even this tiny drop is burdensome. It seems to him, stupidly, that this is prison and that he is better off by himself because—he is completely free. And you know, even though he is flayed alive for this freedom, obtain no work, starves to death, and his freewill is equal to nothing—all the same, it seems to this eccentric fellow that his free will is better.[38]

Dostoevsky differentiated between the illusion of freedom and true freedom and maintained that one may pursue either of them driven by one of the two innate and inherently opposing forces. The first force is a result of what Dostoevsky calls the law of personality and the second, the law of nature. The tendency of the force obeying the law of personality is to create every possible opportunity for the ego to enlarge and to assert itself whilst the tendency of the force obeying the law of nature is to strive for inner perfection by radiating love outwardly and by availing oneself to the service of others. The first pursuit, according to Dostoevsky, eventually leads to isolation, envy, slavery, and self-destruction even though it may initially give the illusion of enrichment and fulfilment. The second pursuit, on the other hand, may seem to lead to the renunciation of freedom at the outset, but eventually brings one to true freedom and joy. Dostoevsky believed that it is impossible to

---

[38] Ibid. p. 382.

pursue true freedom with human endeavour alone, for the ego always stands in the way:

> And thus man strives on earth towards an ideal opposed to his nature. When a man has not fulfilled the law of striving towards the ideal, that is, has not through love sacrificed his ego to people or to another person… he suffers and calls this condition a sin. And so, man must unceasingly feel suffering, which is compensated for by the heavenly joy of fulfilling the law, that is, by sacrifice. Here is the earthly equilibrium. Otherwise, the earth would be senseless.[39]

According to Dostoevsky, only Jesus Christ could vanquish the ego and love human beings as himself, and in doing so, Christ, "the ideal of man in the flesh"[40], confirmed that the "the highest use a man can make of his personality, of the full development of his ego—is, as it were, to annihilate that ego, to give it totally and to everyone, undivided and unselfishly. In this way, the law of the ego fuses with the law of humanism, and in this fusion both the ego and the all (apparently two extreme opposites), mutually annihilate themselves one for the other, and at the same time each attains separately, and to the highest degree, their own individual development."[41] It is also this notion of development which persuaded Dostoevsky about the continuation of life after death and beyond the earth: "It is completely senseless to attain such a great goal if, up on attaining it, everything is extinguished and disappears, that is, if man will no longer have life when he attains the goal. Consequently, there is a future paradisiac life."[42]

The second way in which the Bible influenced Dostoevsky's faith in God is his discovery in it of suffering yet morally

---

[39] Ibid. p. 410.
[40] Ibid. p. 407.
[41] Ibid. p. 407.
[42] Ibid. p. 409.

upright personalities with whom he strongly identified, such as Jacob, Job, Jeremiah, and Jesus. Brought up by a harsh and exacting father, troubled by a fragile psyche most of his life (in the words of *the Underground Man*, by an acute consciousness), condemned to death and having had to undergo a mock execution at the age of 28, exiled to Siberia to serve an eight years prison term with hard labour, afflicted by a humiliating and stupefying epilepsy, and having been a lone voice in defending Christianity and human freedom amidst disillusioned Russian and European humanists, atheists, communists, nihilists, and socialists, Dostoevsky's own life was full of suffering and tragedy, not least his multiple personal losses, including that of a brother and a beloved daughter, and his own chronic illness.

In the Bible, the physically unimpressive Jacob receives a divine covenant and assurance of protection (Genesis 29:13-15), but does not distinguish himself in any earthly affair. In spite of a promise given by God, he undergoes one danger after another and experiences one tragedy after another. At a young age he flees from his home to avoid the revenge of a brother whom he has deceived and serves a crafty father-in-law for twenty years.[iv] When, after twenty years he finally returns to his homeland, he loses his beloved wife in childbirth along the way. Then his daughter is raped. In his old age Jacob loses the son he loves more than life itself and refuses to be comforted saying "I shall go down to the grave…mourning (Genesis 37:35)". "My years have been few and difficult," he tells Pharaoh shortly before he dies (Genesis 49:9).

Job, prosperous and respected in his community, is another biblical character who made a lasting impression on Dostoevsky. The book is an experiment with human freedom and faithfulness to God amidst trials and tribulations. Can a human being love God disinterestedly, without expecting anything in return? The book of Job seems to answer in the affirmative. In the story of Job, God himself testifies before the heavenly hosts to Job's blameless existence. Yet the devil reproaches Job alleging that Job chooses to be virtuous for his own advantage and God grants leave to the Devil to test Job. Within a short period of time Job loses his entire possession, his ten children, and his health. Unaware of the heavenly drama, Job is left alone to make sense of his suffering. His friends allude that Job is being punished because of a sin he has committed and not confessed, but Job rejects this accusation. He is not aware of any wrongdoing on his part and points to people in his surrounding who lead an ungodly life and yet go on living unmolested. Indeed, he emphasises, the ungodly are the most powerful, the richest, and, perhaps, the most carefree. Besides, if God were to punish human beings for the sin they commit, Job wonders, who then can stand confident and blameless before God, for human beings are inherently imperfect. But speaking of uprightness in human terms only, Job contends, he considers himself blameless and believes that God unjustly inflicts him with pain. Even though Job regards himself inadequate to challenge divine justice and is terrified by the divine majesty, he never ceases to question and complain about the unfairness of his treatment. In the end, despite unrelenting pain and a persistent feeling of forlornness, Job refuses to disown or blaspheme God.[v]

In the story of Job, Dostoevsky sees human beings' dignity elevated to the highest place and their capacity to love God disinterestedly as having been convincingly demonstrated. He also sees human beings as free and responsible beings that are capable of making good choices. For Dostoevsky, the Book of Job confirms also human beings' divine privilege to approach God as equals and defend themselves before him (a pattern repeated in the lives of Jeremiah and Jonah).

Another suffering biblical figure with whom Dostoevsky strongly identifies is Jesus himself. He labels him as "beautiful" and as the "ultimate ideal", a person whose steadfast character had been tested by intense and enduring misunderstanding, rejection, and persecution. Dostoevsky was fascinated by the fact that Jesus often foresaw his suffering and death on the cross but chose to confront death rather than escape from it (the epilogue Dostoevsky chose for his final and most consequential book, *The Brothers Karamazov*, is taken from the *Gospel of John* and reflects this very fact). Referring to a painting by Holbein depicting the dead body of Christ right after it was taken from the cross, the consumptive Ippolit (in *The Idiot*) writes the following:

I believe artists usually paint Christ, both on the cross and after He has been taken from the cross, still with extraordinary beauty of face. They strive to preserve that beauty even in His most terrible agonies. In [Holbein's] picture there's no trace of beauty. It is in every detail the corpse of a man who has endured infinite agony before the crucifixion; who has been wounded, tortured, beaten by the guards and the people when He carried the cross on His back and fell beneath its weight, and after that has undergone the agony of crucifixion, lasting for six hours at least.... It's true it's the face of man only just taken from the cross—that is to say, still bearing traces of warmth and life. Nothing is ridged in it yet, so that there's still a look of suffering in the face of the dead man, as though He were still feeling it... Yet the face has not been spared in the least. It is simply nature, and the corpse of a man, whoever he might be, must really look like that after such suffering... In the picture the face is fearfully crushed by blows, swollen, covered with fearful, swollen and blood-stained bruises, the eyes are open and squinting: the great wide-open whites of the eyes glitter with a sort of deathly, glassy light ... Looking at such a picture, one conceives of nature in the shape of an immense, merciless, dumb beast, or more correctly, much more correctly, ... in the form of a huge machine of the most modern construction which, dull and insensible, has aimlessly clutched, crushed, and swallowed up a great priceless being, a being worth all nature and its laws, worth the whole earth, which was created perhaps solely for the sake of the advent of that being.[43]

Elsewhere Dostoevsky indirectly relates his own suffering to that of Christ's when he describes the ordeal of a convicted criminal who is dealt out capital punishment. A footman idly comments to Prince Myshkin (in *The Idiot*) that it is a good thing at least that there is not much pain in death by a guillotine. Prince Myshkin instantly disagrees with this observation and gives a passionate and lengthy explanation about the immeasurable cruelty of the procedure and the absence of any correction or rehabilitation element in it. He then adds:

You may lead a soldier out and set him facing the cannon in battle and fire at him and he'll still hope; but read a sentence of certain death over that same soldier, and he will go out of his mind or burst into tears. Who can tell whether human nature is able to bear this without madness? Why this hideous, useless, unnecessary outrage? Perhaps there is some man who has been sentenced to death, been exposed to this torture and has been told 'you can go, you are pardoned.' Perhaps such a man could tell us. It was of this torture and of this agony that Christ spoke, too. No, you can't treat a man like that![44]

That person, who had been sentenced to death and was pardoned, is, of course, Dostoevsky himself. On April 23, 1849, Dostoevsky was arrested along with 34 members of a literary

---

[43] FDIDI pp. 374-375.
[44] Ibid. p. 22.

circle known as the Petrashevsky Circle for conspiring against the Tsar and the Russian Orthodox Church. Dostoevsky's papers, manuscripts, and books were confiscated on the spot and within months, he, along with his friends, was sentenced to death by firing squad. On December 22, 1849, Dostoevsky was brought out blindfolded to Semyonov Square in St. Petersburg to be executed. There the sentence of death was read to the convicts and they were told to kiss the cross. Relating the incident to his brother in a letter, Dostoevsky later relates "our swords were broken over our heads, and our last toilet was made; then three were tied to the pillar for execution. I was the sixth. Three at a time were called out; consequently, I was in the second batch and no more than a minute was left me to live."[45] When the 'prepare to fire!' was announced and the executioners aimed their rifles to fire, at that instance a messenger from the Tsar rode into the square waving a white flag and declared that he had brought an official pardon from the Tsar Nicholas I. It had later been discovered that the pardon was already agreed upon the previous day, but with an order that it was to be announced only at the last possible second.

The influence of the Bible aside, Dostoevsky could find no adequate reason for a life excluding God. Even the most elementary impulses (the fear of death and the natural inertia to exist) are indefensible to Dostoevsky and all human moral and social values become not only baseless but also meaningless without God. "Not to believe in God and immortality," writes Joseph Frank, a Dostoevsky scholar and biographer, "... is to be condemned to live in an ultimately senseless universe, and the charterers in his great novels who reach this level of self-awareness inevitably destroy themselves because, refusing to

---

[45] Pisma p.128 (December 22, 1849).

endure the torment of living without hope, they have become monsters in their misery."⁴⁶

Whilst Dostoevsky accepts God as a loving father ("all the essence of Christianity ... that is, the whole conception of God as our Father and of God's gladness in man, like a father's in his own child—the fundamental idea of Christ!"⁴⁷), he also recognises the intellectual difficulties the belief necessarily entails. He articulates these difficulties with extraordinary intellectual candour and aloofness. How is it possible to reconcile the idea of love with the cosmic reality that fervidly contradicts it; the undeserved and perpetual suffering of the entire creation; man's inability to comprehend the divine mind; and his acute awareness of his inevitable, irreversible, painful, and humiliating end? "This little word 'why' has covered the whole universe like a flood ever since the first day of creation ... and every minute all nature cries to its Creator: 'why?' And for seven thousand years it has received no answer," resignedly observes Captain Lebyadkin in *The Devils*.⁴⁸ The words of the dying Ippolit in *The Idiot* reverberate with a familiar sense of forlornness: "But this I do know for certain. If I have once been allowed to be conscious that 'I am,' it doesn't matter to me that there are mistakes in the construction of the world, and that without them it can't go on. Who will condemn me after that, and on what charge? Say what you like, it is all impossible and unjust."⁴⁹

In the *Brothers Karamazov*, Ivan takes a similar position: "I accept God and ... his wisdom, his purpose—which are utterly beyond my ken; I believe in the underlying order and the meaning of life; I believe in the eternal harmony in which they say we shall one day be blended. I believe in the Word to which

---

⁴⁶ JF pp. 219-220.
⁴⁷ FDIDI p. 203.
⁴⁸ FDDEV p. 184.
⁴⁹ FDIDI p. 380.

the universe is striving, and which itself was 'with God', and which itself is God and so on, and so on, to infinity. ... Yet ... in the final result, I don't accept this world of God's ... I don't accept it at all."[50]

Likewise, *The Underground Man* regards consciousness as a great existential burden and laments that acute consciousness leads to the realisation of the futility of human activity, any activity. What one normally takes as a primary cause or a fundamental reason for living (such as the pursuit of justice) immediately drags after itself another, still more primary cause, and so on, to infinity, nullifying the significance of all secondary activities. But human beings, according to *The Underground Man*, cannot afford to be inactive, for otherwise the alternative is sheer madness. So, they elevate secondary causes to primary causes in self-deception and pursue them wholeheartedly. The price they pay is self-mockery, self-spite, and, in the end, self-destruction.

All things considered, to Dostoevsky intellectual difficulties mainly lead, not so much to the rejection of God, but to the rejection of suffering. And he could not imagine a world in which love and freewill are possible without admitting suffering. Consequently, he regarded suffering as insufficient reason to reject God. Dostoevsky populated his books with characters in whom suffering produces different effects. In such characters as Father Zossima, Prince Myshkin, and Alexei Karamazov who bear their portion of the weight of care, to borrow an expression from Longfellow, "that crushes into dumb despair one half the human race"[vi], suffering produces compassion towards fellow sufferers and readiness to share the burden and grief of others. In such characters as Ivan Karamazov, Raskolnikov, and Nicholas Stavrogin, suffering induces rebelliousness and a desire to shatter established moral laws. And in such characters as Ippolit, *The Underground Man*,

---

[50] FDBRO p. 213.

and Smerdyakov, suffering produces withdrawal, callousness, distrust, spite, and envy. Once having rejected God and everything that logically follows (morality and eternal life), Raskolnikov and Smerdyakov take their ideas to the extreme and dispassionately murder and rob people whose existence they find offensive. Ivan Karamazov, too, consents to the idea that it is acceptable for one reptile to devour another (and in essence, human beings are no different from a reptile. Moreover, Ivan maintains that every other person on earth nurses a death wish towards his neighbour, an assertion later well developed by Freud). The consumptive Ippolit dreads the last, lonely, and cheerless days of his life and entertains the possibility of murdering a few people on the street before he dies, if for no other reason then so that he may be taken care of in a prison hospital and die there with "dignity".

Alexei and Ivan Karamazov feel strongly towards suffering children (Indeed, one of the reasons for Ivan to reject "this world of God" was on account of suffering children). However, Ivan's compassion for children is an idea, an abstract concept. In real life, Ivan, true to his confession ("I could never understand how one can love one's neighbours. It's just one's neighbours, to my mind, that one can't love, though one might love those at a distance. ... For anyone to love a man, he must be hidden, for as soon as he shows his face, love is gone."[51]), stays aloof. In contrast, Alexei finds himself in the midst of children, not only sharing in their grief and suffering but also bringing with him much yearned hope and courage. Dostoevsky, too, besides carrying his portion of the weight of care to the end of his life, made his readers partake in the suffering of others. From the first book he wrote at the age of 23 (*Poor Folks*) to the last book he wrote at the age of fifty-nine, shortly before he died (*The Brothers Karamazov*), Dostoevsky

---

[51] FDBRO p. 214.

never once omitted from his books a moving story about suffering people. Readers of Dostoevsky remember the vividness with which the suffering of such characters as Katerina Ivanovna Marmeladova and her children in *Crime and Punishment*, Marya Timofeevna Lebyadkina in *The Devils*, and Ilyusha and his family in *The Brothers Karamazov* are related. And, perhaps, with the final words of Alexei Karamazov, after the burial of Ilyusha, Dostoevsky was sharing his own final and most cherished sentiments about children and childhood:

You must know that there is nothing higher and stronger and more wholesome and good for life in the future than some good memory, especially a memory of childhood, of home. People talk to you a great deal about your education, but some good, sacred memory, preserved from childhood, is perhaps the best education. If a man carries many such memories with him into life, he is safe to the end of his days, and if one has only one good memory left in one's heart, even that may sometime be the means of saving us. Perhaps we may even grow wicked later on, may be unable to refrain from a bad action, may laugh at men's tears and at those people who say … 'I want to suffer for all men,' and may even jeer spitefully at such people. But however bad we may become—which God forbid— yet, when we recall how we buried Ilyusha, how we loved him in his last days, and how we have been talking like friends all together, at this stone, the cruellest and most mocking of us— if we do become so will not dare to laugh inwardly at having been kind and good at this moment! What's more, perhaps, that one memory may keep him from great evil and he will reflect and say, 'Yes, I was good and brave and honest then!'[52]

---

[52] Ibid. pp. 716-717.

Tolstoy

Tolstoy believed in a God who created everything that exists with an express purpose, but rejected the claim that God interferes with his creation in extraordinary ways. As far as human beings are concerned, Tolstoy believed that God has endowed them with the desire, as well as the capacity, to seek, understand, and do his will (and thereby discover true happiness). Therefore, his belief excludes the possibility of miracles and prophecies and the existence of celestial agents who convey divine revelations and messages to human beings. Tolstoy also rejected the divinity of Christ and the biblical claims concerning his miraculous conception, ministry, resurrection, and ascension. At the same time, however, Tolstoy rejected claims such as the idea that God is disinterested in human choices and actions; and that existence is an accidental and purposeless phenomenon. Instead, he maintained that God can reveal the meaning and purpose of life to people in the same way that scientific truths can be revealed to exceptionally gifted people; in this respect, he regarded the teaching of Jesus (particularly, the *Sermon on the Mount*) as unique in its insights, truthfulness, relevance, and scope, and maintained that the only way through which the true meaning and significance of human existence can be understood is by accepting and applying this teaching. Furthermore, Tolstoy firmly believed in prayer and an afterlife. Tolstoy is perhaps the most committed of the four persons, whose ideas are examined in this book, with regard to the belief he professed, living out his life, as far as was humanly possible, according to his understanding of the *Sermon on the Mount*. But how did Tolstoy reconcile some apparent contradictions in his theology? For example, if God does not interfere with his creation, what is the purpose of prayer? If there is no such thing as divine revelation, whence does the teaching of Jesus get its exclusive moral authority?

It took Tolstoy more than half a century to develop, refine, and synthesize his beliefs, and all of the books he wrote after the age of thirty-five, fiction and non-fiction alike, vividly portray this process. Historically, this process can be divided into four time periods, all of which can be recognised in Tolstoy's literary works. Moreover, in 1880, Tolstoy published an autobiographical book entitled *Confession* wherein he relates his rediscovery of Christianity as his religion. In it, too, an unmistakable parallel can be drawn between his personal life and the stories of the characters he relates in three of his mature novels, which he published prior to his conversion to Christianity, namely, *The Cossacks*, *War and Peace*, and *Anna Karenina*. Indeed, one is struck by the stark resemblance between the Tolstoy we discover in *Confession* and the major characters in these books (Dmitri Andreich Olenin in *The Cossacks*, Pierre Bezukhov in *War and Peace*, and Konstantin Dmitrievich Levin in *Anna Karenina*). They resemble Tolstoy in, among other things, their privileged social standing, their disenchantment with the idyllic aristocratic lifestyle, their internal restlessness and intense search for the meaning of their life, their deep and unsatisfied desire to be good and to attain perfection in all aspects of their lives, the reclusive nature of their ultimately preferred lifestyle, and the peace of mind they eventually attain by believing in God.

During his adolescence and early adulthood, Tolstoy's life was largely devoid of spirituality and a desire for it, featuring instead feelings of intense internal conflicts and contradictions. Even though Tolstoy was baptised into a Russian Orthodox family and as a boy received instruction about the beliefs and practices of the Church, he never truly believed in them. Rather he merely "accepted with confidence"[53] what he was instructed.

By the time he was fifteen, however, Tolstoy consciously stopped believing in the doctrine of the Orthodox Church and abandoned going to church and observing rituals such as prayer and fasting. In his own words, he did not really reject God or Christ; he simply could not define his belief with any certainty. Instead, he paid unusual attention to the study of philosophical works and literature. At the age of twenty-six, Tolstoy was already a proficient, famous, respected, and rich writer.

Externally, the young Tolstoy was leading a reckless life, gambling, partying, carousing, frequenting brothels, and wasting money on a grand scale. At the time he was writing *The Cossacks*, Tolstoy was deeply in debt after losing a large sum of money on cards. Dissatisfied with himself as well as with life in general, he decided to leave St. Petersburg for good and go to Caucasus. The similarity between Tolstoy's mental condition and that of Olenin's (in *The Cossacks*) and Pierre's (in *War and Peace*) during this period is striking. In *The Cossacks*, Olenin wastes his fortune on cards and becomes disenchanted with life. Then he rejects city life (Moscow) and decides to move to Caucasus where he wishes to lead a simple, hardworking life. On his way to Caucasus, he painfully admits to himself that his past life has been a deception and at that a parasitic, aimless, and joyless one. By contrast, the vast majority of people outside of his social circle lead a hard and burdensome life, producing what the gentry greedily and thanklessly consumed and persevering only through a simple faith they have in God. Olenin promises himself a new life, one dedicated to the service of others. Once in Caucasus, however, he realises the feebleness of his new philosophy of life when he falls in love with a Cossack girl who is betrothed to another man. This love, in its beauty, dignity, and equanimity, is something he has never experienced before.

---

[53] LTCON p. 9.

I love this woman; I feel real love for the first and only time in my life. I know what has befallen me. I do not fear to be degraded by this feeling, I am not ashamed of my love, I am proud of it. It is not my fault that I love. It has come about against my will. I tried to escape from my love by self-renunciation ... but thereby only stirred up my own love and jealousy. This is not the ideal, the so-called exalted love which I have known before; not that sort of attachment in which you admire your own love and feel that the source of your emotion is within yourself and do everything yourself. I have felt that too. It is still less a desire for enjoyment: it is something different. Perhaps in her I love nature: the personification of all that is beautiful in nature; but yet I am not acting by my own will, but some elemental force loves through me; the whole of God's world, all nature, presses this love into my soul and says, "Love her." I love her not with my mind or my imagination, but with my whole being. Loving her I feel myself to be an integral part of all God's joyous world. I wrote before about the new convictions to which my solitary life had brought me, but no one knows with what labour they shaped themselves within me and with what joy I realised them and saw a new way of life opening out before me; nothing was dearer to me than those convictions... Well! ... love has come and neither they nor any regrets for them remain! It is even difficult for me to believe that I could prize such a one-sided, cold, and abstract state of mind. Beauty came and scattered to the winds all that laborious inward toil, and no regret remains for what has vanished! Self-renunciation is all nonsense and absurdity![54]

---

[54] LTCOS pp. 312-313

The "new convictions" to which Olenin refers here and now deems as false and superficial embody his central philosophy that the meaning of life consists of living for the service of others. "That is pride, a refuge from well-merited unhappiness, and salvation from the envy of others' happiness: 'Live for others, and do good!'—Why? When in my soul there is only love for myself and the desire to love her and to live her life with her? Not for others… I now desire happiness."[55]

Similarly, Pierre's life in *War and Peace* begins with recklessness, disorder, and a tendency towards self-destruction. He at the same time deeply wishes to overcome his destructive impulses and to transform his life and make it useful to others. Mirroring his state of mind, he establishes two types of friendships, one of which strongly draws him into heavy drinking, orgy, and sexual debauchery, whilst the other prompts him to undertake a calm, reflective, and thoughtful analysis of the meaning of life. The first relationship culminates in an unhappy marriage with a wife who embodies the philosophy of life upon which the friendship is established. Beautiful, worldly, shallow, and unfaithful, his wife, and the life he leads with her, drives Pierre to limitless frustration, uncontrollable rage, and all-consuming sadness. The second friendship, and its philosophy, equally frustrates Pierre in its impotence to change the misery of the world and to bring an immediate consolation to himself as well as the people who are dear to him.

The philosophy upon which Pierre's second friendship is established faithfully reflects the philosophy to which Tolstoy himself subscribed at the time. Its essential concept is *the pursuit of perfection*, perfection in all domains of human activity: physical, mental, moral, and professional. This type of aspiration was not borne of Tolstoy's eccentricity; rather it reflected the prevailing outlook of the intelligentsia in contemporary Russia and across

---

[55] Ibid. p. 313.

Western Europe. At least ideologically, this was also the belief subscribed to by members of the "upright" aristocratic, literary, and intellectual circles to which Tolstoy belonged. This belief asserts that everything is subject to growth and development; everything strives towards a perfection the characteristic of which is governed by natural laws. One is but a part of the whole and if one knows as much as possible about the whole and the laws pertaining to its development, then one will discover his true place in the whole and his true worth.

But Tolstoy, like Pierre in *War and Peace*, was a person who would not settle for a vague and abstract philosophy. The more he pursued perfection, the more precisely he wanted to know of its nature. As far as physical and mental developments are concerned, Tolstoy observes in his *Confession,* the nature of perfection may easily be determined. Thus, physical perfection means health, physical strength, and fitness; likewise, mental perfection, though boundless, entails acquiring as much knowledge as possible and understanding the essence and significance of the things being studied. This type of knowledge can be determined by natural inclination, human curiosity, and experimentation. But when it comes to moral and professional perfection, determining their exact nature was not straightforward for Tolstoy. What does it mean to be good, and why should one be good? And as a writer, why should he write and what should he write about? These questions require tangible and measurable answers.

One may write in order to educate one's readers ("What do I know and what can I teach?"[56]), in order to express oneself, out of necessity so that one may earn a living and lead an independent life; all of which are reasonable answers, but none of them proved sufficient for Tolstoy. He diligently sought answers in books and through personal discussions with the

---

[56] Ibid. p. 16.

most brilliant minds his country produced at the time, but none of them was able to satisfy him. He also travelled around Europe searching for an answer, but there, too, he was unsuccessful in his quest. Thus, the first period of his life, a semi-tranquil life, comes to an end, giving rise to a period of intense, relentless, and desperate searching for the meaning and purpose of life.

The second period of Tolstoy's spiritual odyssey lasted about a decade. Outwardly he carried out everyday activities as usual (out of habit, as he puts it) and even became highly successful as a writer (he completed *War and Peace* and *Anna Karenina*), but internally he abandoned all interest in life except the singular wish to discover the purpose of his existence. Readers familiar with *Anna Karenina* can comprehend Tolstoy's condition by relating it to the life and struggle of Konstantin Levin.

By this time Tolstoy had abandoned city life altogether and moved to Yasnaya Polyana, to his ancestral estate located 200 kilometres away from Moscow—his "inaccessible literary stronghold"[57], as he puts it, leading a more or less reclusive life, in the same way Konstantin Levin abandons Moscow and lives on his country estate and leads a solitary and hard-working life. Interestingly, this period coincided with the culmination of the development of Tolstoy's physical body, which he knew also mirrored the development process of his intellectual faculties. Instead of growth, he now perceived that his body began to shrink, his muscles to loosen, and his teeth to fall out, contradicting the assertion that everything develops in infinite space and time. The life philosophy, which once seemed rational and adequate, now appeared to him not only shallow and useless but also painfully deceptive.

"Can it be that I have overlooked something, that there is something which I have failed to understand? Is it not possible

---

[57] SMLAN p. 308

that this state of despair is common to everyone?"[58] Tolstoy pondered for a long time and desperately sought for an explanation in all categories of knowledge. "I did not search casually, out of mere curiosity, but painfully, persistently, day and night, like a dying man seeking salvation."[59] After ten years of tireless search, Tolstoy classically summarised the kind of knowledge that was offered to him. The natural sciences, he explains, provide plausible theories as long as they address questions surrounding the origin of the material phenomena and the laws that determine and govern the relationships between these phenomena, but when it comes to the purpose and meaning of life, as to why one should be living and to which end one should be aspiring, they have nothing to offer.[vii] Speculative philosophy, on the other hand, pretends to address the transcendental aspect of life, whereas in reality the answer it provides can be summarised as follows: The entire humanity lives and develops itself on the ground of spiritual principles from which also it derives its ideals. These ideals manifest themselves in religion, art, and the formation of states. These ideals always rise higher and higher; humanity strides to the highest steps of goodness. Man is a part of humanity and, therefore, his occupation should be in acquiring knowledge and in helping fellow mankind to actualise their ideals.

Indeed, not only did Tolstoy realise the insufficiency of science and philosophy to offer him any definite and conclusive answer, but he also realised that none of his predecessors, who had set out before him in search of a rational answer to the meaning and purpose of life, had ever returned with one. On the contrary, their conclusion was that life has no purpose, summarising their findings with such statements as: 'We move closer to the truth only to the extent that we move further from

---

[58] LTCON p. 33.
[59] Ibid. p. 33.

life'[60]; 'all is vanity'; 'life is suffering'; and 'everything is an illusion'. Socrates. Solomon. Buddha. Schopenhauer. As if involuntarily agreeing to these statements, Tolstoy, too, was nursing the same sentiment: "Life is an evil and a cruel practical joke someone permitted himself to play on me," he writes in his autobiography.[61] Yet, he was deeply disappointed in science and philosophy as well as with himself that he repeatedly struggled with the idea of ending his own life.

His pursuit of perfection, which started seemingly innocuously, eventually led him to a confrontation with death itself. "The same happens to me what happens with anyone who is suffering from some terminal disease," confesses Tolstoy. At first there occur insignificant signs of indispositions which the patient does not give much attention to. Then they occur more frequently, intensely, and with them a ceaseless agony. The pain grows, and then hardly has the patient time to look around himself, he realises that the indispositions he took for mere trifles have become the most significant realities for him.[62] The full significance of this confession and the spectrum of agony it abstracts can be appreciated by referring to *The Death of Ivan Ilyich*, a book Tolstoy wrote at about this time.

As science and philosophy were unable to give him an adequate explanation, Tolstoy turned his attention to real people, first to the people of his own calibre, the aristocracy, the intellectuals, the liberal thinkers, and the artists. To his great consternation, however, Tolstoy was unable to learn anything from them except the "tactics" they adopted over time in order to survive. The first tactic, he observes, is blissful ignorance. People who adopt this tactic waste their time by pursuing inconsequential goals, not thinking about their ultimate end. The second tactic is Epicureanism, the philosophy of employing one's whole

---

[60] LTCON p. 43.
[61] Ibid. p. 29.
[62] Ibid. p. 26.

existential potential for the pursuit of pleasure, for, they say, life is short and unpredictable. The third tactic is suicide. Tolstoy points out that so many intellectuals in Russia and Europe who had realised the futility of life subsequently put an end to their misery by taking their own lives, because they could not abide living without a meaning for their existence. And there were people like himself who thoroughly "understood" the futility of life, but went on living out of cowardice. The fate of these people was, Tolstoy observes, suffering, shame, and lack of self-respect.

Interestingly, throughout his search for an explanation to the question of life, Tolstoy had also been examining the soundness of his reasoning and whether it consisted of any faulty components. For example, he asked himself whether what he hitherto considered to be the realisation of the futility of life could merely be the realisation of the futility of his own life and not life as an abstract totality. Secondly, he wondered whether this realisation could simply be the first stage of consciousness that life is in fact the most significant existential affair to which he should pay his whole attention. Eventually, he accepted the possibility that finding no meaning for life should not necessarily lead to the conclusion that life has no meaning at all. Secondly, he also realised that whereas in reality he was searching for a purpose that goes beyond the present, the timely, the causal, and the perishable life, his investigation was merely limited to the life that is inherently causal and bound by time and space. The attempt to fit the eternal into the temporal and the infinite into the finite was, to Tolstoy, like "a deaf man judging the meaning and worth of music by the appearance and the movements of the musicians".[63] Thirdly, the conclusion he arrived at concerning the practical side of life, based on the observation of the lives of few people in his

---

[63] LTKNI2 p. 80.

own social and professional milieu, could not be representative of the lives of millions of people who had lived in the past and those who were now living around the world. According to Tolstoy, the majority of people on earth find sufficient reasons to exist and to make sure that life continues. These people cannot be collectively ignorant, unreasonable, cowardly, or selfish, or cannot be merely driven by an accidental impulse which propels them to exist. In fact, the multitudes of peasants to whom he was drawn and for whom he had developed natural affection were hard working, sacrificial, and uncomplaining. Not only did they find a reason for living, but also considered the reason to be good. As a result, they could get up each morning and face the day with renewed strength. The aristocracy and the intelligentsia, by contrast, Tolstoy observes, led a perpetually idle, parasitic, greedy, and miserable existence. This realisation further strengthened Tolstoy's conviction that the senselessness of his own life and the lives of the people in his immediate circle did not necessarily provide an authentic representation of life *per se*.

Furthermore, Tolstoy was compelled to critically question and scrutinise the quintessential characteristics of what he had so far regarded as being rational and irrational for accepting or rejecting various explanations about life. For example, his main reason for disregarding the religious explanations when he was young was that they did not sound reasonable to him. Now the middle-aged writer observed that there were many conditions in life which do not lend themselves to logical reasoning. If, for example, a man finds a bean next to a sack containing beans, he will deduce that the bean must have fallen from the sack. Other than regarding his explanation as the simplest and the most likely explanation, no logical inference (inductive or deductive) will justify the rationality of his explanation. Still, many a time human beings find this type of explanation not only reasonable and satisfactory but also indispensable in the course of everyday life. So, what if what he so far considered unreasonable and irrational were indeed reasonable after all? Specifically, what if some of the biblical claims about the purpose of human life were true in the literal sense of the word, and how would they change his views of life or give meaning to his own life if he were to earnestly accept and apply them? Tolstoy was ready to re-examine them with an unbiased attitude, thus bringing to a close the second period of his odyssey, as he puts it, with a change of attitude towards religion.

The third period of Tolstoy's life lasted about three years during which time he applied his intellectual strength to the study of the Scriptures. Parallel to his study, he also consulted and had interminable discussions with a large number of priests, bishops, pastors, monks, and theologians of different churches, denominations, and movements. But the biblical explanations of the origin of man, the fall, sin, hell, judgement, redemption, death, and the resurrection, were indigestible to Tolstoy because they were, as he understood them, in direct contradiction with scientific evidence and common sense. Likewise, he found the explanations and expositions he received from Christian scholars on these matters equally incomprehensible and troublesome. They all believed in "a wicked and senseless God who has cursed the human race and devoted his own Son to sacrifice, and a part of mankind to eternal torment," Tolstoy laments in *The Kingdom of God is within You*.[64] Such people, Tolstoy maintains, cannot believe in the God of love. "The man who believes in a God, in a Christ coming again in glory to judge and to punish the living and the dead, cannot believe in the Christ who bade us turn the left cheek, judge not, forgive these that wrong us, and love our enemies."[65] Similar statements of faith, such as the Trinity, the

---

[64] LTKIN p. 79.
[65] Ibid.

creation of the world in seven days, and the existence of angels and demons, deeply confused and troubled Tolstoy. No person in his right mind would accept these types of statements, Tolstoy maintains.

At the same time, however, Tolstoy discovered in the teaching of Jesus priceless truths in the light of which human life obtains a profound meaning and relevance:

> Look at the private life of separate individuals; listen to those valuations of acts, which men make in judging one another; listen, not only to the public sermons and lectures, but also to those instructions which parents and educators give to their charges, and you will see that, no matter how far the political, social life of men … is from the realisation of Christian truths in private life, it is only the Christian virtues that are by all and for all, without exception and indubitably, considered to be good, and that the anti-Christian vices are by all and for all, without exception and indubitably, considered to be bad. Those are considered to be the best of men who renounce and sacrifice their lives in the service of humanity and who sacrifice themselves for others; those are considered to be the worst who are selfish, who exploit the misery of their neighbour for their personal advantage.[66]

So how could Tolstoy accept the teaching of Jesus, which makes numerous references to the Old Testament and contains numerous claims pertaining to direct divine intervention in the form of miracles and prophesies, without accepting the rest of the Bible? He explains that the Bible, including the teaching of Jesus, makes sense only if one considers it as a work of man and not as a book directly revealed to human beings by extraordinary means. If one were to accept this assertion, Tolstoy maintains, it is possible to separate the authentic claims

---

[66] Ibid. pp. 206-207.

of the Bible from the spurious and speculative ones, and to find explanations as to why and how the spurious and speculative claims found their way into the Bible.

If one takes the Bible as a work of man, it is then natural for it to be imperfect, Tolstoy explains, because the people who produced it could but have limited insight about life, God, and history. Besides, exceptionally gifted leaders such as Moses, Jesus, the prophets, and the early apostles could not have convinced their followers to accept the demands of their teaching without ascribing supernatural origin to them, for the level of obedience, sacrifice, commitment, and discipline they demanded of their subjects were contrary to innate human tendencies:

> If Christianity had been offered to men in its real, and not [in] its corrupted, form, it would not have been accepted by the majority of men, and the majority of men would have remained alien to it… But, having received it in its corrupted form, the nations who received it were subjected to its certain, though slow, action, and by a long experimental road of errors and of sufferings resulting therefrom are now brought to the necessity of acquiring it in its true sense.[67]

Tolstoy goes on to state that the timeless truths which can be found in the Bible were not results of extraordinary divine revelations, as the biblical authors alleged, instead, they were revealed to exceptionally insightful people, who had committed their lifelong devotion to the pursuit of truth, justice, and divine love, in the same way scientific facts were revealed to exceptionally insightful and committed people:

> This property of foreseeing the path on which humanity must travel is in a greater or lesser degree common to all men, but there have always, at all times, been men, in

---

[67] Ibid. p. 192.

whom this quality has been manifested with particular force, and these men expressed clearly and precisely what was dimly felt by all men, and established a new comprehension of life, from which resulted an entirely new activity, for hundreds and thousands of years.[68]

Unlike scientific revelations, moral revelations, Tolstoy asserts, have the tendency to forcefully induce particular devotions on the common persons to those who have been the channels of revelations. Depending on the scope and relevance of the revelations, they may even induce devotions akin to religion, for now a new path of life or a new perspective to life or even a new purpose for life is laid out for them. This, according to Tolstoy, explains why his followers considered Jesus as the Son of God:

> To this demand responds the peculiar ability of humanity to segregate certain people who give a new meaning to the whole of human life—a meaning from which results the whole new activity which is different from the preceding one. The establishment of the new life-conception, which is proper for humanity under the new conditions into which it is entering, and of the activity resulting from it, is what is called religion.[69]

Tolstoy maintains that even though God wishes to have a relationship with human beings and that human actions and decisions matter to him, he, nevertheless, does not employ extraordinary ways to interact with them. A belief in extraordinary divine revelation, divine intervention, and divine grace undermines the price that has to be paid to pursue perfection and goodness, and relieves human beings from being accountable to their actions. The faculties with which God has endowed human beings are sufficient in themselves for human

---

[68] Ibid. p. 90.
[69] Ibid. p. 89.

beings to discover God's will for their life, to find happiness in their discovery, and to earn God's approval.

Tolstoy identifies parallels between the development of his own comprehension of the essence and meaning of life and its fulfilment in the acceptance of Christianity, on the one hand, and the development of the consciousness of religion in human beings (society) as a whole, on the other.

> We know three ... conceptions of life: two of them humanity has already outlived, and the third is the one through which we are now passing in Christianity. There are three, and only three, such conceptions, not because we have arbitrarily united all kinds of life-conceptions into these three, but because the acts of men always have for their base one of these three life-conceptions, because we cannot understand life in any other way than by one of these three means. The three life-conceptions are these: the first—the personal, or animal; the second—the social, or the pagan; and the third—the universal, or the divine.[70]

The first conception pertaining to the purpose of life, according to Tolstoy, reflects the values of an individual at the infancy of his moral development and humanity as a historical and cultural entity at the infancy of its moral development. At the centre of this conception are human lust and its gratification. So what is considered as good and the purpose of life according to this conception is the gratification of lust. "The savage recognizes life only in himself, in his personal desires. The good of his life is centred in himself alone. The highest good for him is the greatest gratification of his lust. The prime mover of his life is his personal enjoyment. His religion consists in appeasing the divinity in his favour, and in the worship of imaginary personalities of gods, who live only for personal ends"[71].

---

[70] Ibid. p. 90.

As the moral consciousness of human beings, both as individuals and as a collective entity, developed, the second conception of life emerges giving greater value to the social organisation than to the individual. In other words, the life and fulfilment of the individual consists primarily of the preservation of the social organisation. "A pagan, a social man, no longer recognizes life in himself alone, but in the aggregate of personalities—in the tribe, the family, the race, the state—and sacrifices his personal good for these aggregates. The prime mover of his life is glory. His religion consists in the glorification of the heads of unions—of eponyms, ancestors, kings, and in the worship of gods, the exclusive protectors of his family, his race, his nation, his state"[72].

The third conception of life is a result of the further development and maturation of human moral consciousness, according to Tolstoy. At this stage, human beings no longer recognise life in terms of their individual or collective personalities, but in the source of the everlasting, immortal life, in God. Their primary aim is to discover God's will in their life. They are not only willing, but also ready, to sacrifice their personal and domestic and social well-being to do God's will. The prime mover of their religion is love and their religion is the worship in deed and in truth of the beginning of everything, of God. "The whole historical life of humanity is nothing but a gradual transition from the personal, the animal life-conception, to the social, and from the social to the divine"[73].

With this conviction Tolstoy closed the third period of his life and began the fourth, during which time he publicly rejected, and was excommunicated from, the Russian Orthodox Church. His sole preoccupation was to wholeheartedly live out his life

---

[71] Ibid. p. 91.
[72] Ibid.
[73] Ibid.

according to the truth of the *Sermon on the Mount*. He became an outspoken pacifist, disowned his property, including the copyright of all his books, and led a simple life.

---

[i] When Freud states that under certain conditions the boundary between the ego and the external world becomes blurred and a person may disown his or her own feeling or thought as something foreign or alien to him or her, perhaps he had Daniel Schreber in his mind. Schreber, a familiar name for many psychiatry students, was a 42 year old, highly successful and respected judge when one morning he woke up with a strange feeling that it would be pleasurable to succumb to the idea of taking the role of a woman in a sexual intercourse. Schreber was disturbed and distraught by the thought and was convinced that it must have originated from outside, and not within his mind. One plausible explanation he found was that someone (his doctor) must have been employing telepathy on him to invade and insert the idea into his mind. Schreber's condition was subsequently diagnosed as dementia praecox and as his condition recurred and worsened, Schreber presumed that his illness was the act of divine punishment, as God was using divine rays to transform him into a woman. Freud, who at the time did not have a personal interview with Schreber, had nevertheless read his Memoirs, and drew his own conclusion about Schreber's illness. Thus, according to Freud, Schreber was suffering from repressed homosexual tendencies, which were first directed towards his father and then towards his brother. Freud maintains that both God and the doctor were objects of displacement for the psychic externalisations of the secret sexual wishes the judge felt at infancy.

[ii] Joseph Frank contests Freud's analysis of Dostoevsky and attributes the pathological shyness and nervousness from which Dostoevsky suffered all his life rather to "the paternal insistence on scholastic achievement as a moral obligation, and as the only defence against grinding poverty and loss of status." Moreover, he refers to the absence of any source material which shows the existence of an early evidence of epilepsy from which Dostoevsky suffered in later life. "The 'facts' that Freud adduces can be shown to be extremely dubious at best, and at worst simply mistaken; the case history Freud constructed in the effort to 'explain' him in psychoanalytic terms is

purely fictitious (JF p. 21, pp. 45-49)".

[iii] It was Max Planck who first offered Einstein a professorial position in Berlin. The two had a fruitful cooperation and a cordial collegial relationship for nearly three decades. Einstein would later write the following for Planck's memorial service: "A man to whom it has been given to bless the world with a great creative idea has no need for the praise of posterity. His very achievement has already conferred a higher boon upon him. Yet it is good — indeed, it is indispensable — that representatives of all who strive for truth and knowledge should be gathered here today from the four corners of the globe. They are here to bear witness that even in these times of ours, when political passion and brute force hang like swords over the anguished and fearful heads of men, the standard of our ideal search for truth is being held aloft undimmed. This ideal, a bond forever uniting scientists of all times and in all places, was embodied with rare completeness in Max Planck. Even the Greeks had already conceived the atomistic nature of matter and the concept was raised to a high degree of probability by the scientists of the nineteenth century. But it was Planck's law of radiation that yielded the first exact determination — in of other assumptions — of the absolute magnitudes of atoms. More than that, he showed convincingly that in addition to the atomistic structure of matter there is a kind of atomistic structure to energy, governed by the universal constant h, which was introduced by Planck. This discovery became the basis of all twentieth century research in physics and has almost entirely conditioned its development ever since. Without this discovery it would not have been possible to establish a workable theory of molecules and atoms and the energy processes that govern their transformations. Moreover, it has shattered the whole framework of classical mechanics and electrodynamics and set science a fresh task: that of finding a new conceptual basis for all physics. Despite remarkable partial gains, the problem is still far from a satisfactory solution (AEIDE pp.78-79).

[iv] Dostoevsky, who suffered shortage of money, lived with excruciating insecurity all his life, and endured the bitter and humiliating persecution of creditors, must have strongly identified with Jacob when the latter accuses his father-in-law with the following words: "I have been with you for twenty years now. Your sheep and goats have not miscarried, nor have I eaten rams from your flocks. I did not bring you animals torn by wild beasts; I bore the

loss myself. And you demanded payment from me for whatever was stolen by day or night. This was my situation: The heat consumed me in the daytime and the cold at night, and sleep fled from my eyes. It was like this for the twenty years I was in your household (Genesis 31:38-41)."

[v] Job doesn't seem to believe in an afterlife, which makes his suffering more painful and his uprightness more honourable. His repeated remarks about death suggest that life ends there: "Remember that my life is a breath; my eye will never again see good. The eye of him who sees me will behold me no more; while thy eyes are upon me, I shall be gone. As the cloud fades and vanishes, so he who goes down to [the grave] does not come up; he returns no more to his house, nor does his place know him anymore." (Job 7: 7-10). "Are not the days of my life few? Let me alone, that I may find a little comfort before I go whence I shall not return, to the land of gloom and deep darkness, the land of gloom and chaos, where light is as darkness!" (Job 10:20-22). "But man dies, and is laid low; man breathes his last, and where is he?" (Job 14:12). In another place Job seems to contradict these verses by suggesting the continuation of life after death: "For I know that my Redeemer lives, and at last he will stand upon the earth; and after my skin has been thus destroyed, then from my flesh I shall see God, whom I shall see on my side, and my eyes shall behold, and not another." (Job 19:25-27). Bible translators, however, warn that the last verses are difficult to accurately translate (refer to the comments to this verses in the NIV Bible).

[vi] The Goblet of Life: Longfellow, H.W., 1843. *Ballads and other poems.* Moxon.

[vii] Perhaps Einstein had Tolstoy in mind when, half a century later, in a speech he delivered to Princeton students, he said the following: "For the scientific method can teach us nothing else beyond how facts are related to, and conditioned by, each other. The aspiration toward such objective knowledge belongs to the highest of which man is capable, and you will certainly not suspect me of wishing to belittle the achievements and the heroic efforts of man in this sphere. Yet it is equally clear that knowledge of what is does not open the door directly to what should be. One can have the clearest and most complete knowledge of what is, and yet not be able to deduct from that what should be the goal of our human aspirations. Objective knowledge provides us with powerful instruments for the achievements of certain ends, but the ultimate goal itself and the longing to

reach it must come from another source. And it is hardly necessary to argue for the view that our existence and our activity acquire meaning only by the setting up of such a goal and of corresponding values. The knowledge of truth as such is wonderful, but it is so little capable of acting as a guide that it cannot prove even the justification and the value of the aspiration toward that very knowledge of truth. Here we face, therefore, the limits of the purely rational conception of our existence. (AESCI pp. 41-42)."

Part II
The Purpose of Human Life

In this part I shall examine the response of my subjects to the question of whether human life has a definite purpose. Freud observes that the question of whether or not human life has a purpose has been asked time and again; that it has never been met with a satisfactory answer; and that perhaps it does not admit of such an answer. Freud proposes instead an examination of the behaviour of human beings and an investigation into what they demand of life and what they wish to attain in it. This way, he argued, it is possible to practically determine the purpose and object of human life. According to Freud, human beings fundamentally desire to be happy and to remain so. Moreover, he identifies two fundamental and opposing human instincts—the sexual instinct and the instinct of death and destruction—the gratification of which is indispensable to human happiness. The first instinct manifests itself primarily in the form of sexual love, while the other manifests itself in the form of inward and outward aggression. The natural tendency of the instinct of sex is to preserve the organic substance and to bind it into ever-larger units whereas the tendency of the instinct of death is to dissolve these units and to reinstate their antecedent inorganic state. These two instincts are inherently opposed to one another, and what can be perceived as a normal state of mind is the result of the tension between them being maintained at equilibrium. Freud claims that the value human beings attach to anything with which they come into contact depends on its relation to these two primary instincts.

Einstein believed that since human life is causally dependent on infinite primary and secondary causes, it cannot have a definite purpose, but that human beings are uniquely endowed with the faculty of consciousness and a "cosmic religious feeling" which give their existence the illusion of purpose. This illusion can give meaning to life if human beings aim to (1) pursue knowledge, desiring to comprehend the mind of God and to love God, and (2) develop a sense of duty desiring to serve others rather than being served by others. On the contrary, he argues, human selfishness and human passions can obscure and eventually destroy the illusion of purpose and make existence intolerable.

Dostoevsky believed that human life has a definite purpose but maintained that this question cannot be answered rationally and definitely because life on earth is incomplete, providing merely a glimpse of and being the temporary aspect of, the true and everlasting life. According to Dostoevsky, the comprehension of the purpose of human existence must therefore necessarily entail faith. He compared human life with a seed that is taken from a different world and planted on earth. Without the knowledge of the other world, it is impossible to sufficiently understand the tree and its significance as well as the direction towards which it grows. Dostoevsky believed that the Bible contains unique and trustworthy revelations about the purpose of human life as well as the other world. In his great books Dostoevsky created rebellious characters who reject the biblical ideas of human freedom, love, and immortality; in doing so, however, they also reject the existence of good and evil and undertake practical experiments, which involve living a life contrary to biblical ideals. In the process, they obliterate commonly accepted notions of beauty, human dignity, compassion, and justice. In the final analysis, these characters make life on earth impossible, for themselves and those they interact with.

Tolstoy too believed that human life on earth has a purpose, but that the quality of one's own life determines whether, and to what extent, this purpose may be discovered. He refers to the falsity of everyday human life and how it tends to obscure the ability to discover and appreciate truth. He introduces great and sudden changes in the lives of his major characters in order to bring them into the consciousness of the significance of life. Through this process, some of them engage with God and begin to internalise the *Sermon on the Mount*, which becomes their purpose in life; some of them succeed in adapting their life style to their circumstances and continue to live without ever discovering the true essence and worth of their life; still others become more convinced and acutely conscious of the futility of life and put an end to their own.

Freud

The question whether human life has a definite purpose, Freud writes in *Civilisation and Its Discontents*, has been asked times without number, has never received a satisfactory answer, and perhaps, does not admit of such an answer. Freud proposes instead an indirect approach to address the question, which is, to investigate the behaviour of human beings and what they demand of life and wish to attain in it. This investigation yields an objective outcome, Freud maintains. Accordingly, human beings' primary purpose is to be happy and to remain so. Happiness, Freud maintains, has two essential features, namely, the attainment of pleasure and the avoidance of pain. When the aim is the avoidance of pain, happiness corresponds to peace. Depending on the psychological disposition of a person, one may pursue both of these goals with equal or variable intensity or one of them exclusively. The pursuit of happiness is an innate and strong tendency in human beings and manifests itself right from infancy. Freud broadly classifies the obstacles which frustrate this aim into four categories, two of them innately related to personal constitutions and the other two arising from the external world. Thus, firstly, happiness is intrinsically ephemeral; the longer it lasts the further diluted it becomes and the less appealing it is for human beings. For happiness to attain its most desirable intensity it has to be instantaneous, since human beings are so constituted that they can only enjoy intense contrasts. From this it follows that the capacity to experience happiness on a perpetual basis is constrained from the outset by human nature. Secondly, happiness requires the proper acquisition of sensory information (even the love of books or the love of music involve the senses of sight and hearing, respectively); but the biological faculties by which pleasurable feelings can be experienced are subject to deterioration and dissolution.

Thirdly, powerful and pitiless forces from the external world (nature) assail or constantly threaten to assail human beings and their dearest objects of pleasure. "It is true that nature would not demand any restrictions of instinct from us, she would let us do as we liked; but she has her own particularly effective method of restricting us. She destroys us—coldly, cruelly, relentlessly, as it seems to us, and possibly through the very things that occasioned our satisfaction."[1] Fourthly, human beings experience pain from their relations with other fellow human beings. "We never have so little protection against suffering as when we are in love; we are never so desolate as when we have lost the object of our love or its love for us."[2] Freud classically concludes that human beings are inclined to be unhappy rather than to be happy; indeed, "one is inclined to say that the intention that man should be 'happy' has no part in the plan of 'creation'".[3]

So, human existence is tasked from the very outset with achieving two types of goals, primary and secondary. The primary goals are the gratification of instinctual needs whereas the secondary goals are the removal or avoidance of obstacles which stand between human beings and the primary goals. Over the course of time, these two types of goals intermingle with each other so often and in such a complex manner that it is not easy to cleanly distinguish one from the other. Indeed it is out of psychological necessity that primary goals should be absorbed or modified by secondary goals in order to make existence tenable. According to Freud, the impediment or failure of this process often leads to psychological disorders such as neurosis, paranoia, delusion, hysteria, and psychosis.

In the same way that a quantum physicist strives to identify the basic particles constituting an atom, Freud, too, tried to

---

[1] PRPHI (Freud, S. *The Future of an Illusion*) p. 115.
[2] SFCIV p. 20.
[3] Ibid. p. 14.

determine the primary instinctual needs, the gratification of which is vital for human happiness and healthy mental development. Freud asserts that there are two such fundamental instinctual needs; all the other needs being either the modifications or the masking of them or needs which are derived from them. The first is associated with the sexual instinct and the second is associated with the instinct of death. These two instincts are inherently opposed to one another and what we perceive as a normal state of being is the result of the tension between these two forces being maintained at equilibrium. When the equilibrium is disturbed, it creates ambivalence, and ambivalence manifests itself in the form of a sense of guilt and anxiety. The natural tendency of the sexual instinct is to preserve the organic substance and to bind it into ever-larger units, whereas the tendency of the instinct of death is to dissolve these units and to reinstate their antecedent inorganic state. The typical manifestation of the instinct of death is aggression, inward (directed towards self) as well as outward (directed towards others). "The reality behind all this, which many would deny, is that human beings are not gentle creatures in need of love, at most able to defend themselves if attacked; on the contrary, they can count a powerful share of aggression among their instinctual endowments. Hence, their neighbour is not only a potential helper or sexual object, but also someone who tempts them to take out their aggression on him, to exploit his labour without recompense, to use him sexually without his consent, to take possession of his goods, to humiliate him and cause him pain, to torture and kill him."[4]

Human beings are equally aggressive towards themselves, Freud maintains, and proposes different models by which he attempts to explain the interrelationship between inward aggression, on the one hand, and self-consciousness, fear of

---

[4] Ibid. P. 48.

punishment, sense of guilt, and conscience, on the other. According to these models, inward aggression is the redirection of an outward aggression by the psychological processes of *internalisation* and *identification*. (I shall return to this subject shortly in more detail).

Freud rejects the existence of absolute right and wrong, good and bad, as well as the existence of an intrinsic capacity in human beings to appreciate goodness and beauty[i]. In the psychic realm what human beings consider as good amounts to the gratification of their instinctual needs whereas the bad consists of the obstacles hindering them from achieving this gratification. Seemingly intrinsic values such as the love of justice and beauty or the love of children or humanity in general can be explained in terms of the basic instincts, Freud claims. Likewise, regrets or remorse for harms or wrongs done to others arise not because the transgressor has an innate capacity to recognise and acknowledge a wrong for what it is worth rather because of fear of punishment and the loss of love:

> In the first place, if we ask how a person comes to have a sense of guilt, the answer we receive cannot be gainsaid: one feels guilty (pious people would say "sinful") if one has done something one recognises as 'evil'. Then we realise how little this tells us. ... Even a person who has done no wrong may consider himself guilty—which raises the question of why in this case the intention is equated with the deed. Both cases presuppose that we have already recognised evil as reprehensible, as something that should not be carried out. How do we arrive at such judgement? We may reject the notion of original—as it were, natural—capacity to distinguish between good and evil. Evil is often far from harmful or dangerous to the ego; it may even be something it welcomes and takes pleasure in. Here, then is a pointer to

an outside influence, which determines what is to be called good or evil. As a person's own feelings would not have led him in this direction, he must have a motive for submitting to this outside influence. This is easily discovered in his helplessness and dependency on others; it can best be described as a fear of loss of love. If he loses the love of a person he depends on, he is no longer protected against various dangers; above all, he is exposed to the risk that this more powerful person will demonstrate his superiority by punishing him. At first, then, evil is something for which one is threatened with loss of love; it must therefore be avoided. Hence, it hardly matters whether one has already done something wrong or merely intends to; in either case the danger arises only if the supervising authority finds out, and in either case the authority would behave in the same way. This state of mind we call a 'bad conscience', but it really does not merit the name, for at this stage consciousness of guilt is clearly no more than a fear of loss of love, a social anxiety.[5]

Freud returns to his theory of the murdered primal father to explain the emergence of justice. The primal family, where only the father enjoyed instinctual freedom and all the other members lived in slavish thraldom, represents the extreme social condition in which a minority enjoys cultural privileges whilst the majority is denied them. The primal father must certainly have been a terrifying figure, exhibiting the utmost degree of aggression and cruelty when his pleasure was affected, which eventually induced the brothers to unite and revolt against him. The strength of this united body then opposed as *right* the strength and rule of the father, who was condemned as a *brute*, mirroring the age old struggle and revolt

---

[5] Ibid. pp. 61-62.

of the oppressed masses against the oppression and brutality of the minority or the individual tyrant. After the primal father had been defeated and savagely murdered and thus removed from power, the brothers decided to renounce individual power for the sake of communal rule, warranting a peaceful and sustainable coexistence. "The replacement of the power of the individual by that of the community is the decisive step towards civilization," Freud explains. "Its essence lies in the fact that the members of the community restrict themselves in their scope for satisfaction; whereas the individual knew no such restriction. Hence, the next requirement of civilisation is *justice*—that is, the assurance that the legal order, once established, shall not be violated again in favour of an individual."[6]

Freud refers to the additional inhibitions the brothers introduced upon their community following the murder of the primal father (monogamy and the prohibition of sexual relations within one's own family) to explain how the love of children and humanity developed therefrom. Accordingly, these loves are essentially erotic attractions by nature, but the ego, anticipating conflict, frustration, loss, and pain in pursuing pleasure, is forced to curb its sexual desire and transform genital love into a more acceptable and attainable familial love and friendship (broadly speaking, into affection). Freud calls this type of transformation *aim-inhibited* love. The love of humanity, Freud alleges, is likewise an aim-inhibited love, but here, unlike familial love, the ego aims to free itself from attachment to a particular object and chooses to love all human beings equally and "unconditionally". The underlying motivation may be different. For example, the ego may be afraid of being rejected by its love object or it may be afraid of losing it. In either case, by aiming to love instead of being loved

---

[6] Ibid. p. 32.

and by shifting its attachment from a concrete object to an abstract concept or entity, the ego avoids the uncertainties and disappointments of sexual love.

In the same manner, Freud identifies a connection between beauty, that is, "the beauty of human forms and gestures, of natural objects and landscape, of artistic and even scientific creations,"[7] and sexual instinct. Whilst he admits that psychoanalysis does not offer a definite answer as to the exact nature of this connection, he insists nevertheless that the enjoyment of beauty contains an erotic element in it. The ecstasy which can be experienced from the appreciation of beauty, Freud maintains, is derived from the realms of sexual sensation. "The love of beauty is a perfect example of a feeling with an inhibited aim. Beauty and attraction are first of all the attributes of a sexual object."[8]

The two primary instincts are impossible to gratify in their natural form. Indeed, right from the beginning human beings learn to replace the *"pleasure principle"* by the *"reality principle"*, because the path to pleasure leads them to suffering and anxiety. The *reality principle*, on the other hand, is a mechanism by which the demands of the basic instincts are reconciled with or moderated by the demands of external surroundings and involves the masking and inhibition of the original aim when it becomes unattainable.

> The programme for attaining happiness, imposed on us by the pleasure principle, cannot be fully realised, but we must not—indeed cannot—abandon our efforts to bring its realisation somehow closer. To reach this goal we may take very different routes and give priority to one or the other of two aims: the positive aim of gaining pleasure or the negative one of avoiding its opposite. On neither

---

[7] Ibid. p. 20.
[8] Ibid.

routes can we attain all we desire. Happiness, in the reduced sense in which it is acknowledged to be possible, is a problem concerning the economics of the individual libido. There is no advice that would be beneficial to all; everyone must discover for himself how he can achieve salvation. The most varied factors will come into play and direct his choice. It is a question of how much real satisfaction he can expect from the external world, how far he is led to make himself independent of it, and, finally, how much strength he feels he has to change it in accordance with his wishes. Apart from the external conditions, what will be decisive here is the individual's mental constitution.[9]

Freud categorised the human psychic constitution in the following way, even though a clean separation between these categories is difficult to make: the erotic, the narcissistic, and the "man of action". The erotically disposed person places emotional relations with others before everything else. The narcissist, who is the most self-sufficient of the three personality types, places independence from any external object or persons above everything else and seeks internal gratification through the inner workings of "his own soul". The "man of action" never abandons the external world in which he or she can assert his or her power.
The classification gives a hint as to which of the two basic instincts is predominant in a person. In the erotically disposed, the sexual instinct is dominant (hence, the outstanding artist and the saint are essentially erotically disposed, according to Freud); in the narcissist, the tension between the instincts of love and death tends to be at a balance (the successful narcissist most likely becomes a brilliant scientist or a philosopher later in

---

[9] Ibid. pp. 20-21.

life); in the "man of action", the dominant instinct is the instinct of death (or aggression). When successfully internalised, the instinct of death can become constructive and even indispensable, Freud explains, in which case it can be directed towards subduing nature as well as leading an organisation, a mission, a political party, or a country.

Freud offers several hypotheses to explain how the instinct of aggression, despite its inclination to disintegrate and destroy life, can become innocuous or even amenable to life. These hypotheses assume the existence of a superego, which emerges early in life as an extension of the ego and closely censures the ego's attitudes and actions. Freud assumes that human beings' apparent harshness towards themselves can best be explained by regarding their harshness either as a redirected or inverted aggression, which they must have once disposed towards others and the external world, or as the internalisation of an external aggression directed towards them. In the first hypothesis, the instinct of aggression is activated when first the child experiences prohibitions at the hands of a parent (or an authority) as it attempts to gratify an important need (masturbation). The frustration produces intense anger and a desire to take revenge, but this desire, too, must be forfeited, for the child is physically weak to execute its desires. To discharge its aggression, a psychological faculty will automatically emerge in the child by extending its ego to become the superego. When this is achieved, the ego takes the place of the parent through the process of identification and the superego, assuming the role of the child, punishes the ego (now the representation of the parent) with the same propensity to harsh aggressiveness towards the ego that the ego would have liked to enjoy against the parent. So, the aggression once directed outward (towards the parent) is now directed inward (towards self) by the complex interplay of the psychological mechanisms of internalisation, displacement, and identification.

The second hypothesis maintains the same source-sink relationship in the transfer of aggression in the psychic realm (aggression is still directed from the superego (the source) towards the ego (the sink)) but reverses the roles taken by the ego and the superego (it will become clear later that this model is particularly proposed to explain the existence of a superego in women). As in the first model, the superego is the aggressor but here it comes into being as a result of the child absorbing into itself the invulnerable authority of the parent. Other approvals, aspirations, criticisms, and prohibitions the child upholds as standards and ideals in its early stages of psychological development are likewise absorbed and contribute to the constitution of the superego. The ego remains what it always was whereas the external authority is now represented by the superego, through the process of internalisation. The aggression with which the superego assails the ego is therefore the aggression of the parent. The aggression of the superego, however, is harsher and can be provoked even by ill intentions even though they are not yet committed. This is because the superego, existing in the same mental sphere wherein the ego resides, is omnipresent and omniscient and sees and knows everything upon which the ego is intent or wishing to do, whereas the external authority can punish only wrongs that are actually committed. The aggression of the superego in both theories is further reinforced by the ego's secret wish for punishment, which is produced by the awareness of guilt. Essentially, it, too, is a form of aggression, an inwardly directed death instinct.

The difficulty of discharging the basic instinctual impulses, due to prohibitions imposed by external and internal aggressions, compels the ego to invent socially acceptable and personally economical alternative channels and to accommodate a certain degree of perpetual privation. Thus, neurosis is a psychological disorder arising from the ego's inability to invent new ways or to tolerate the privation. Indeed, the psychological state of human beings, strictly speaking, is never to be regarded as *normal* or *abnormal*, for the boundary between these two states is never distinct nor permanent, this becoming easier to notice when the demand of the basic impulses stand in a stark contrast with socially and culturally defined behavioural thresholds. "The neuroses exhibit on the one hand striking and far-reaching points of agreement with those great social institutions, art, religion and philosophy," writes Freud in *Totem and Taboo*. "But on the other hand they seem like distortions of them. It might be maintained that a case of hysteria is a caricature of a work of art, that an obsessional neurosis is a caricature of a religion and that a paranoia delusion is a caricature of a philosophical system."[10]

Freud, who for much of his life, experienced first-hand the aggression and brutality of the Nazis, believed that one of mankind's greatest sources of grief is the unbridled gratification of the instinct of death through external and internal aggression, in direct contradiction to his earlier claim that the gratification of the instinct of death can be pleasurable to them. He himself did not see a contradiction in this, though, for he maintains that human beings enjoy inflicting pain on others, but normally do not enjoy it when pain is inflicted upon them. Moreover, Freud is "pro-life", even though he does not explain why gratifying the instinct of life is good but gratifying the instinct of death is bad. In order for life to prevail, Freud offers two recommendations: Firstly, a certain degree of sublimation of the death instincts is required so as to reduce external conflict and, secondly, the ego should be trained to trust and rely on the superego (as long as the demands of the latter are reasonable), so as to avoid internal conflict. Considering their

---

[10] SFTOT p. 55.

inaptitude for discipline and hard work, however, Freud warned, human beings may not be able to fully succeed to transform aggressive impulses into productive impulses; in which case, coercion should be admissible, so that the masses can be induced (by punishment) to renounce aggression. But Freud sees difficulties with the implementation of coercion. Technically, individuals in possession of exceptional intellectual endowment and who manage to willingly renounce aggression and are looked upon by the masses as their role model, should be entrusted with the power to subdue the masses; these individuals, however, for fear of losing their influence over the masses, will eventually give way to their demand more readily than the masses give way to them. For this reason, the leaders should be fully independent and disinterested. But these are character traits no human being possesses.

Furthermore, Freud asserts that in the same way the superego comes into being in an individual psyche, it also comes into being in the collective psyche of a group of people living together or in a society having shared values. In the absence of such a superego strict laws and direct coercion is the only means to bridle outward aggression originating from within the society itself, but as the society's superego develops, its member collectively internalise the common values and laws (approvals and disapprovals), and the social superego begins to exercise inward coercion when these are violated. Whereas the superego of a child predominantly absorbs the authority of its parents, the social superego absorbs the authority of its powerful personalities which make strong impression in its collective consciousness:

> The superego of a cultural epoch has an origin not unlike that of the individual; it rests upon the impression left behind by the personalities of great leaders, people who were endowed with immense spiritual or intellectual power or in whom some human striving found its

strongest and purest, and hence often most one-sided, expression. In many cases the analogy goes even further, in that in their lifetime these figures were quite often, though not always, mocked and abused by others, or even cruelty done to death, just as indeed the primeval father did not attain divinity until long after he was done to death. The most poignant example of this fateful link is the figure of Jesus Christ—unless this figure is mythological and was called into being on the basis of an obscure memory of that primeval event.[11]

Thus, in the same way the personal superego may impose unreasonable demands and restrictions upon the ego, the cultural superego, too, may impose upon the ego unreasonable demands and restrictions, without taking its psychological constitution into consideration, which then becomes a sources of immense grief:

> The study and treatment of neuroses lead us to level two reproaches against the individual superego: in the severity of its precepts and prohibitions it shows too little concern for the happiness of the ego, in that it fails to take sufficient account of the forces that oppose compliance with them, the instinctual strength of the id, and the difficulties that prevail in the real environment. For therapeutic purposes we are therefore often obliged to oppose the superego and attempt to lower its demands. We can make quite similar objections to the ethical demands of the cultural superego. This too is insufficiently concerned with the facts of man's physical constitution; it issues a commandment without asking whether it can be obeyed. It assumes that it is psychologically possible for the human ego to do whatever is required of it, that the ego has absolute

---

[11] Ibid. p. 78.

control over the id. This is an error. Even in people who are called normal, control of the id cannot be increased beyond certain limits. To demand more is to provoke the individual to rebellion or neurosis, or to make him unhappy. The commandment 'Love thy neighbour as thyself' is the strongest defence against human aggression and an excellent example of the un-psychological manner in which the cultural superego proceeds. It is impossible to keep this commandment; such a huge inflation of love can only lower its value, not remove the problem. ... How potent an obstacle to civilisation aggression must be if the defence against it can cause as much unhappiness as the aggression itself![12]

Among the prohibitions causing the greatest frustration and, hence, the greatest grief, in human beings, are cultural prohibitions on the sexual instinct. Freud admits that these prohibitions are not entirely the work of the social superego. Indeed, the importance of the sexual life of civilised people as a source of happiness, and hence, as a means to fulfil the purpose of life, has perceptibly diminished, not only due to cultural pressure, but also "something inherent in the function itself denies us total satisfaction and forces us on to other paths."[13] Freud refers to the various psychological maladies to which modern human beings are exposed due to sexual deprivation and pointedly attacks Christianity for its insistence on monogamy, as a result of which, Freud claims, the sexual life of civilised society is seriously disabled and is becoming atrophied in the same way organs like our teeth and our hair seem to be. "After all, the sexual life of civilised man has been seriously damaged; at times one has the impression that as a function it is subject to a process of involution, such as our teeth and our

---

[12] SFCIV p. 79.
[13] Ibid. p. 41.

hair seem to be undergoing as organs. One is probably entitled to suppose that its importance as a source of happiness—and therefore as a means to fulfil our purpose in life—has perceptibly diminished."[14] A return to greater possibilities of happiness would be possible, Freud purports, if the restrictions imposed upon the sexual instincts were to be abolished or greatly relaxed.[ii]

Since the time of Freud, the world has witnessed great cultural and sexual revolutions and yet it is a matter of dispute whether human beings have indeed achieved the great possibility of happiness which Freud had hoped. Furthermore, Freud's theory about the two basic human instincts, on the basis of which, as we have seen, many of his other theories are established, does not apply with equal significance to men and women. Indeed, Freud himself had admitted that he had established his theory essentially based on his observation and understanding of the male sex. At best, Freud regarded women as the *Dark Continent* (*der Schwarzer Kontinent*) in which case one can plausibly suppose that it cannot be known whether and to what extent the instincts of life and death are at work in women, and whether the life of women has an entirely different purpose. In some of the significant articles Freud published on women, most notably in his *Female Sexuality* (1931), he makes several claims about women which appear to have compatibility issues with his basic instincts and the purpose of human life. For example, Freud claims that even though up to the age of three or thereabout sexual development in both boys and girls is essentially masculine in nature (i.e., it is "active"), after the age of three, the sexual consciousness of a girl undergoes a fundamental transformation when she realises that her clitoris will not develop to become a penis. This realisation invokes in her feelings of failure (she feels as though she were a failed

---

[14] Ibid.

boy), inferiority, and envy, and a capacity for jealousy far surpassing that of a boy. An adult woman likewise regards herself as a castrated man. The consequence is far-reaching. To begin with, as a result of the "degeneration" of her clitoris into a "residual penis", Freud purports, the woman transits from being sexually active to being sexually passive and emotionally submissive[iii]. Secondly, whereas in a boy the superego emerges primarily as a result of the internalisation of parental disapproval of his masturbation and the threat of punishment by castration, this fear does not exist in a girl since she already feels castrated. Hence, her superego must come into existence as a consequence of something else, namely, from her experiences of upbringing and fear of losing her parents' love. Subsequently, the woman's superego "never becomes so inexorable, so impersonal, so independent of its emotional origins" and she "shows less sense of justice than man, less inclination to submission to the great exigencies of life, is more often led in her decisions by tender or hostile feelings."[15]

His outlook on female sexuality also obliged Freud to revise his theory of the Oedipal complex where he attempted to cohesively combine his hypothesis about the two basic instincts with his hypothesis about the child's desire (1) to have sexual relationship with its mother, (2) to regard its father as its rival, and (3) to nurse a death wish towards its father. The Oedipal complex essentially assumes that the child is masculine. Freud maintains that whereas the girl's pre-oedipal sexual attraction is towards her mother as well, after her discovery that she will not have a penis like a boy and that her genitalia will be invisible, she will reject her mother as her love object and transfer her sexual fantasy towards her father instead. But her detachment from her mother and attachment to her father is neither a seamless nor a painless process. As it were, it is at once an

---

[15] PG p. 516.

emotionally laborious and a complicated process. Obliged thus to perform two difficult tasks at the same time, as Peter Gay summarises, the woman is only too likely to suffer erotic shipwreck. "She becomes masochistic and humourless, gives up sex altogether and clings to her masculine traits, resigns herself to submissive domesticity."[16]

In conclusion, Freud's claim that the main purpose of human life is the gratification of the two basic instincts suffers from two types of contradictions. The first contradiction arises when Freud advised to nurture the instinct of life (the sexual instinct) and to sublimate or suppress the instinct of death (aggression) without giving sufficient reason as to why the gratification of the first instinct is desirable and the gratification of the second instinct is undesirable. The second contradiction arises due to the difficulty of giving equal significance to the two basic instincts in men and women as a result of which the two sexes seem to have different pursuits (or even purposes) in life.

---

[16] Ibid. p. 519.

Einstein

"What is the meaning of human life, or, for that matter, of the life of any creature?" asks Einstein rhetorically in an article he published in 1934. "To know an answer to this question means to be religious. You ask: Does it make any sense, then, to pose this question? I answer: The man who regards his own life and that of his fellow creatures as meaningless is not merely unhappy but hardly fit for life."[17] Elsewhere, he attempts to offer his view on the meaning of life: "Without deeper reflection one knows from daily life that one exists for other people, first of all for those upon whose smiles and well-being our own happiness is wholly dependent, and then for the many, unknown to us, to whose destinies we are bound by the ties of sympathy. A hundred times every day I remind myself that my inner and outer life are based on the labours of other men, living and dead, and that I must exert myself in order to give in the same measure as I have received and am still receiving."[18]

Einstein maintains that whether or not a human life has a meaning depends on how the individual conceives of his or her own life in relation to the lives of fellow human beings. A primitive human being in this regard is one whose life is entirely devoted to the gratification of instinctual needs. Whilst Einstein accepts that the gratification of basic needs is a legitimate and indispensable goal, he regards it nevertheless as an elementary goal. In this respect, the infantile and isolated consciousness of the primitive person regards self and its immediate demands as the most vital concerns in which all its awareness should be invested. Other people, depending on their distance from the self, are interesting to it insofar as they can be employed as tools by which the needs of the self can be

---

[17] AEIDE p. 13.
[18] Ibid. p.8.

gratified. Einstein terms this experience as a *delusion*. Consequently, for Einstein, the significance of every human endeavour and success, science, art, religion or even the cultivation of virtue, depend on the extent to which they are able to free the individual from the bondage of self and to empower them for the service of others:

> When we survey our lives and endeavours, we soon observe that almost the whole of our actions and desires is bound up with the existence of other human beings. We notice that our whole nature resembles that of the social animals. We eat food that others have produced, wear clothes that others have made, live in houses that others have built. The greater part of our knowledge and beliefs has been communicated to us by other people through the medium of a language, which others have created. Without language our mental capacities would be poor indeed, comparable to those of the higher animals; we have, therefore, to admit that we owe our principal advantage over the beasts to the fact of living in human society. The individual, if left alone from birth, would remain primitive and beast like in his thoughts and feelings to a degree that we can hardly conceive. The individual is what he is and has the significance that he has not so much in virtue of his individuality, but rather as a member of a great human community, which directs his material and spiritual existence from the cradle to the grave. A man's value to the community depends primarily on how far his feelings, thoughts, and actions are directed toward promoting the good of his fellows. We call him good or bad according to his attitude in this respect.[19]

The transition of the human mind from its initial and infantile state of disconnectedness from the rest of the universe to a

---

[19] Ibid. p. 13.

state of unity with the universe requires the exercise of four types of freedoms, Einstein explains: freedom from self, freedom of expression, freedom of time, and freedom of independence. The attainment of freedom from self begins by first realising that the gratification of the basic instinctual impulses is insufficient to make human beings happy. "In order to be content, human beings must also have the possibility of developing their intellectual and artistic power to whatever extent accords with their personal characteristics and abilities."[20] Einstein realised that intellectual and artistic pursuits may not necessarily make human beings happier or nobler or more socially amenable, but he was also persuaded that without intellectual and artistic nourishments no true liberation from self could be attained.

Freedom of expression is vital, according to Einstein, first and for most, to sustain life on earth. "Those instrumental goods which should serve to maintain the life and health of all human beings should be produced by the least possible labour of all."[21] But this goal requires the free, fast, and unrestricted dissemination of all types of scientific knowledge. "By freedom I understand social conditions of such a kind that the expression of opinions and assertions about general and particular matters of knowledge will not involve dangers or serious disadvantages for him who expresses them. This freedom of communication is indispensable for the development and extension of scientific knowledge, a consideration of much practical import."[22] Whereas putting laws in place to uphold freedom of expression is an essential step, Einstein insists that it is insufficient, for it equally requires the intellectual and emotional readiness of the members of the

---

[20] Ibid. P. 31.
[21] Ibid.
[22] Ibid. pp. 31-32.

society to accommodate differences and dissent, and to examine new and untried ideas.

The other dimension of freedom Einstein considers vital for the spiritual nourishment of the individual is freedom of time. He states that the human effort required to gratify physical needs and to support one's life should not reach to the extent that it deprives the individual the time as well as the strength he needs to pursue personal activities. Perhaps Einstein was recalling an argument between Lida and the phlegmatic painter in Chekhov's *The House with the Mezzanine* when he wrote his piece about freedom of time. In the story, Lida, the young, beautiful, and assiduous aristocrat, tries hard to improve the facilities of the local health care centres and to educate the poor children of her village, but for the landscape painter, the activities of this selfless young lady are a sickening reminder of the ignorance and perpetual self-deception of the gentry.

"Last week Anna died in childbirth. If there had been a dispensary nearby, she would still be alive..." she challenges him...

"What matters is not that Anna died in childbirth, but that all these Annas, Mavras, Pelageyas bend their backs from early morning till dark, get sick from overwork, tremble all their lives for their hungry and sick children, fear death and sickness all their lives, get treated all their lives, fade early, age early, and die in dirt and stench; their children grow up and start the same tune... The whole horror of their situation is that they have no time to think of their souls, no time to remember their image and likeness; hunger, cold, animal fear, a mass of work, like a snowslide, bar all the paths to spiritual activity, to what precisely distinguishes man from animal and is the only thing worth living for. You come to their aid with hospitals and schools, but that doesn't free them from bondage, but, on the contrary, enslaves them still more, because, by introducing new prejudices in their life, you increase the number of their needs, not to mention that they must pay ... for their little pills and primers, and that means bending their backs even more."

"...it's impossible to sit with folded arms... The highest and holiest task for a cultured person is to serve his neighbour, and we try to serve as we can..." Lida defends herself.

"Dispensaries, peasant literacy, book with pathetic precepts and jokes cannot diminish either ignorance or mortality, any more than the light from your windows can illuminate this huge garden," is the response the painter gives her. "The people must be free from heavy physical labour ... their yoke must be lightened, they must be given a respite, so that they don't spend their whole lives at the stove, the washtub, and in the field..."[23]

Lastly, and perhaps, the most important type of freedom for Einstein is the freedom of independence or individuality. Einstein labels the freedom of expression and the freedom of time as outward expressions of human freedom but freedom from self and the freedom of independence he regards them as inward freedom. The completeness of the individual's synthesis into the universal consciousness paradoxically requires their intellectual and artistic independence. Only a mind which can establish and maintain its originality, autonomy, and uniqueness can truly and uniquely nourish the universal body:

> It can easily be seen that all the valuable achievements, material, spiritual, and moral, which we receive from society have been brought about in the course of countless generations by creative individuals. Someone once discovered the use of fire, someone the cultivation of edible plants, and someone the steam engine. Only the

---

[23] ACSTO pp. 190-191.

individual can think, and thereby create new values for society, nay, even set up new moral standards to which the life of the community conforms. Without creative personalities able to think and judge independently, the upward development of society is as unthinkable as the development of the individual personality without the nourishing soil of the community. The health of society thus depends quite as much on the independence of the individuals composing it as on their close social cohesion.[24]

Einstein did not need to look far and wide for a concrete example by which he could demonstrate the essence and value of mental and emotional independence. His own academic carrier was distinctly marked by originality, intellectual independence, and a series of audacious ventures into questioning and challenging well-established scientific traditions and fundamental axioms. As in his professional life, his personal life, too, was marked by unmistakable emotional aloofness and independence. He not only was aware of his detached scientific and emotional personalities, but also accepted them as healthy and necessary parts of his being:

> My passionate sense of social justice and social responsibility has always contrasted oddly with my pronounced lack of need for direct contact with other human beings and human communities. I am truly a "lone traveller" and have never belonged to my country, my home, my friends, or even my immediate family, with my whole heart; in the face of all these ties, I have never lost a sense of distance and a need for solitude—feelings which increase with the years. One becomes sharply aware, but without regret, of the limits of mutual understanding and consonance with other people. No doubt, such a person loses some of his innocence and

---

[24] AEIDE pp. 13-14.

unconcern; on the other hand, he is largely independent of the opinions, habits, and judgments of his fellows and avoids the temptation to build his inner equilibrium upon such insecure foundations.[25]

Einstein's elaborate elucidation of the various aspects of human freedom appears to be remarkable given his commitment to causal determinism, which excludes freewill and rests on the claim that the behaviours and actions of human beings are determined by natural laws. Indeed, Einstein himself was aware of this contradiction when he wrote: "I do not at all believe in human freedom in the philosophical sense. Everybody acts not only under external compulsion but also in accordance with inner necessity."[26] He turns to Schopenhauer to explain how he reconciles causal determinism with his notion of human freedom by quoting: "A man can do what he wants, but not want what he wants."[27] In this sense, he accommodates philosophical contradictions in the same way that he accommodates in physics the wave-particle duality of light and the massless nature of photons, which nevertheless have momentum and energy; namely, by accepting the limitation of the human mind to comprehend the divine mind.

Einstein was not the first determinist who nevertheless accommodated the idea of human freedom. Indeed, Spinoza, the great determinist devoted an entire chapter (Part IV) in his *Ethics*, where he unfolds in meticulous detail and precision his proof of the compatibility of causal determinism with human freedom and the notion of human bondage.

Even though Spinoza rejects the biblical view of God, he maintains that the human mind and body are expressions of one and the same thing, which is the essence of God. The only difference between the mind and the body is that the former is

---

[25] Ibid. p. 8.
[26] Ibid.
[27] Ibid.

causally determined or conditioned by *Thought* whereas the latter is causally determined by *Extension* (the reader may recall that *Thought* and *Extension* are the two attributes of God by which he can be conceived). In the same way the two attributes of God do not causally interfere with one another, Spinoza maintains, the body and the mind are independent of one another. The popular belief that the mind governs the body or the body influences the mind is a misconception as far as Spinoza is concerned. The temptation to regard the two entities as interdependent arises, Spinoza asserts, because they both ultimately point to one end, which is God, the prime cause of everything. In reality the body does not determine the mind's ability to think nor does the mind determine the body's capacity for motion or rest. For every physical motion the body undergoes there is a corresponding idea of that motion happening in the mind simultaneously, independently of the body's action[iv]:

> ...mental decision on the one hand, and the appetite and physical state of the body, on the other hand, are simultaneous in nature; or rather, they are one and the same thing which, when considered under the attribute of Thought and explicated through Thought, we call decision, and when considered under the attribute of Extension and deduced from the laws of motion-and-rest, we call a physical state (Part III, Proposition 2).[28]

For example, when the body feels hungry, the mind simultaneously conceives of the idea of hunger, because both the feeling and the idea of hunger have God as their causal source. When the body has fed enough, the mind conceives at the same time the idea of satisfaction. As the attribute Extension is the primary cause of all physical phenomena, so is the attribute Thought the primary cause of all ideas arising in or

---

[28] BSCOM p. 281.

conceived by the mind. Thus, the mind's conception of what is taking place in itself or outside of itself and the corresponding decisions to deal with them are both determined by, and subject to, infinite causes and effects in the realm of ideas. The mind does not and cannot choose what or how to think. It is not free to do so, because it does not possess absolute or freewill. Instead, it is determined to will in one way or another by a cause which is also determined by another, and this again by another, and so on to infinity. The same is true of emotions. In the same way definite causes are assignable to ideas and physical phenomena, definite causes are assignable to emotions, Spinoza maintains. Hence, an understanding of these causes and their properties leads to the understanding and the proper perception of emotions. And yet, Spinoza specifies two conditions under which the mind can either attain a certain degree of freedom or suffer the penalty of bondage:

> The supreme reward of the Divine Law is the law itself, namely, to know God and to love him in true *freedom* with all our heart and mind. The *penalty* it imposes is the deprivation of these things and bondage to the flesh, that is, an inconstant and irresolute spirit (*Theological-Political Treaties*).[29]

The two conditions referred to here are the passive and active states in which a human mind can be found. According to Spinoza, an active mind is one, which has adequate knowledge about all the links between a thing or an idea and its primary cause. A mind which does not possess adequate knowledge is passive. Passiveness with regard to something or some situation arises when the mind is incapable of conceiving it in its entirety without the aid of someone or something else. In which case, the mind does not simply accept its limitation and content itself with incomplete knowledge; instead, it makes up for the

---

[29] Ibid. p. 429.

missing knowledge by applying the faculty of imagination. Let us suppose, for example, someone is viewing a house under construction. If this person knows the intention of the builder, if for example, the person has seen the blueprint of the house, then the person can tell whether the construction is completed or not. If, the construction is completed, he or she can state that the house is perfect. Otherwise, the person can state that the house is imperfect. Here the semantics of *perfection* and *imperfection* are simply associated with the completion and incompletion of the house, respectively, with respect to the intention of the builder. But if the person does not have the blueprint in the hand or does not know what the builder intends to do with the house, all he or she can do is compare the house with the image of their ideal house and judge whether the house is perfect or not perfect. In this case, the word perfection is not the same as completion. The house may be completed and still the person may regard it as an imperfect house.

This appears to have been the original meaning of these terms. But when human beings began to form general ideas and to devise ideal types of houses, buildings, towers, and so on, and to prefer some models to others, it came about that each called "perfect" what he saw to be in agreement with the general idea he had formed of the said thing, and "imperfect" that which he saw at variance with his own preconceived ideal, although in the builder's opinion it had been fully completed. There seems to be no other reason why even natural phenomena (those not made by human hand) should commonly be called perfect or imperfect. For human beings are desirous to form general ideas both of natural phenomena and of manmade, and these ideas they regard as models, and they believe that Nature (which they consider does nothing without an end in view) looks to these ideas and holds them before herself as models. So when they see something occurring in Nature at variance with their preconceived ideal of the thing in question, they believe that Nature has then failed or blundered and has left that thing imperfect. So we see that human beings are in the habit of calling natural phenomena perfect or imperfect from their own preconceptions rather than from true knowledge. ... Nature does not act with an end in view; that the eternal and infinite being, whom we call God, or Nature, acts by the same necessity whereby it exists. ... Therefore, just as he does not exist for an end, so he does not act for an end; just as there is no beginning or end to his existing, so there is no beginning or end to his acting. What is termed a "final cause" is nothing but human appetite insofar as it is considered as the starting point or primary cause of something. ... human beings are commonly ignorant of the causes of their own urges ... they are conscious of their actions and appetites but unaware of the causes by which they are determined to seek something (*Ethics*, Part IV, Preface).[30]

As far as the human mind is concerned, its major sources of knowledge can be either the links leading to the attribute of Extension or the links leading to the attribute of Thought. The former primarily relies on sensory perception whereas the latter relies on rational analysis. Spinoza regards sensory knowledge inferior to rational knowledge. For the ordinary mind, the body is its source of knowledge, through its interaction with the external world and the affects resulting from the interaction. Spinoza collectively regards as the affects (*affectus*):
a) the actions which the body exerts on other objects,

---

[30] Ibid. pp. 320-321.

b) the actions which are exerted on the body by other objects, and,
c) the resulting emotional experiences.

The affects generate qualitative sensory information, which is imprecise, unordered, conflicting, and random, and is limited in scope to spatial and temporal dimensions only. As a result, the knowledge the mind can obtain from this information is inherently inadequate for establishing definite ideas about the body as well as the external world. An idea about something becomes definite when the mind determines not only what the thing is but also how and why it exists. A definite idea enables the mind to grasp the true significance of the thing with respect to eternity. Spinoza insists that for the mind to establish definite ideas, it has to set itself free from the influence of the affects and rely on discursive and inferential reasoning.

In order to indicate the inadequacy of sensory knowledge (or, in general, knowledge coming from experience) and how it can become a cause of bondage, Spinoza makes a careful analysis of the human emotions and how they are related to the mind. Accordingly, human beings are driven by an innate impulse (conatus) to indefinitely preserve their existence. This impulse is an integral component of their essence and expresses itself in the form of physical or mental activities. Spinoza calls it *will* when it is regarded with respect to the mind and *appetite* (appetitus) when it is regarded with respect to both the body and the mind (as long as the mind is conscious of the appetite). The human mind has the unique ability of perceiving the state of the body, but this ability brings with it freedom and oppression.

Any perception of the mind pertaining to the state of the body as a whole can be interpreted in terms of the existential impulse. If this impulse is threatened, the mind perceives it as pain. If it is strengthened or reinforced, the mind perceives it as pleasure. If this impulse is undergoing its natural course (desiring and seeking), the mind can perceive it as appetite or desire (cupiditas), depending on its own level of consciousness. If the mind perceives the condition of the body but itself is unaware of its perception, it is simply understood as an appetite. But if the mind is conscious of the condition of the body and its own awareness, then it is understood as desire (cupiditas). Any perceived emotion by the mind can be translated into either pleasure or pain with the accompanying idea of the cause and timing of the emotion. For example, hope means an uncertain pleasure and fear means an uncertain pain. When a hope is fulfilled, it is transformed into confidence and when a fear comes to pass it is transformed into despair.

Spinoza identifies some challenges in relying on emotions as a source of knowledge. Firstly, emotions do not merely convey the state of the body to the mind but they also influence the mind to undergo a state transition. This is because whatever increases or diminishes the activity of the body, the idea of the same thing (in the realm of thought) increases or diminishes the power of the mind to think. In other words, if the mind perceives that the body is undergoing pain, with that perception it transits from an active state to a passive state. The transition produces mental distress, which is the equivalence of physical pain. Secondly, since perception is directional (what is visible to person A may not be visible to person B if the two are standing at different locations), the mind's perception of the state of the body may be incomplete or inaccurate as a result of which wrong emotions (as ideas) can be produced. Thirdly, wrong emotions stir wrong desires that tend to oppose the existential impulse and eventually endanger its aim to subsist. Because the body can be assailed by too many external and potentially uncontrollable and incomprehensible causes (forces), reliance on emotions as primary indicators of the true state of the mind or of the body or of reality in general makes the mind passive and inconstant. Spinoza refers to this condition as *bondage*.

The only way to set the mind free from the bondage of emotions is to pursue virtue. Spinoza uses virtue and power synonymously. Both mean vesting the mind with adequate (rational) knowledge, so that it can transcend into an active state ("By virtue and power I mean the same thing; that is virtue, insofar as it is related to man, is man's very essence, or nature, insofar as he has power to bring about that which can be understood solely through the laws of his own nature[31]").[v] An active mind may not change the course of events, as they are causally determined by God, but understands the necessity and significance of their occurrence and embraces them with equanimity. It is neither inordinately despondent nor overconfident of its fortune, whether it is bad (painful) or good (pleasing); instead, it rejoices in its internal harmony and serenity. Spinoza calls this state blessedness, as opposed to bondage.

But knowledge produces a more desirable fruit, the love of God ("The mind's highest good is the knowledge of God, and the mind's highest virtue is to know God"). For Spinoza, love is a state of recognition and union. When we know something adequately, we recognise not only its essence, but also its causal link to its primary cause, one of God's attributes. Therefore, knowledge is a channel by which we get to know God intimately. The recognition entails the identification of eternity, necessity, order, intelligence, and perfection (completion). And in the end, knowledge produces acceptance.

Spinoza's definition of love, strictly speaking, rules out a disinterested love towards our neighbour. We love our neighbour for selfish reasons, for he is useful to us ("To act in absolute conformity with virtue is nothing else in us but to act, to live, to preserve one's own being (these three mean the same) under the guidance of reason, on the basis of seeking

---

[31] Ibid. p. 323 (*Ethics*, Part IV).

one's own advantage (Ethics, Part IV, Proposition 24)")[32] Disinterested love is possible towards God only, Spinoza maintains. Knowing that no action, inaction, attitude, or circumstance induces God to change the course of nature in our favour, we love him for what he truly is, without expecting anything in return. Besides, Spinoza asserts that a weak emotion can be consumed by a strong emotion. Thus, as we grow more and more knowledgeable of God, our attachment to people, to things, and to self, grows weaker and weaker; in the end, it is inevitable that the love of God consumes all other loves, and at this stage man is said to be truly blessed. In this sense only Spinoza accommodates the concept of freedom applicable to the human mind.

Einstein's proposal to set human beings free from the confinement of everyday life is fundamentally in accord with Spinoza's *Ethics*. Developing a cosmic religious feeling essentially means to be able to comprehend beyond the tangible, material universe and all our ideas thereof. "I want to know how God created this world," he explains his deepest interest in his scientific quest. "I am not interested in this or that phenomenon, in the spectrum of this or that element. I want to know his thoughts. The rest are details."[33] At the same time, however, Einstein, unlike Spinoza, who is optimistic about the capacity of the human mind, realises the limit of human intellect; which is why he likens the attitude of even the most intelligent human being towards God to that of a child's which admires a multitude of books in a big library. The child realises that each book is written by someone but does not understand the content of each book. Moreover, Einstein realised that a cosmic religious feeling alone is insufficient for the attainment of human blessedness. Insofar as human beings

---

[32] Ibid. p. 333.
[33] TF p. 177.

are social beings, the bondage or freedom of their fellow human beings necessarily affects them. Thus, human beings' greatest destiny is to serve others, Einstein emphasised repeatedly. This requires the identification of the need of others in oneself and the need of oneself in others. Consequently, Einstein's conception of human freedom involves the knowledge (love) of God and the service (love) of fellow human beings. If one considers these two as an abstract totality of human endeavour, Einstein claims, they are compatible with the essential theology of Moses and Jesus for both of whom the greatest commandment is to love God unreservedly and to love one's neighbour as one loves himself or herself.

Dostoevsky

Dostoevsky's belief about the purpose of human life reflects the Christian theology of sin, rebellion, suffering, sacrifice, redemption, and ultimate reconciliation with God. Dostoevsky conveys these notions both in small and big terms in all his novels. Interestingly, the characters in whom a major redemption work unfolds and comes to fruition, if at all, either have a difficult relationship with their earthly fathers or are fatherless[vi], epitomising both Dostoevsky's traumatised experience with his earthly father and the innate brokenness of human fatherhood in general and the disunity it begets in human personal and social life. Often this vital and shared fate attracts the characters, both consciously and unconsciously, towards each other and binds them together towards a common destiny, which is, (1) their redemption from sinfulness and death, and unity with one another as well as with God, or (2) their common destruction.

In *Crime and Punishment*, the two main characters, Raskolnikov and Sonia, are both fatherless and struggle in life because their fathers have left nothing to their family as a means of support. Sonia's father has died recently, after having led a wasteful and guilt-ridden existence. Sonia is driven to prostitution by her stepmother, whilst poverty compels Raskolnikov to drop out of the university and to commit murder. Sonia's image of fatherhood is restored when she looks up to God and accepts him as her ultimate and true father, whereas the image of God as a father figure is obliterated in Raskolnikov because of his poor image of earthly fathers. In *The Idiot*, the three main characters, Prince Myshkin, Nastasya Filipovna, and Rogozhin, are all fatherless. The epileptic and destitute Prince is an orphan and has very little recollection of his parents whereas Nastasya Filipovna is born into an aristocratic family, but she, too, becomes an orphan whilst still a child, and falls under the protection of a man of questionable character. Dostoevsky does not state it explicitly, but from the numerous hints he gives, it is reasonable to conjecture that her protector has sexually abused her since her formative years. She is consumed by shame and rage and suffers from a compulsion for self-destruction. Rogozhin's father has died shortly before the story begins. He has been a highly successful businessman, but also a cold, harsh, and exacting father. His relationship with his impulsive son has never been good, partly on account of Rogozhin's unbridled passion towards Nastasya Filipovna. The son finally runs away from home fearing for his life, but a month hardly passes before the father dies, leaving his son more than a million roubles as an inheritance.

Prince Myshkin and Rogozhin are intensely attracted towards Nastasya, the former out of pity and the latter out of sexual love. Perhaps in this scenario, more so than anywhere else in any other of Dostoevsky's novels, Freud's two innate and opposing human instincts, the *instinct of life* and the *instinct of destruction*, are ostensible to behold. Nastasya feels the Prince's pity as a force of strength investing her with the courage to forgive the past, to embrace the future, and to renew her faith in humanity. But this force cannot be received without first destroying the Prince, for she knows that pity alone cannot hold the two together forever. Rogozhin's love, on the other hand, diminishes her to the rank of a mere sexual object and forcibly binds her to the lurid past from which she desperately wishes to escape; this compounds her sense of inferiority and exacerbates her tendency to self-lacerate, fuelling her rage at the world and at herself and helplessly drawing her towards self-destruction.

In *The Devils*, one of the two main characters, Nicholas Stavrogin, grows up without a father. The other, Peter Verkhovensky, does not see his father, Stepan Verkhovensky, until he comes of age. Stepan Verkhovensky is employed to instruct the young Nicolas and to guide his social and intellectual developments, and indeed succeeds in "touching some of the deepest chords" in the heart of his pupil, and in stirring in him "the first and still vague sensation of that eternal and sacred longing which many a chosen spirit, having once tested and experienced it will never afterwards exchange for some cheap feeling of satisfaction."[34] Unfortunately, his liberal and unexamined ideas prove inadequate to the task of stilling the cravings of the young man, so that he is left with an abiding sense of emptiness and a want of meaning in his life.

In *The Brothers Karamazov*, Dostoevsky further develops the problem of earthly fatherhood, providing a more complete picture of its complex aspects and demonstrating the serious and disastrous consequences it has in the emotional, mental, and spiritual development of children. There are five main characters in *The Brothers Karamazov*—Fyodor Pavlovich Karamazov, the father, his three legitimate sons (Dmitri, Ivan, and Alexei), and Pavel Fyodorovich Smerdyakov, who is believed to be the illegitimate son of Fyodor Pavlovich Karamazov, but the latter neither admits nor seriously denies this fact; nor does Dostoevsky offer a definite answer to his readers. But Smerdyakov is informally adopted into the Karamazov household from infancy.

Fyodor Pavlovich Karamazov is "one of those senseless persons who are very well capable of looking after their worldly affairs and, apparently, nothing else"[35]. His dearest worldly affairs are money and women, for whose sake he goes to a great length and suffers ineffable humiliation. He destroys two marriages (both women lose their lives on account of him), abandons his three sons from childhood, and irredeemably tarnishes his dignity. At the beginning of the book, we find him

---

[34] FDDEV p. 54.
[35] FDBRO p. 3.

relentlessly scheming as how to seduce the woman with whom his son Dmitri is in love. It suffices to examine a single chapter (*The Old Buffon*) to realise the extent to which the father has fallen. He is inept at establishing any form of relationship because he neither recognises nor regards boundaries. He is intensely aware of the inferiority of his position and of his inadequacy to transform it. Each encounter with a fellow human being is to him a new descent into painful and embarrassing mockery, blasphemy, and buffoonery. He finds delight in humiliating himself as well as others.

Dmitri Karamazov, the eldest son, is wild and impulsive, although honest and generous. He has inherited the sensuality of his father, which is his constant trap and torment. If one were to scrutinise the lives of both men, one would be able to detect the onset and predict the outcome of a particular bad habit. Both of them are attracted to women and alcohol and easily succumb to dissipation. Dmitri is aware and fearful of his weakness, while Fyodor Karamazov has long given up all resistance. Within both of them is a desire to experience and submit to God. Whereas in the father this desire has degenerated into aimless inquiry and perpetual mockery, it remains strong and persistent in Dmitri. The old man's inherent sense of inferiority disrobes him of his sense of self-respect. Dmitri, on the other hand, tries to overcome his inferiority by maintaining a strong sense of dignity and a habitude of interminable self-reflection and self-reproach. The old man clings to money as his prime source of security and self-worth, whereas Dmitri disdains money altogether and wastes it on a grand scale.

Ivan Karamazov is the most intelligent member of the Karamazov family. He is young, educated, charismatic, independent, and proud. Emotionally, he is reserved and mildly depressed and distrustful of any form of emotional expression. He despises the excessive dissipation and lewdness of his father and his brother Dmitri and reacts to them by wishing both his father and his brother death ("one reptile will devour the other. And serve them both right, too."[36]). Ivan is an atheist and rejects the assertion that human suffering has a purpose. He believes that youth's curiosity carries one up to the age of thirty but beyond that life becomes an unbearable burden and, therefore, should be extinguished. But in spite of his gloomy outlook on life, Ivan is thoroughly a Karamazov and he is aware of it.

Alexei Karamazov is the hero of the book, but not in the usual sense of the word. Except for his excellent character, Alexei does not accomplish anything remarkable. But he is the lone flicker of light in a setting which is otherwise clouded by doubt, abject poverty, greed, mistrust, contention, rancour, and never ending division (between family members as well as members of the society). Wherever he goes, Alexei takes with him desperately wished for compassion, peace, moderation, forgiveness, hope, and unusual cheerfulness. Whereas people respect Ivan for his intellect, they respect Alexei for his heart; they are afraid of Ivan, but they are not afraid of Alexei at all; they are fearful of expressing their opinion in Ivan's presence, however they feel free and confident with Alexei.

Insofar as Alexei Karamazov can be taken as the hero of *The Brothers Karamazov*, Pavel Fyodorovich Smerdyakov is certainly its antagonist. Insofar as Alexi Karamazov is not a hero in the usual sense, Smerdyakov, too, does not enter into any conflict with the hero in the usual sense. In fact, we only find them in the same social setting twice, and even then, only briefly. The conflict between them is a conflict of values, signifying a battle between good and evil in the deepest spiritual sense.

Smerdyakov is the son of a mentally retarded woman who used to wander barefoot on the streets of the town. She is found to

---

[36] FDBRO p. 125.

be pregnant, but no one knows who the father is. One warm night in May, the servant of Fyodor Pavlovich Karamazov finds her groaning with pain in his master's garden.

> But the gate from the yard into the garden was locked at night, and there was no other way of entering it, for it was enclosed all round by a strong, high fence. Going back into the house, Gregory lighted a lantern, took the garden key … went into the garden in silence. There he heard at once that the groans came from the bathhouse that stood near the garden gate, and that they were the groans of a woman. Opening the door of the bathhouse, he saw a sight which petrified him. An idiot girl, who wandered about the streets and was known to the whole town by the nickname of Lizaveta Smerdyastchaya (Stinking Lizaveta), had got into the bathhouse and had just given birth to a child. She lay dying with the baby beside her. She said nothing, for she had never been able to speak.[37]

The woman dies, but the servant raises the child (Smerdyakov) in the household of Fyodor Pavlovich Karamazov. There are many hints and clues that can be pieced together by which one may assert that the Old Karamazov is indeed his biological father, but Dostoevsky refuses to give a definite answer.

Smerdyakov is described as a deeply insulted and injured personality. Cheerless, sullen, arrogant, implacable, and spiteful, his childhood passion is to hang and bury cats with diabolic solemnity. He is utterly incapable of showing or accommodating any humane emotions. He is moderately intelligent, but exceptionally perceptive and controlled. He understands the deepest motives and weaknesses of his victims and applies his whole mental strength to trap and destroy them. Smerdyakov is an atheist and a nihilist and incurably envious.

---

[37] FDBRO p. 84.

Being acutely self-conscious of the inferiority of his social position, he fails to acknowledge and appreciate the generosity and kindness of his guardian parents and of the simple girl who loves him and devotedly serves him.

The Brothers Karamazov is a parricide story and the struggle of his four sons to come to terms with inherited sin. The story takes place in a small town, so that the characters have ample opportunity to encounter each other. Dostoevsky wisely exploits each encounter to reveal new personality traits in his characters that can only be revealed through the encounter. (We are told plenty about Kuzma Samsonov but we may not know him for what he truly is until his brief encounter with Dmitri Karamazov.[38]) The greed and lasciviousness of the Old Karamazov excites the indignation of Dmitri Karamazov beyond measure. The intellectual aloofness of Ivan exacerbates the deep sense of inferiority in Smerdyakov and provokes spite and profanity in Fyodor Karamazov. The meekness and simplicity of Alexei Karamazov, on the other hand, kindle even in the old man a gentler spirit and a readiness to admit his wrongdoings, an attitude Fyodor Karamazov is barely capable of experiencing.

Interestingly, the Karamazovs do not know each other very well. The three legitimate sons are brought up in different places and by different people and never meet their father before they come of age. Speaking of Dmitri, Dostoevsky tells us that after the death of his first wife the father completely abandons his son, "not out of malice or matrimonial grievances, but simply because he [forgets] him."[39] The same will be the fate of Ivan and Alexei.

The only person who establishes a long-term relationship with Fyodor Karamazov is Smerdyakov. The boy grows up in his

---

[38] Ibid. pp. 334-343.
[39] Ibid. p. 5.

house to become his personal cook and confidant. The old man shows unusual sensitivity and something resembling compassion towards Smerdyakov. This reclusive and sullen boy eventually wins the trust of his master and begins to share intimate and personal secrets. He will effectively exploit these assets to murder the old man and to indubitably implicate Dmitri Karamazov in the murder.

Shortly after he becomes an adult and decides to enter a nearby monastery, Alexei Karamazov comes to town to receive a blessing from his father whom he has never met or seen before. Interestingly, the old man receives Alexei affectionately, consents to his wish, and invites him to come and visit him occasionally.

The relationship between the old man and Dmitri Karamazov is the most unharmonious relationship in the book. Dmitri Karamazov grows up in the belief that his father owes him a property belonging to his mother. Relationship between father and son is first established when Dmitri, who has been in the military, visits his father to claim his property. The father immediately recognises that his son is of an impulsive and coarse temperament; and that he is extravagant, having a vague and exaggerated expectation about his inheritance. He agrees to pay him the money in several instalments, a term the son readily accepts. Money starts to trickle in but with each arrival Dmitri is asked to sign some "incomprehensible" documents. Before long he learns with great consternation that he has actually received from his father all the money his property is worth and is no longer entitled to receive any more money. Thus Dmitri's dream of leading an independent life once he retires from the military comes to an end. Shortly before the fateful incident (the murder of Fyodor Karamazov), Dmitri comes to town once again to settle matters with his father, but soon father and son enter into bitter contention for a woman the father initially hires to corrupt his son.

During that time, Ivan Karamazov, who has just graduated from a university in Moscow and is intending to embark upon an extended trip to Europe, comes to town to visit his father "who had ignored him all his life, hardly knew him, never thought of him, and would not under any circumstances have given him money, though he was always afraid that his sons Ivan and Alexei would also come to ask him for it.[40]" No one knows the purpose of his visit but the young man decides to stay with his father and the two seem to be on the best possible terms.

Dmitri and Alexei immediately form a strong, spontaneous, affectionate, and cheerful bond. The big brother repeatedly expresses yearning to see his little brother whom he considers an angel and to whom he freely confesses his worst transgressions and wild jealousy. Alexei equally loves his brother and suffers with him because he sees the same distractive impulse in himself.

Dmitri and Ivan already know each other (though they have never seen one another before the fateful gathering). Dmitri once entrusts his fiancée Katerina Ivanovna to Ivan when he is still in the military and she is living in Moscow, where Ivan also studies. Soon Ivan and Katerina fall in love with each other, but Katerina refuses to acknowledge his love because she is proud and guilt-ridden. Dmitri, who regards himself as morally and intellectually unequal to both of them, passively encourages the love affair and quietly drifts away from his fiancée. The two are never truly in love with each other, on account of the insincerity of the foundation upon which their relationship is established. Ivan regards his brother as a "brute" and a "reptile" while Dmitri regards Ivan as a "riddle" and a "tomb".

Smerdyakov, though moderately intelligent, is by no means an original thinker. He does not have a philosophy of his own;

---

[40] Ibid. P. 12.

instead he absorbs Ivan's philosophy of life and interprets it literally. Ivan maintains that the conception of virtue originates from man's belief in immortality. If the belief were to be destroyed in man, then his entire notion of virtue, that living force which upholds the life of the world, would collapse completely. In which case nothing would be immoral, everything would be lawful, including cannibalism. Then egoism becomes the most natural and rational principle of life. Since Smerdyakov rejects God and immortality, he also rejects virtue.

Because Smerdyakov grows up in the servants' quarter, all the Karamazov brothers take him for a servant. Dmitri uses him as a spy and as an informer and often mistreats and terrifies him because of his jealousy and overpowering rage. Ivan keeps him at a distance and turns cold on his eagerness to show off his cleverness and his grasp of complex ideas. But Smerdyakov pays them, with the exception of Alexei Karamazov, in kind. He accepts Ivan's theory about virtue and decides to murder and rob the old man. First he entices Ivan into giving his consent, albeit implicitly, to the murder. Thereby Smerdyakov destroys Ivan's assumed intellectual independence and disinterestedness. Secondly, he skilfully manipulates the outrageous contention between the old man and Dmitri and through premeditated misinformation and misguidance ensnares Dmitri to take full responsibility for the murder.

The Brothers Karamazov is overtly a crime story, a story about the murder of a father and his falsely accused son. Its core theme, however, is deeply spiritual, dealing with sin, atonement, and redemption. This is apparent from the biblical verse Dostoevsky chose for the epigraph of the book, which is taken from the Gospel of John (John 12:24, KJV):

> Very truly I tell you, unless a kernel of wheat falls to the ground and dies, it remains only a single seed. But if it dies, it produces many seeds.

Readers who are acquainted with the New Testament would agree that in this verse Jesus is speaking about the inevitability of his own death, as a sacrifice for sin. Twice previously and at least once afterwards (John 3:14, John 8:28, John 12:32), we find Jesus speaking about his death on the cross and the redemptive power of his death, and foretelling that his death will bring many believers into the path of everlasting life. Joseph Frank, who is a scholar and biographer of Dostoevsky, asserts that Dostoevsky's theology of man is consistent with Eastern Orthodoxy rather than Augustinian (Western) tradition. Hence, according to Frank, whereas the Augustinian tradition regards man as "having fallen into irredeemable sin from a state of perfection before the fall", Eastern orthodoxy regards man as "having emerged into earthly life still imperfect and unformed."[41]

In my view, the Augustinian theology does not claim that sin is irredeemable. Indeed, St. Augustine in his *Confession* unequivocally declares that Jesus died to redeem sinners from eternal damnation. Furthermore, a closer investigation of *The Brothers Karamazov* reveals that Dostoevsky's theology of human life coincides with the theology of St. Augustine as well as Luther. This might sound ironic, considering Dostoevsky's repeated and harsh criticism of the Catholic and the Lutheran Churches in his books, and his unwavering devotion to and extravagant elevation of the Russian Orthodox Church. Yet, his criticism has to be regarded in its proper context. In the same way Prince Myshkin separates the catholic establishment (Catholicism) from the Catholic believers (in *The Idiot*) and directed his attack towards the former, Dostoevsky's quarrel with the Catholic and Lutheran Churches (particularly, with the Catholic Church) must be understood as a consequence of his strong disapproval of what he perceived as their unbiblical

---

[41] JF p. 411.

existential philosophy, namely, asserting influence through political and financial strength as opposed to through faith in Jesus Christ.

In *The Brothers Karamazov*, of the four people who are directly connected with the story and die, two of them, Father Zossima and the boy Ilyusha, die of natural causes. Fyodor Pavlovich Karamazov and Smerdyakov, however, die of unnatural causes. Smerdyakov, the illegitimate son of the old Karamazov and who was born in his garden, murders his father, whom he has been serving as a cook and confidant for a long time, and commits suicide. One may reasonably deduce that the epigraph of the book refers to these two characters.

The garden in which Smerdyakov is born is an allusion to the Garden of Eden where first sin, through the disobedience of Adam and Eve, entered into the world, according to the Old Testament (Genesis 3). In the same way the Bible does not explain how the Tempter made its way into the Garden to deceive Adam and Eve, Dostoevsky, too, does not tell us how Stinking Lizaveta managed to enter into the Karamazov Garden on that fateful day in May when she gave birth to her son. All we know is that "the gate from the yard into the garden was locked at night, and there was no other way of entering it, for it was enclosed all round by a strong, high fence."

The Bible maintains that after the fall (the disobedience of Adam and Eve), sin took permanent residence in the human soul, influencing its tendencies, motives, desires, and actions. The Bible also maintains that all the descendants of Adam and Eve inherit the sinfulness of Adam, the primal father. For example, when the prophet Nathan confronted King David after his adultery with Bathsheba and the death of her husband (2 Samuel 12), the King referred to his inherited sin during his prayer and confession in Psalm 51:5:

Surely I was sinful at birth, sinful from the time my mother conceived me.

The Apostle Paul in his epistles further develops the idea of inherited sin. Accordingly, in his Epistle to the Romans (6-8), Paul identifies two distinct entities which the human soul (personality) consists of, namely, the Old Man (παλαιὸς ἄνθρωπος) and the Flesh (σάρξ). There is also a third entity, which is not inherently a part of the human personality but resides in it and exercises control over both the Old Man and the Flesh. Paul describes the third entity as Sin and ascribes to it several properties which can be ascribed to an intelligent being only. Thus Sin is personified as a deceiver and a liar, a vicious slave master who rules and pays a terrible wage and eventually kills.

The Flesh resembles Freud's *ego*; it is through the Flesh a person's identity finds an expression. It consists of the intellectual and emotional faculties as well as the conscience. The Old Man, on the other hand, is an inherited personality bequeathing the Flesh its innate tendencies, motives, instincts, and desires. In other words, whereas the Flesh has a capacity to will and to desire, the Old Man generates an instance of a will and a desire in the Flesh; the Flesh has a capacity for motivation, but the old man generates a particular motive, and so on. The Old Man descends directly from Adam, the first man who admitted Sin into the human race. Sin resides in the Old Man and extends its rule to the Flesh. In the same way Freud's ego is the servant of largely unconscious and uncontrollable forces in the mind, the Old Man, too, is merely a servant of Sin whose control over the Old Man is complete, making the Old Man irredeemable. In his Epistle to the Ephesians (4:18-19) the Apostle Paul describes the Old Man as one who has been darkened in his understanding and has lost all sensitivity, having completely given itself over to sensuality, impurity, and greed. The Flesh exhibits similar attributes but it can be redeemed and regenerated. For this to happen, however, two conditions must be fulfilled, namely, the Old Man must relinquish its control over the Flesh by dying and the Flesh must surrender to God its control of the mind (φρονοῦσιν). When the Old Man dies, Sin loses its dwelling place in the mental realm and, consequently, its control over the Flesh entirely and the mind gains its true freedom and begins to comprehend spiritual reality.

The personalities of the main characters in Dostoevsky's *The Brothers Karamazov* fit into Paul's model of the human personality. The old Karamazov and Smerdyakov can be taken as representations of Paul's Old Man and Sin, respectively. Both of them will have to die, for there is no redemption for them. Their corruption is complete. Moreover, in Paul's model, Sin exists as long as the Old Man exists, it does not have a life of its own. Likewise, shortly after the death of the Old Karamazov, Smerdyakov commits suicide. The sensualist Dmitri Karamazov and the intellectual Ivan Karamazov can be regarded as representations of the faculties of emotion and intellect within the Flesh (or the natural man), respectively. They both feel disconnected, disunited, forlorn, and directionless, and suffer in their own way, but in the end they will be redeemed, after the death of the Old Karamazov and Smerdyakov. Alexei Karamazov, who is the full brother of Ivan Karamazov, is essentially the representation of the regenerated or the spiritual mind in Paul's model. The spiritual mind, according to Paul, attains genuine freedom by submitting to God.

In order to appreciate the magnitude of influence Smerdyakov exercises on the family of Karamazov, it is useful to consider the strength of the different bilateral relationships they form. Altogether one can consider ten distinct bilateral relationships in the family. The Old Karamazov maintains a strong relationship with Smerdyakov and Dmitri (a strong contention with Dmitri), a mild relationship with Ivan (largely negative) and a weak relationship with Alexei (largely positive). Dmitri maintains a strong relationship with the Old Karamazov, Smerdyakov, and Alexei; he is weakly related to Ivan through his fiancée, Katerina Ivanovna. Other than her, however, the two have little in common. They rarely come into conversation. Whilst Dmitri's relationship with Alexei is affectionate, with the Old Karamazov and Smerdyakov his relationship is intensely hostile. He regards them both with immeasurable contempt. Ivan has strong relationships with Smerdyakov and Alexei. His relationship with Smerdyakov is almost equal but opposite in its intensity to his relationship with Alexei. Smerdyakov exerts a destructive force on Ivan whereas Alexei's unconditional love and confidence in his brother exerts a force of life in Ivan. Alexei maintains a strong relationship with his two brothers, Dmitri and Ivan, and a distant relationship with his father. He maintains no relationship with Smerdyakov (he is almost indifferent to him). Thus, Smerdyakov maintains strong relationships with the Old Karamazov, Dmitri, and Ivan. He manages to destroy the Old Karamazov, to corrupt Ivan (morally), and to have Dmitri condemned as a parricide.

Smerdyakov carefully and skilfully sets up a plot and prepares Dmitri Karamazov to murder his father. When he realises that the plot is not moving as planned (Dmitri has no desire to kill his father), he carries out the murder himself, and still manages to indubitably implicate Dmitri in the murder. The entire chain of events, before and after the murder, piece by piece, work in favour of Smerdyakov and condemn Dmitri Karamazov as the parricide. Except for the brothers no one will be able to discern the truth about the murder, but the brothers shall know the truth, each in his own way. Dmitri knows because he has not killed his father. Ivan, who in the beginning is firmly convinced of Dmitri's crime, has in the end to learn the truth from Smerdyakov himself, after three separate interviews. Alexei knows from the very beginning, not objectively, but because of his faith in his brother Dmitri and because of his conviction that Smerdyakov is an incarnate of evil. The knowledge acquisition process of the brothers is consistent with Paul's personality types, namely, the source of knowledge for the Flesh is experience; for the carnal mind, it is rational enquiry, and for the spiritual mind, it is faith.

At the time Dostoevsky was writing *The Brothers Karamazov*, Tolstoy published *Anna Karenina*. Dostoevsky's reaction to *Anna Karenina* was mixed. Whereas he regarded the story of Levin appallingly passive, shallow, and egoistic, he was deeply moved by the story of Anna. From the review Dostoevsky wrote, it is possible to understand why he was moved: in the story of Anna, Dostoevsky discovered the same theme which had preoccupied him for a long time, namely, the problems of sin, suffering, self-destruction, forgiveness, and redemption:

> In Anna Karenina a view of human guilt and criminality is presented. People are taken in abnormal circumstances. Evil exists antecedently. Seized in a vortex of falsehood they commit crimes and inevitably perish. It deals, as we see, with a favourite and very ancient European theme. But after all how is the question solved in Europe? It is there solved always in one way. The first reply is that the law has been given, written, formulated, and constituted, during thousands of years. Evil and good are always defined and weighted. He who does not follow it, he who infringes it, pays with liberty, property, or life—pays literally and inhumanly. The other contrary reply is: Since society is abnormally arranged, it is impossible to hold individuals responsible for the consequences. Therefore, the culprit is not responsible and crime does not yet exist. To have done with crime and human guilt we must end the abnormality of society and its arrangements. The

world of West Europe offers no other replies to the problem of man's guilt and delinquency.

But ... [Tolstoy's] view clearly considers that no abolition of poverty, no organising of labour, will save humanity from abnormalities, and consequently from guilt and delinquency. This is expressed with terrible profundity and force in an immense psychological study of the soul of man, and with a realism of artistic presentation unequalled among us. It is made so clear and intelligible as to be obvious, that evil lies deeper in humanity than our Socialist physicians imagine—that no arrangement of society will eliminate evil; that the human mind remains the same, abnormality and sin proceed from it, and that finally, the laws of the soul of man are still so unknown, so unimagined by science, so undefined, and so mysterious, that there are not as yet, and cannot be, physicians or ultimate judges, but there is only He, who says 'Vengeance is mine, I will repay.' To Him alone all the secrets of this world and the ultimate fate of man are known.

And that he may not perish in despair through failing to understand his path and destiny, man is here shown the way of escape. It is indicated with genius in the wonderful scene in the earlier part of the novel, where the heroine is at death's door and the culprits and enemies are transformed into higher beings, into brothers forgiving one another everything—into beings who by mutual and complete forgiveness free themselves from falsehood, guilt, and crime, and thereby justify themselves with full consciousness that they have acquired a right to do so. But further in the last part of the novel, in that dark and terrible picture, followed up step by step, of the fall of a human soul, there is so much instruction for a human judge and for him who holds the scales and weights, that in fear and amazement he will certainly exclaim: 'No, Vengeance is not always mine, and I cannot repay!' and he will not inhumanly hold a miserably fallen offender guilty for having spurned the issue long since indicated by the light or even for having consciously rejected it.[42]

One might as well take this as a synopsis of Dostoevsky's own book, *The Brothers Karamazov*.

If my assertion that Dostoevsky's characters typify the personality model of the Apostle Paul can be taken as a plausible assertion, then it is possible to draw three conclusions. First of all, Dostoevsky is optimistic about human destiny. Both the human emotion (symbolised by Dmitri) and the mind (symbolised by Ivan) shall be saved from damnation, even though their salvation comes at a high price and after they have both been exposed to intense suffering. This is symbolised by the suffering to which both Dmitri and Ivan are exposed after the murder of their father. To Dmitri, the events leading to his trial, the unified misperception with which the public regards him, the humiliating and callous prosecution process and his conviction, and the severe sentence he is given by the criminal justice system are all a transition from one mental and emotional agony to another. In addition to the agony arising from being falsely accused, Dmitri is steadily assaulted by doubt concerning the existence of God and about the sincerity of his faith in God. Ivan likewise undergoes a mental breakdown after the murder of his father. As his philosophy of life collapses under the pressure of a consuming guilt and an acute self-consciousness, Ivan begins to believe that he is visited by the Devil who puts to him a steady stream of overwhelmingly absurd and hideous questions which Ivan neither ignores nor is able to answer. He will be saved from an imminent mental

---

[42] AM pp. 399-401.

breakdown by acknowledging his inadequacy and defencelessness and by turning to Alexei for help.

Secondly, Dostoevsky views intellectual corruption (sin) as deadlier than emotional sin. Dmitri Karamazov may be unruly, extravagant, sensual, and coarse, but he will not be the one who will murder the Old Karamazov. During his third and last interview with Ivan, Smerdyakov pronounces his verdict as to the real parricide: "Are you still trying to throw it all on me, to my face? You murdered him; you are the real murderer, I was only your instrument, your faithful servant, and it was following your words I did it." Smerdyakov is referring to Ivan's assertion that it is a natural law for one reptile to devour another. What Ivan considers as a philosophical plausibility, Smerdyakov puts into practice. Smerdyakov goes on to tell Ivan what he thinks of him:

> You are very clever. You are fond of money… You like to be respected, too, for you're very proud; you are far too fond of female charms, too, and you mind most of all about living in undisturbed comfort, without having to depend on anyone—that's what you care most about.… You are like Fyodor Pavlovich [Karamazov], you are more like him than any of his children; you have the same soul as he had.[43]

Thirdly, the Old Karamazov puts his complete trust in Smerdyakov and enjoys the delicious food he cooks for him. He even develops a feeling akin to compassion towards Smerdyakov. All the brothers, however, regardless of their philosophy of life and natural disposition, intuitively find in Smerdyakov an unusual and ominous evil. When Dmitri hears for the first time that Smerdyakov committed suicide, he cries out: "He was a dog and died like a dog![44]" With this

---

[43] FDBRO p. 587.
[44] Ibid. p. 615.

Dostoevsky seems to suggest that human beings, unless they are completely corrupt like the Old Karamazov or Smerdyakov, may not be able to agree on what should be regarded as good, but they cannot help but establish a unified understanding of evil to make coexistence possible. At an individual level, the perception of evil is unified likewise. The faculties of emotion and intellect and, in Dostoevsky's view, of spirit, have the same perception of evil. This idea also seems to suggest that evil was not originally inherent to human nature, even though it is now a part of human nature.

Tolstoy

"Man cannot live without having a definite idea of the meaning of his life, and always, though often unconsciously, conforms his acts to this meaning which he ascribes to his life," writes Tolstoy in *The Kingdom of God is within You*.[45] In the same way, Tolstoy maintains, human beings "living under the same conditions cannot help but have a conception about the meaning of their collective life and the activity resulting therefrom."[46]

But to each individual the discovery of the meaning of life is not like a movement towards an immovable or a definite target. "As an individual, entering into a new age, invariably changes his comprehension of life, and a grown man sees its meaning in something else than in what a child sees it, so an aggregate of people, a nation, inevitably, according to its age, changes its comprehension of life."[47]

Nevertheless, it is not that life can have multiple meanings or that different people living under different social and cultural conditions can discover or define different meanings for their life. For Tolstoy there is but one ultimate goal for human life, which is establishing and maintaining a loving relationship with God, the essence of which is manifested in the recognition and the carrying out of God's will wholeheartedly. The evolution to which Tolstoy refers is not the target but the mental lens through which it is perceived and the alignment of one's aspirations and actions with the target.

According to Tolstoy, both the search for the meaning of life and the alignment of one's action with the perceived meaning, when they occur consciously and habitually, define the essence

---

[45] LTKIN p. 88.
[46] Ibid.
[47] Ibid.

of the religion of the person. So, "religion, in the first place, is not, as science thinks, a phenomenon which at one time accompanied the evolution of humanity, and later became obsolete, but is a phenomenon always inherent in the life of humanity, and is in our time as inevitably inherent in humanity as at any other time. In the second place, religion is always a determination of the activity of the future, and not of the past, and so it is obvious that the investigation of past phenomena can in no way include the essence of religion."[48]

Doubtless, Tolstoy's philosophy of religion attained its final form when he was already an old man. His biographer Aylmer Maude maintains that it had passed through multiple and difficult stages of development, consisting of frequent and considerable contradictions and revisions. It is interesting to closely examine his novels in order to establish how the evolution to which he referred actually took place in his own mind.

Indeed one common feature we find to be present in Tolstoy's major characters is their relentless search for the meaning of life. Often there exists a state of dichotomy (as opposed to internal peace and unity) within his characters arising from one of the following conditions: (1) They find no tangible purpose for their life or (2) there is a fundamental misalignment between what they perceive as the ultimate goal in life and the reality of their day to day living. Often this state of dichotomy persists for a long time unperceived while their actions are conditioned and propelled by appetency. For some of them (such as Prince Stepan Arkadyevich Oblonsky) this appetency predominates over all other needs throughout their life and, therefore, they will never be able to discover the truth about life. Others are aware of the dichotomy but can neither determine its origin not find a remedy for it. These characters

---

[48] Ibid.

will try many things to attain inner harmony and fulfilment, but they will not be successful, because, even though they succeed in defining a purpose for their life, this purpose is either quintessentially evanescent or incompatible with what Tolstoy views as the true purpose of life. The theme in question can be illustrated by considering one particular chapter from *Anna Karenina*.

Towards the end of the book a train in Moscow departs from the Kurskaya Railway Station, taking with it a celebrated writer and philosopher, a famous professor, a count and respected military officer as well as several young volunteers who are travelling to fight the Ottoman Turks along with their Serbian and Montenegrin brothers. In the city they leave behind, the prevailing topic of public discussion is about the shameful handling of the Christian Slavs by the Turks and the brave struggle of the Slavs for their liberty; and how Russia, as a Christian nation, should put one of the commandments of Jesus—to love one's neighbour as oneself—into practice. The Russian Empire itself has not declared war on the Ottoman Empire, but the aristocracy unreservedly rally to assist the brothers by creating public awareness, by raising funds, and by recruiting volunteers. Several lectures, conferences, table talks, dinners, and balls are being organised and famous people are invited to educate the public on the subject. The media, which usually maintains a strong dislike and opposition towards the gentry, now shows solidarity with them, and extensively publishes articles on the question of the Slavs. Externally, the city as a whole seems to be gathering a concerted momentum for a sacred and tangible cause, but when the true motive of the individuals is scrutinised, it has little to do with loving and assisting a neighbour.

The celebrated philosopher has been toiling on a book project for six years, but when the book is finally published, public response is disturbingly cold; neither the scholars on the subject nor the general public nor the literary critics pay attention to it. The philosopher experiences disappointment on two fronts. Firstly, whilst writing the book, he had an occupation, a sense of purpose, and sincerely believed that he was making a contribution to the scientific community. With the completion of the book, however, he feels empty and aimless. Secondly, the failure of the book represents for him not merely the failure of a singular book, but the failure of a lifetime endeavour as a scholar and duty-conscious member of the society. Fortunately, at about this time, the question of the Slavs takes prominence in the popular consciousness and experts are sought everywhere to explain it. The philosopher, who once tentatively raised the question, seizes the opportunity and makes himself useful.

The Count, Count Vronsky, has tried the army, horse breeding, horse racing, politics, and painting as the primary interests in his life; nevertheless he has not found whole-hearted contentment in any one of them. Now the Serbian war affords him a new hope, a new beginning, and a new purpose in life. He is going there to fight, taking with him a squadron of soldiers at his own expense.

The other volunteers have a similar past. Referring to one of them, a retired officer, Tolstoy gives the following account: "One could see that this man had tried everything. He had worked for the railway, and as a steward, and had started his own factory, and talked about it all using learned words needlessly and inappropriately."[49]

Tolstoy often subjects his major characters to great and sudden changes under the burden of which they realise the existence of a great dichotomy in their life. For some of them the greatness of the upheaval brings them face-to-face with the inevitability

---

[49] LTANN p. 776.

of death (the word "death" appears more than 200 times in *War and Peace*, 107 times in *Anna Karenina*, and 50 times in *The Death of Ivan Ilyich*). Furthermore, the upheavals admitted into the lives of the characters Tolstoy created prior to his conversion to Christianity are distinctly different from the ones admitted to those characters he created after his conversion, vividly reflecting the shift in Tolstoy's own state of mind. The characters he created prior to his conversion usually have sufficient time to grapple with and make sense of the changes surrounding their life whereas this is not the case for the characters he created after his conversion, hinting at the sense of urgency Tolstoy felt to communicate his post-conversion convictions.

In *War and Peace*, Prince Andrew Bolkonsky and Count Pierre Bezukhov, despite material blessing and professional success, are both discontented with their lives. The creation of these two characters coincides with the period during which Tolstoy himself was relentlessly searching for the meaning of life. Indeed having carefully studied the biography and autobiography of Tolstoy, I find myself compelled to conclude that Count Pierre Bezukhov and Prince Andrew Bolkonsky represent the two sides of Tolstoy himself, the one representing the mystical and the other the rational sides of Tolstoy. Count Pierre, like Tolstoy, is clumsily built, carries about him an air of distraction and indifference; exhibits conspicuous inaptitude for small talk in society and frequently circumvents established social customs. Externally, he is of an impulsive nature, often finding himself in bad company and doing terrible things against his best judgment. Privately, however, Pierre is deeply thoughtful and unusually selfless, compassionate, and faithful. Prince Andrew appears to be the exact opposite of the count, being a rational and analytic person whose idea of perfection lies in the ability to explain all the facts of life reasonably, considering important only what is rational, and applying the standard of reason to everything. He tends to be severe in his judgement both of others and of himself and disposes a cynical attitude towards life.

Quintessentially, however, Prince Andrew and Count Pierre are both driven in life by the same insatiable and abiding thirst for discovering the meaning of life and for attaining perfection, even though their understanding of perfection is slightly different. Pierre's pursuit of perfection begins when he joins the Freemasons after he entered into an unhappy marriage, being persuaded that moral uprightness is an end in itself, and that a respect for one's duties leads to the development of honourable character. Pierre will eventually abandon the pursuit of this goal on account of the many obstacles affecting his life including his impulsive nature, indulgence in carousing, unhappy marriage, and the lack of commitment on the part of fellow freemasons. But Pierre's ability to objectively analyse his own situation can be demonstrated by examining how well he evaluates the attitudes of his fellow freemasons:

He divided the Brothers he knew into four categories. In the first he put those who did not take an active part in the affairs of the lodges or in human affairs, but were exclusively occupied with the mystical science of the order: with questions of the threefold designation of God, the three primordial elements—sulphur, mercury, and salt—or the meaning of the square and all the various figures of the temple of Solomon. Pierre respected this class of Brothers to which the elder ones chiefly belonged … but he did not share their interests. His heart was not in the mystical aspect of Freemasonry. In the second category Pierre reckoned himself and others like him, seeking and vacillating, who had not yet found in Freemasonry a straight and comprehensible path, but hoped to do so. In the third category he included those Brothers (the majority) who saw nothing in Freemasonry but the external forms and ceremonies, and prized the strict performance of these forms without troubling about their purport or significance ... Finally, to the fourth category also a great many Brothers belonged, particularly those who had lately joined. These according to Pierre's observations were men who had no belief in anything, nor desire for anything, but joined the Freemasons merely to associate with the wealthy young Brothers who were influential through their connections or rank, and of whom there were very many in the lodge.[50]

Pierre's frustration with Russian Freemasons[vii] coincides with Emperor Napoleon's invasion of the Russian Empire and the conquest of Moscow, presenting Pierre with an unwelcomed opportunity to explore his purpose in life, including assassinating Napoleon himself. Indeed, Pierre takes this particular mission very seriously and pursues it wholeheartedly, but it, too, will in the end be frustrated when Pierre is taken captive by the French army and is stripped off his freedom, wealth, and everything he possesses, including the certainty of his very existence.

Prince Andrew's yearning for perfection does not have an identifiable origin, but its first manifestation comes in the form of a calm but inward and unceasing obsession to make history, the consequence of which should be profound and lasting. The prince is convinced that only individuals with extraordinary strength, resolve, and courage, such as Emperor Napoleon, who, at the time, is subduing much of Europe with his swift and impressive military and diplomacy victories and is setting out to conquer the Russian Empire, can make history. Seeing his destiny in frustrating Napoleon's dream, he enlists in the army, becomes an officer in the *Third Coalition*, and demonstrates to himself as well as to his regiment his great

---

[50] LTWAR p. 341-342.

aptitude for leadership and unquestionable courage. But a day arrives when the French army suddenly and masterfully outmanoeuvres Prince Andrew's regiment and opens a fierce and bloody battle from which the unwary Russian soldiers, overcome by panic and confusion, and having abandoned their guns, flee. Whereupon, Prince Andrew, filled with indignation and shame, seizes the battle flag and rushes into the battlefield, beseeching the retreating soldiers at the top of his voice to return to the battlefield and fight. He has hardly made a few steps forward when he realises that he has been wounded in the stomach and cannot carry himself any further. It is during a brief moment of consciousness that Prince Andrew realises the futility of his longing to distinguish himself and to make history. Gazing at the vast and magnificent sky from where he has fallen on the ground and struggling to remain conscious, it occurs to him for the first time that no single individual, however intelligent and chivalrous, can be truly great compared to the magnificence and prominence of creation:

> Above him there was now nothing but the sky—the lofty sky, not clear yet still immeasurably lofty, with grey clouds gliding slowly across it. "How quiet, peaceful, and solemn; not at all as I ran," thought Prince Andrew— "not as we ran, shouting and fighting, not at all as the gunner and the Frenchman with frightened and angry faces struggled for the mop: how differently do those clouds glide across that lofty infinite sky! How was it I did not see that lofty sky before? And how happy I am to have found it at last! Yes! All is vanity, all falsehood, except that infinite sky. There is nothing, nothing, but that.[51]

Shortly before Prince Andrew slips into unconsciousness, Napoleon, Prince Andrew's hero and idol, makes a brief stop

---

[51] Ibid. p. 217.

nearby, and seeing the Prince lying in his blood and the battle flag beside him, and thinking that the Prince is already dead, Napoleon praises the gallantry of his death:

> Prince Andrew understood that this was said of him and that it was Napoleon who said it… But he heard the words as he might have heard the buzzing of a fly. Not only did they not interest him, but he took no notice of them and at once forgot them … at that moment Napoleon seemed to him such a small, insignificant creature compared with what was passing now between himself and that lofty infinite sky with the clouds flying over it. At that moment it meant nothing to him who might be standing over him, or what was said of him; he was only glad that people were standing near him and only wished that they would help him and bring him back to life, which seemed to him so beautiful now that he had today learned to understand it so differently.[52]

But this epiphany, other than giving him a fresh impulse to cling to life, does not lead the Prince to any particular revelation. In the long run he recovers from his wound, peace is established once again between the two countries and Prince Andrew goes on with his life, experiencing mostly tragic but also a few happy days. His wife dies of childbirth leaving him with their infant son and thus bringing to an end his unhappy marriage; he finds his first true love but is bereft of her once again, for the girl he loves, impatient of waiting, betrays him; Emperor Napoleon invades the Russian Empire for the second time and the Prince, too, joins the army for the second time, fights bravely in combat, and sustains a serious injury. During his final days on earth, Prince Andrew believes he has discovered not so much the meaning of life, but what gives meaning to life—which is love.

---

[52] Ibid. p. 226.

> Love hinders death. Love is life. All, everything that I understand, I understand only because I love. Everything is, everything exists, only because I love. Everything is united by it alone. Love is God, and to die means that I, a particle of love, shall return to the general and eternal source.[53]

This newly discovered philosophy of love, however, characteristic of the Prince's nature, is essentially eccentric, for it manifests itself in the rejection of life and the love of humanity[viii]:

> During the hours of solitude, suffering, and partial delirium he spent after he was wounded, the more deeply he penetrated into the new principle of eternal love revealed to him, the more he unconsciously detached himself from earthly life. To love everything and everybody and always to sacrifice oneself for love meant not to love anyone, not to live this earthly life. And the more imbued he became with that principle of love, the more he renounced life and the more completely he destroyed that dreadful barrier which, in the absence of such love, stands between life and death. When during those first days he remembered that he would have to die, he said to himself: "Well, what of it? So much the better!"[54]

Sadly, the rational Prince dies not of his injury but of the lack of will to cling to his earthly life, having found no sufficient reason for it.

Neither does Pierre find a definite answer[ix] to the meaning of life, but finds meaning in love, believing that love is the only glue that holds together the entities of life. With the discovery and acceptance of love he discovers happiness. Unlike Prince Andrew, Pierre's concept of love fully admits love in all its

---

[53] Ibid. p. 775.
[54] Ibid. pp. 773-774.

dimensions. Indeed, Pierre will measure the significance of all his future activities based on their nearness to his concept of love:

> Often ... Pierre recalled this period of blissful insanity. All the views he formed of men and circumstances at this time remained true for him always. He not only did not renounce them subsequently, but when he was in doubt or inwardly at variance, he referred to the views he had held at this time of his madness and they always proved correct. "I may have appeared strange and queer then," he thought, "but I was not so mad as I seemed. On the contrary I was then wiser and had more insight than at any other time, and understood all that is worth understanding in life, because... because I was happy." Pierre's insanity consisted in not waiting, as he used to do, to discover personal attributes which he termed "good qualities" in people before loving them; his heart was now overflowing with love, and by loving people without cause he discovered indubitable causes for loving them.[55]

In *Anna Karenina*, Levin, Kitty, Anna, Karenin, and Vronsky are also exposed to upheavals. Levin's first encounter with an upheaval comes to pass at the deathbed of his brother who has been ill for a long time and finally succumbs to a slow, painful, and humiliating death. Yet the patient refuses to give up his life and clings to every flicker of hope until the very end. The experience impels Levin to question first the meaning of suffering and then the meaning of life itself.

> From that moment when, at the sight of his beloved brother dying, Levin had looked at the questions of life and death for the first time through those new convictions, as he called them, which imperceptibly,

---

[55] Ibid. p. 886.

during the period from twenty to thirty-four years of age, had come to replace his childhood and adolescent beliefs, he had been horrified, not so much at death as at life without the slightest knowledge of whence it came, wherefore, why, and what it was. The organism, its decay, the indestructibility of matter, the law of conservation of energy, development, were the words that had replaced his former faith. These words and the concepts connected with them were very well suited to intellectual purposes, but they gave nothing for life, and Levin suddenly felt himself in the position of a person who had traded his warm fur coat for muslin clothing and, caught in the cold for the first time, is convinced beyond question, not by reasoning but with his whole being, that he is as good as naked and must inevitably die a painful death. From that moment on, though not accounting for it to himself and continuing to live as before, Levin never ceased to feel that fear at his ignorance. Moreover, he felt vaguely that what he called his convictions were not only ignorance but were a way of thinking that made the knowledge he needed impossible.[56]

Kitty's first encounter with an upheaval comes on the day when the person she loves and expects to propose to her (Count Vronsky) publicly humiliates her by rejecting her in favour of another woman (Anna). That same incident brings Anna and Vronsky together and irreversibly changes their social standing. Anna, a married, society woman who yearns for true love, refuses to be discreet about her affair, and gives herself completely to Vronsky. The discovery of his wife's unfaithfulness compels the obtuse statesman, Alexei

---

[56] LTANN pp. 785-786.

Alexandrovich Karenin, to peer into life for the first time and realise the false foundation upon which he has established his happiness and his fame and the bottomlessness of the abyss into which he must now descend.

Alexey Alexandrovich was not a jealous man. Jealousy, in his opinion, was insulting to his wife, and a man ought to have trust in his wife. Why he ought to have trust—that is, complete assurance that his young wife would always love him—he never asked himself; but he felt no disturbance, because he had trust and told himself that he had to have it. But now, though his conviction that jealousy was a shameful thing and that one ought to have trust was not destroyed, he felt that he stood face to face with something illogical and senseless, and he did not know what to do. Alexei Alexandrovich stood face to face with life, confronting the possibility of his wife loving someone else besides him, and it was this that seemed so senseless and incomprehensible to him, because it was life itself. All his life Alexei Alexandrovich had lived and worked in spheres of service that dealt with reflections of life, and each time he had encountered life itself, he had drawn back from it. Now he experienced a feeling similar to what a man would feel who was calmly walking across a bridge over an abyss and suddenly saw that the bridge had been taken down and below him was a bottomless deep. This bottomless deep was life itself, the bridge the artificial life that Alexei Alexandrovich had lived.[57]

In his *Confession*, Tolstoy admits that during his desperate and relentless search for the meaning of life, he was often overwhelmed by doubt and haunted with a sense of forlornness

---

[57] Ibid. pp. 142-143.

that he thought he was left with only three alternatives: (1) living on as before, but now with an abiding sense of self-deception; (2) suicide; or (3) surrendering to God. Alexei Alexandrovich Karenin and Vronsky choose self-deception and go on with their life, always managing to alleviate secondary goals as primary goals, so that they can push the hour of Armageddon always a day away. Kitty surrenders to God. Levin and Anna grapple for some time with suicide, Anna finally giving in. There is a stark similarity between the alternatives Tolstoy presents the characters in *Anna Karenina* and the alternatives with which he himself felt he was left with at the time he was writing *Anna Karenina*. Here are some verses taken from *Anna Karenina* and *Confession*:

> And, happy in his family life, a healthy man, Levin was several times so close to suicide that he hid a rope, lest he hang himself with it, and was afraid to go about with a rifle lest he shoot himself."—*Anna Karenina*.[58]

> So [Levin] lived, not knowing and not seeing any possibility of knowing what he was and why he was living in the world, tormented by this ignorance to such a degree that he feared suicide, and at the same time firmly laying down his own particular, definite path in life."—*Anna Karenina*.[59]

> "Death!" [Anna] thought. And she was overcome with such terror that for a long time she could not realize where she was, and for a long while her trembling hands were unable to find a match and light another candle in place of the one that had burned down and gone out.

---

[58] Ibid. p. 789.
[59] Ibid. p. 791.

"No, anything—only to live! I do love him. He does love me. It was and it will be no more," she said, feeling tears of joy at the return to life running down her cheeks. And to save herself from her fear, she hastily went to him in the study.—*Anna Karenina.*[60]

And in such a state of affairs I came to a point where I could not live; and even though I feared death, I had to employ ruses against myself to keep from committing suicide.—*Confession.*[61]

The horror of the darkness was too great, and I wanted to be free of it as quickly as possible by means of a rope or a bullet. It was this feeling, more powerful than any other, that was leading me toward suicide.—*Confession.*[62]

My question, the question that had brought me to the edge of suicide when I was fifty years old, was the simplest question lying in the soul of every human being, from a silly child to the wisest of the elders, the question without which life is impossible; such was the way I felt about the matter. The question is this: What will come of what I do today and tomorrow? What will come of my entire life —*Confession.*[63]

No one prevents us from denying life, as Schopenhauer has done. So kill yourself, and you won't have to worry about it. If you don't like life, kill yourself. If you live and cannot understand the meaning of life, put an end to it; but don't turn around and start talking and writing about

---

[60] Ibid. p. 752.
[61] LTCON p. 29
[62] Ibid. p. 33.
[63] Ibid. p. 34.

how you don't understand life. You are in cheerful company, for whom everything is going well, and they all know what they are doing; if you are bored and find it offensive, leave. After all, if we are convinced of the necessity of suicide and do not go through with it, then what are we, if not the weakest, most inconsistent, and, to speak quite frankly, the most stupid of all people, fussing like foolish children over a new toy?
—*Confession*.[64]

Thus I was saved from suicide. When and how this transformation within me was accomplished, I could not say. Just as the life force within me was gradually and imperceptibly destroyed, and I encountered the impossibility of life, the halting of life, and the need to murder myself, so too did this life force return to me gradually and imperceptibly.—*Confession*.[65]

Anna never comprehends the source of the dichotomy in her life and desperately seeks remedies for it in the wrong places. When she finds none, existence becomes too terrible to face and she refuses to roll the boulder of life any further:

And the candle by the light of which she had been reading that book filled with anxieties, deceptions, grief and evil, flared up brighter than ever, lit up for her all that had once been in darkness, sputtered, grew dim, and went out for ever.[66]

Eventually, three seemingly inconsequential incidents persuade Levin to abdicate his rational inquiry pertaining to the meaning

---

[64] Ibid. 53-54.
[65] Ibid. 75.
[66] LTANN p. 768.

of life in favour of faith in God. The first incident occurs when his wife undergoes a painful and lengthy labour during which time Levin, who until then considers himself an unbeliever, prays, and while praying believes. The experience not only gives Levin peace of mind but also reminds him of his childhood faith in God and joy in life. After his wife's delivery, however, Levin fails to find the same strength of conviction in him to continue on the path of faith; instead he picks up the old rational path and goes on tormenting himself with endless analysis and doubt. And yet, he finds it difficult to acknowledge that his prayer experience has been a delusion and that his momentary belief was merely a manifestation of helplessness and self-deception. "He was in painful discord with himself and strained all the forces of his soul to get out of it."[67]

The second incident occurs during a prosaic conversation with a farmer who maintains that living for God and not for the belly makes life worth living. After reflecting for a while upon the words of the farmer, Levin realises that there are certain truths which are universally accepted even though they are not explainable to the rational mind. For example, no one would regard living for one's belly as heroic whilst many regard selflessness as an admirable character. Where does such an understanding come from? Moreover, was it through rational analysis that he arrived at the knowledge that he must love his fellow human beings rather than oppress and take advantage of them? As a child when he was told to love his "neighbour" he gladly believed it, for he was told what was already in his soul. Who then discovered this truth? Levin is certain that this discovery does not come through rational analysis. Indeed, through rational analysis human beings seem to discover the opposite: that existence is a struggle and the law of survival justifies the oppression of all who hinder the satisfaction of

---

[67] Ibid. P. 787.

one's desire, but the law of loving one's neighbour could not be discovered by reason, because it is unreasonable.[x]

The third incident involves the children of his sister-in-law who, in the absence of the grown-ups, were cooking raspberries over a candle and pouring milk into each other's mouth. When their mother and Levin catch them in action and the mother scolds them by telling them that the food and cups they are playing with have been obtained with a high price and through hard labour and difficulty, and that they are destroying the very substance by which they are existing, the children cannot believe what they are hearing, for they cannot conceive that the funny game they have invented can in any way be harmful. Levin asks himself, were the children left alone to procure or make cups for themselves and to milk the cows, would they still be playing the same game? He answers his own question with a negative. Indeed, they would die of hunger. In the same way, Levin maintains, if human beings were to be left alone with their passions and thoughts and without the conception of God and good and evil, they would destroy themselves; they reject God and question moral values simply because they are spiritually provided for, exactly like the children of his sister-in-law.

Levin's acceptance of the existence of God and his decision to live for God coincides with Tolstoy's own conversion to Christianity. In his post-conversion books, the characters whom Tolstoy introduces to great and sudden changes are left with limited choice and time.

In *The Death of Ivan Ilyich*, Ivan is a highly regarded official of the Court of Justice who is endowed with intelligence, temperament, character, life style, and degree of success, which his colleagues and friends regard as ideal. With the exception of his difficult marriage[xi] to a demanding and self-absorbed woman, his life, by and large, takes the direction and shape he wishes it to take. He is an agreeable, carefree and contented man. But one day, as he hangs a curtain for his new house, he falls down from a ladder and hurts his side. In the beginning the pain expresses itself almost imperceptibly and Ivan dismisses it and goes on with his life as usual. But the pain persists and grows in intensity, finally becoming terminal. A long, gruesome, and lonely battle ensues, Ivan maintaining that he does not deserve to suffer so much because he has been leading a righteous life. The arbitrariness and meaninglessness of suffering and man's ultimate destiny—death—distresses him to no end and he becomes more and more introspective and emotional. Except Gerasim, the servant boy in his household, no one pays particular attention to his suffering. Indeed his family makes light of it and expressly avoids the subject of death, pretending his illness to be an ephemeral nuisance. Other people around him go on living as usual, mainly preoccupied by appearances, balls, promotions, human networking, and relationships. But Gerasim is different. He is not only selfless and compassionate but also unafraid of death. His relationship with Gerasim prompts Ivan to question, for the first time, whether his life has indeed been righteous and whether his definition of life and death has been accurate. He now clearly sees that the past has all been a deception. All his life he has been reaching for something, trying to fill a void he has never understood very well; he has been living without God, without true mirth and joy, and without a particular reason. His body was alive, but his soul was dead. With this realisation, the inevitability of death ceases to frighten him. He is convinced that he will not miss the sort of life he has once had. As soon as Ivan accepts death as an alternative to a false life, he is stabbed by an external and perceptible force in his chest and side and is transported into the heart of light. As Ivan dies, not only the horror of death, but also death itself disappears.

In *Master and Man*, Vasili Andreevich Brekhunov is a successful village merchant, a family man, and an elder in his parish. Life for him is a bargain, the rule of which one should master to win and to enjoy life. However, one day after St. Nicholas's Day, he sets off with a sledge to a nearby village to purchase a grove. The landowner has asked ten thousand roubles but Vasili Andreevich is hopeful of sealing the deal at seven thousand, even though he is quite certain that the grove is worth three times the price he is offering! Of late, word has reached him, some timber dealers from town were bidding for the grove and unless he made haste, he might not secure it. Determined to entice the landowner on the spot with a payment of three thousand roubles, he decides to travel in a bad and uncertain weather. Owing to his wife's incessant imploring, he takes with him Nikita, the only sober peasant he can find in his household on that day. Nikita, though a valued labourer, known for his industry, dexterity, and strength, has a rough past, for "about twice a year, or even oftener, he had a drinking bout, and then besides spending all his clothes on drink he became turbulent and quarrelsome."[68]

This unfortunate man has been living with a wife who has been unfaithful to him for twenty years, openly having an affair with a cooper who lodges with the family. Both his wife and his master exploit him shamelessly, the master paying him less than half the wage he deserves (even that mostly in kind rather than in cash) and the wife claiming the wage he earns. But since recently, Nikita has vowed not to drink anymore, for he wishes to purchase a horse for his only son when he comes of age.

On the way, the stormy wind increases in intensity and roughness, and snow begins to fall heavily. Twice, the travellers go astray from their road, both times coming to one and the same village, which is about six kilometres away from their

---

[68] LTRAI p. 168.

destination. Upon their second arrival they go to the house of an elderly peasant who receives them warmly, advises them against the journey, and offers them lodging for the night. For by this time it is already dark and the wind has become ferocious. But Vasili Andreevich, anxious to settle the deal that day, declines the offer and, after warming themselves with vodka and tea, the master and his peasant set off in pitch darkness. Before long, however, they go astray once again and this time they find themselves surrounded by a ravine with no hope of crossing it. With the wind howling ever more harshly and the snow falling heavily, the travellers finally decide to spend the night where they are, the landowner taking the sledge as a sleeping box and the peasant preparing a place in the open next to the sledge.

Still warmed by the vodka he has drunk at the elderly peasant's, Vasili Andreevich scarcely realises the gravity of his situation, regarding it as merely a nuisance but momentary inconvenience. As he always does in such situations, he fixes his thought on the one thing that "constituted the sole aim, meaning, pleasure, and pride of his life—of how much money he had made and might still make, of how much other people he knew had made and possessed, and of how those others had made and were making it, and how he, like them, might still make much more."[69]

Satisfied with himself, Vasili Andreevich gradually slumbers. Meanwhile, in the interminable night the snow accumulates massively and almost buries the sledge; the ferocious wind offensively whirls and scatters the snow in and outside the sledge; and the temperature becomes unbearably cold. When finally a wolf howls nearby, the brief slumber of the merchant is interrupted and all of a sudden he realises that compared to all the difficulties and discomforts he has ever been exposed to

---

[69] Ibid. 196.

in his life, this one is different and may cost him his life: "After this Vasili Andreevich could not fall asleep again or even calm himself. The more he tried to think of his accounts, his business, his reputation, his worth and his wealth, the more and more was he mastered by fear..."[70] Overcome by the fear of death, he decides to mount the horse and to get away alone. "The horse will move when he has someone on his back," he reasons. As for Nikita, "it's all the same to him whether he lives or dies. What is his life worth? He won't grudge his life, but I have something to live for, thank God."[71] He gets away, as he intends, but he does not travel far before his horse stumbles and falls, throwing him off its back, and runs away. The incident makes him more vulnerable to the cold temperature; and to his much regret he loses one of his gloves.

Meanwhile, Nikita, from the time he sits down behind the sledge, he does not stir. "Like all those who live in touch with nature and have known want, he was patient and could wait for hours, even days, without growing restless or irritable... The thought that he might, and very probably would, die that night occurred to him, but did not seem particularly unpleasant or dreadful. It did not seem particularly unpleasant, because his whole life had been not a continual holiday, but on the contrary an unceasing round of toil of which he was beginning to feel weary. And it did not seem particularly dreadful, because besides the masters he had served here, like Vasili Andreevich, he always felt himself dependent on the Chief Master, who had sent him into this life, and he knew that when dying he would still be in that Master's power and would not be ill-used by Him."[72]

With great difficulty and with his last strength, Vasili Andreevich follows the horse's track, which leads him back to

---

[70] Ibid. 200.
[71] Ibid. p. 201.
[72] Ibid. pp. 201-202.

the sledge and where also he finds Nikita half frozen and struggling to remain conscious. When Nikita realises that his master has returned, he too uses his last strength and raises his head up and asks the master for forgiveness and begs him to pay to his son or to his wife what the master owes him.

The selflessness of the humble peasant unlocks an overpowering feeling of compassion in the master and makes him forget all his trouble and danger. He decidedly throws himself on the peasant and warms him with his own body and mantle. He remains in that way for "one hour, another, and a third, but he was unconscious of the passage of time." His capacity to give unconditional love fills him with a strange and unspeakable joy and for the first time in his life he attains true unity within himself. The next day villagers find the unfortunate travellers, the master dead and Nikita unconscious but alive.

---

[i] Nevertheless Freud begins his *Civilisation and Its Discontents* by acknowledging the existence of people who are capable of venerating men of exceptional greatness, "although their greatness rests on attributes and achievements which are completely foreign to the aims and ideals of the multitude. One might well be inclined to suppose that after all it is only a minority who appreciate these great men, while the majority cares nothing for them. But the discrepancy between men's opinions and their behaviour is so wide and their desires so many-sided that things are probably not so simple."

[ii] And yet, elsewhere Freud remarks that sexual need does not unite men; it separates them instead. Which is why the sons of the primal father introduced a strict incest prohibition in the first place: "Though the brothers had joined force in order to overcome the father, each was the other's rival among the women. Each one wanted to have them all to himself like the father, and in the fight of each against the other the new organisation would have perished. For

there was no longer any one stronger than all the rest who could have successfully assumed the role of the father. Thus, there was nothing left for the brothers, if they wanted to live together, but to erect the incest prohibition — perhaps after many difficult experiences — through which they all equally renounced the women whom they desired, and on account of whom they had removed the father in the first place. (SFTOT p. 98)"

[iii] In order to accommodate the phenomenon of submissiveness in males and aggression in females, Freud introduced the concept of innate bisexuality. In essence, according to this theory, all human beings exhibit bisexual tendencies but as a result of both external (sociocultural) and internal (psychological) factors, it is often forced to remain latent.

[iv] Einstein, however, rejects Spinoza's claim that the mind and the body are independent from one another. In an article he wrote about the philosopher Bertrand Russell, Einstein finds a middle way in Kant as regards to the theory of knowledge, criticising Spinoza and Hegel, on the one hand, for giving an unlimited penetrative power to thought and, Hume and Berkeley, on the other, for their "naïve" realism.

[v] As far as Spinoza is concerned, virtue has nothing to do with the distinction of good and evil and the valuation and pursuit of good. Instead, it means to acquire the knowledge of natural laws governing causal relationships and to view everything through this knowledge. The basis for virtue, according to Spinoza, is the desire to preserve life indefinitely. Hence, a virtue contradicting the desire to preserve life is inconceivable. As regards the knowledge of good and evil, Spinoza asserts that it is nothing other than the emotion of pleasure or pain insofar as we are conscious of it. The reader may recall the similarity between Freud's definition of good and evil in his *Pleasure Principle* with that of Spinoza's.

[vi] None of the father figures in Dostoevsky's novels are beautiful. The good ones are those who are entirely absent from the stories

because they are long dead. The rest are irredeemably corrupt and fallen. To the first group belong the fathers of Raskolnikov, Zosima, and Prince Myshkin. To the second belong Semyon Zakharovich Marmeladov who is an alcoholic and a squanderer of his family's little wealth; General Ivolgin, a compulsive liar and a drunkard; Captain Snegiryov, a drunkard and a clown; the vain and impotent scholar Stepan Trofimovich Verhovensky whose unexamined ideas his own son takes to their extreme to inflict incalculable pain on innocent people; and Fyodor Pavlovich Karamazov who, amongst all father figures of literary creation, has no equal for squalor, depravity, and meanness.

[vii] Tolstoy summarises Pierre's frustration with the following words: "... he was struck for the first time by the endless variety of men's minds, which prevents a truth from ever presenting itself identically to two persons. Even those members who seemed to be on his side understood him in their own way with limitations and alterations he could not agree to, as what he always wanted most was to convey his thought to others just as he himself understood it. (LTWAR p. 343)."

[viii] Compare this with the philosophy of Socrates at the time of his death to which Tolstoy subscribed at the time he wrote *War and Peace*: "We move closer to the truth only to the extent that we move further from life (Plato's Phaedo, Sec. 62-69)". Tolstoy cites this quote in his *Confession* and adds: "What do we who love truth strive for in life? To be free of the body and of all the evils that result from the life of the body. If this is so, then how can we fail to rejoice when death approaches? (LTCON p. 43.)"

[ix] Tolstoy could have given Count Pierre or Prince Andrew no definite answer, for he himself at this time did not possess one pertaining to the meaning of his own life.

[x] Freud agreed with this observation. As we shall see, in *Civilisation and Its Discontents*, he argues that the seemingly unattainable ideals of Christianity, particularly, its insistence upon loving one's neighbour as

oneself, inevitably aggravates and distorts human aggression and imposes an intolerable burden of guilt.

[xi] As a side remark, perhaps reflecting Tolstoy's struggle within his own marriage, Ivan is the fourth major character experiencing an unhappy marriage: Pierre, Andrew, and Anna being the others. Readers familiar with *The Kreutzer Sonata* will realise in it another case of an unhappy marriage.

Part III
The Significance of the Bible

In this part I evaluate the significance my subjects attach to the Bible as a means of comprehending human existence. Except for Dostoevsky, all the others rejected the divine origin of the Bible. But Dostoevsky argued that the Bible presents characters, stories, and moral values that cannot be found elsewhere; it also presents the ideal *man*, Christ, who has no parallel in beauty and authority in literary creation. Consequently, Dostoevsky trusts the Bible with its claims. All of his major books demonstrate the failure of human beings to provide either personal or social values which can be regarded as superior or worthy alternatives to the ones provided in the Bible. As someone who was intimately acquainted with suffering all his life, Dostoevsky found solace in the experience of fellow sufferers in the Bible, particularly, Job and Jesus, who gave meaning not only to his suffering but also to the suffering of creation.

Tolstoy agreed with Dostoevsky but argued that the Bible also contains doctrines and historical narratives which are contrary to common sense, factually incorrect, and morally hostile to the core teaching of Christ. He maintained that it is possible to separate the authentic claims from the spurious and speculative ones by taking the Bible as the product of human endeavour. This task can be done, Tolstoy purported, by removing or reinterpreting biblical passages which cannot be understood rationally, for to him it seemed illogical for God or Jesus to behave or act in a manner which is contrary to common sense or the highest human aspirations. Moreover, Tolstoy purported that it was possible to take the *Sermon on the Mount* as a reference by which to identify what he regarded as the authentic or original teaching of Jesus. Hence, Tolstoy spent more than a decade attempting to "reproduce" and harmonise" the four Gospels. In doing so, he rejected the supernatural nature, birth, and resurrection of Jesus; removed or reinterpreted the miracle and wonder stories, and attempted to rationally explain the parables and teaching of Jesus.

Freud likewise maintained that the Bible contains a trace of authenticity in the historical accounts about Ancient Israel, its coming into existence, its existence as a sovereign kingdom for many centuries, and its eventual dissolution, but he asserts that these accounts have been deliberately distorted and modified by Bible editors for tendentious reasons. Like Tolstoy, Freud too attempted to reconstruct the Pentateuch (the first five books of the Torah) by applying psychoanalysis. Accordingly, Freud claimed that Moses and the Levites were Egyptians by birth; an Egyptian Pharaoh was the first to accept and adopt monotheism as his state religion; after the death of this Pharaoh and the return of pantheism in Egypt, Moses, who also accepted monotheism, persuaded the Israelites to convert to his religion in exchange for becoming his people and owning their own land; Moses and the Israelites left Egypt peacefully and without the intervention of God and the plagues, but the primitive Israelites eventually murdered Moses in the wilderness, because they could not abide his highly developed and abstract concept of God. Besides psychoanalysis Freud relied on several biblical passages, for he maintained that they contain hints as to what really transpired during the Exodus of the Israelites out of Egypt.

Einstein's causal determinism does not allow for extraordinary divine revelation and intervention, but he never hesitated to express his fascination with Jesus and the prophets: "If one purges the Judaism of the Prophets and Christianity as Jesus Christ taught it of all subsequent additions, especially those of the priests, one is left with a teaching which is capable of curing all the social ills of humanity." With this declaration, Einstein also agreed with Tolstoy that the Bible contains subject matter, which appear to be in conflict with core biblical values.

Except for Freud, all the rest wholeheartedly agree that the central message of the Bible, which may be summarised as to love God and to love one's neighbour as oneself, can be assumed as the highest aim towards which human beings can aspire on earth. But Freud maintained that the commandment to love one's own neighbour as oneself puts an immeasurable burden and a profound sense of guilt on human beings, because it is impossible to fulfil. According to Freud, this commandment does not take the nature and capacity of the human ego into consideration.

Freud

In order to make Freud's view on the Bible comprehensible to the general reader, it is essential to first allow for a brief introduction to the history of Ancient Israel according to the Bible. Around 1876 B.C., the patriarchal figure Jacob and his family (in all, 70 people), fleeing a famine in Canaan, migrated to Egypt where one of Jacob's sons, Joseph, had already secured a prominent position in the court of the Pharaoh. Shortly after their arrival, the Pharaoh himself received them and gave them the region of Goshen (the northern part of Egypt) in which to settle. After about 400 years of peaceful and prosperous sojourn, during the eighteenth dynasty (according to biblical scholars, most probably during the reign of Thutmose III), the Egyptians oppressed and set slave masters over the Israelites and forced them to build Rameses and Pithom as storage cities for the Pharaoh. But around 1446 B.C. (probably, during the reign of Amunhatep II), the Israelites peacefully left Egypt under the leadership of Moses, who, though born to an Israelite family, was raised from childhood by the daughter of Pharaoh. The Bible maintains that God commissioned Moses to lead the Israelites out of Egypt and into Canaan, the Promise Land. When Pharaoh refused to let the Israelites go, God brought upon Egypt ten plagues, including the killing of all the firstborn males in the land of Egypt, and forced Pharaoh to release the Israelites. The final miracle involved the division of the Red Sea, so that the Israelites could cross it, but when the Egyptians tried to do the same, they were drowned because the waters returned to their original place.

After the Israelites left Egypt, the Bible relates, the Israelites arrived at Mount Sinai, where God revealed himself to them and gave Moses the Ten Commandments. From Sinai, the Israelites wandered in the deserts for forty years, before they finally conquered Canaan and settled there. Following the conquest of Canaan, Joshua, the successor of Moses, divided the land to the twelve tribes by lot (ten of the tribes were the descendants of 10 of Jacob's sons and two of them were the descendants of Joseph, Jacob's favourite son). One of the tribes, Levi, however, was not included in the allocation of land, because Moses had set it apart for a priestly duty.

After the conquest of Canaan, the Israelites persisted as a single nation for about 370 years, but during the reign of Kind Rehoboam (930 B.C.), the son of King Solomon and the grandson of Kind David, the Kingdom of Israel was divided into two, north and south. Weary of the heavy taxation and the hard conscripted labour to which his father subjected them, the elders from the northern part, under the leadership of Jeroboam, gathered together and petitioned King Rehoboam to relieve them of their yoke. But the young king was unwilling and, in fact, threatened to make their yoke heavier. Upon hearing the unexpected reply, the ten tribes from the north rebelled against the two southern tribes (the tribes of Judah and Benjamin) and anointed Jeroboam as their king.

From then on, the two kingdoms existed independently, the northern becoming the Kingdom of Israel and the southern becoming the Kingdom of Judah. The northern kingdom persisted as a sovereign kingdom for about 210 years but ceased to exist in 721 B.C., when its capital city, Samaria, was finally conquered and destroyed by the Neo-Assyrian Empire. The Kingdom of Judah, on the other hand, survived as a sovereign kingdom until Jerusalem, its capital city, was vanquished and totally destroyed by the Babylonian King Nebuchadnezzar II in 586 B.C.

The most important claims of the Bible which Freud contests are the claims pertaining to the person and life of Moses and the composition of the population of ancient Israel. Specifically, according to the Bible:

1. Moses is born into an Israelite family during the time when the oppression and persecution of the Israelites reaches peak intensity but Moses is raised by the daughter of Pharaoh who finds him floating on the river Nile inside a wicker basket which was caulked with bitumen and pitch.
2. One day, when Moses is about 40 years of age, he witnesses the mistreatment of an Israelite by an Egyptian, whereupon he sides with the victim and murders the Egyptian. Word reaches, however, the ears of Pharaoh, and Moses, fearing for his life, flees from Egypt and takes refuge in the desert of Midian under the shelter of a Midianite priest who marries one of his daughters off to Moses.
3. After forty years of leading an obscure and insignificant existence as a Shepherd, Moses one day sees a revelation at Mount Sinai and receives a commission from God to lead the Israelites out of Egypt into Canaan where they shall dwell and worship God forever.
4. Moses returns to Egypt and confronts Pharaoh, but Pharaoh is unwilling to let the Israelites go. Indeed, after the confrontation with Moses, Pharaoh intensifies his oppression of the Israelites.
5. Nevertheless, after divine interventions and punishments in the form of a series of plagues, Pharaoh finally lets the people of Israel peacefully leave Egypt along with all their belongings.
6. But as soon as the Israelites are out of Egypt, Pharaoh regrets his decision and pursues the Israelites with chariots and overtakes them at the Red Sea whereupon God divides the sea and lets the people peacefully cross it. But when the Egyptians try to cross the Red Sea, God returns the waters to their original place and drowns them all along their chariots.

7. After the event, Moses leads the people to Mount Sinai where God reveals himself to them with fire, thunder, lightning, dense cloud, and a very loud blast of the horn. There at Mount Sinai, Moses receives the Ten Commandments from God and the People of Israel makes a covenant with God to be his people and to worship him alone.
8. After Mount Sinai, however, the Israelites repeatedly fail to obey and trust God or Moses and repeatedly quarrel with Moses and even attempt to murder him, as a result of which God makes them wander aimlessly in the desert for 40 years.
9. But God is also displeased with Moses on account of his hot temperament and impatience and tells him that he will not enter the Promised Land.
10. After 40 years of wandering in the desert and the death of Moses, the Israelites, under the leadership of Joshua, enter into Canaan and conquer it.

Freud maintains that the Bible contains useful but unreliable historical evidence. He accepts the settlement of the Jewish people in Egypt for a long period of time and their eventual Exodus out of it led by an actual person named Moses, and the authenticity of the description of the personality and temperament of Moses ("Since such a trait does not lend itself to glorification, it may very well be historical truth."[1]). He also accepts the wandering of the Israelites in the wilderness for a long time (he estimates this time to have been fifty to 100 years) and their eventual conquest of the Land of Canaan. Besides, Freud accepts the story of King David as an authentic historical account and admires the latter prophets and psalmists for their excellent poetry, appreciation of beauty, and consistent defence of truth and justice.

---

[1] SFMOS p. 53.

But Freud rejects the miraculous drama described in the Bible surrounding the Exodus of the Israelites and narrated in the Pentateuch, targeting his sternest criticism towards the biblical "editors" (notably, Ezra and Nehemiah) whom he accuses of deliberately distorting the historical accounts for tendentious motives. Specifically, Freud claims the following:

(1) Moses was not the founder of Monotheism; neither did monotheism originate from the Jewish people. It potentially originated in Syria and was exported to Egypt during the reign of Thutmose III.

(2) Moses was not, as the Bible claims, an Israelite. Instead, he was an Egyptian nobleman both by birth and by upbringing.

(3) The exodus out of Egypt did not happen as a result of divine intervention. Instead, conducive circumstances around 1400 B.C. and which lasted for over 17 years gave rise to it.

(4) The composition of the people who left Egypt as well as who entered and conquered Canaan was not, as the Bible claims, homogeneous. Instead, it consisted of Egyptians, Jews, and Midianites.

(5) The Moses who led the Israelites out of Egypt and the Moses of the Mount of Sinai were two different people.

(6) Moses did not die of natural cause. Instead, the Jewish people shamelessly murdered him in a place east of Jordan some time after they left Egypt.

In his book *Moses and Monotheism* Freud gives three major reasons for his claims:

(i) There are two contradictory and incompatible accounts of the personality of Moses given in the Bible. The first account relates the personality of a Moses when he was in Egypt whereas the second account relates the

(ii)   personality of a Moses when he was in the wilderness of Midian.
(ii)   Likewise, there are two contradictory and incompatible accounts of the God of Moses. The first account must be related to the God of Moses the Egyptian and the other to the God of Moses the Midianite.
(iii)   The disintegration of the Kingdom of Israel into two kingdoms during the reign of King Rehoboam is an indication that the Exodus essentially consisted of at least two distinct peoples: Egyptians and Jews, each of which initially had its own God and its own leader which explains the inconsistencies in the personalities of Moses and God.

According to Freud, it was to cover these facts and in order to present a unified, consistent, credible, and favourable account of the history of the people of Israel that the biblical editors first defined a form and into this form they fitted the figure of Moses and the religion he founded. In doing so, they irretrievably changed some of the historical facts, but other facts can still be reconstructed by adopting analytic methods, to which psychoanalysis belongs. Following in the footsteps of the German protestant theologian Ernst Sellin[2], who claims that Moses might have not died of a natural cause; instead, might have been violently murdered by the people he led out of Egypt[3], Freud asserts that unmistakable traces of the violent end of Moses by the Israelites can be found in the Pentateuch itself and in the books of the Prophets.

Consequently, in *Moses and Monotheism* he attempts to reconstruct the Pentateuch by synthesising "evidences" he gathered from the Bible itself and from archaeology, ancient

---

[2] SFMOS p. 59.
[3] E. Sellin. 1922. *Mose und seine Bedeutung für die israelitisch-jüdische Religionsgeschichte.*

history, and psychoanalysis. Freud started writing the book in 1934 and completed it in 1938, one year before he died. However, he admitted to a friend that the figure of Moses had occupied his mind throughout his life.[4] He maintained that understanding Moses was crucial to understand "how the Jew came to be and why he had drawn this immortal hatred on himself."[5]

During the writing of his book, Freud had ample access to high quality research articles and books as well as the opportunity to have personal discussions with prominent researchers and scholars in the fields of archaeology, anthropology, ancient history, theology, and psychology. The University of Vienna, where he held a professorship, provided a prestigious library which was established in 1356.

The main thesis of *Moses and Monotheism* is proving that the original Moses was an Egyptian who first worshiped the Sun God. Freud's hypothesis states that between 1358 and 1350 B.C. he left Egypt with Jewish immigrants to establish his own nation, which should commit itself to a strict monotheism. After he successfully led the Jewish people out of Egypt, however, they violently murdered him in the wilderness. Following the murder, the Israelites wandered in the wilderness for a long time where also they met their kinsmen who did not migrate to Egypt a long time ago. The two people decided to unite their forces and invade Canaan. As a consequence of this merger, a merger of religion also took place, as a result of which the original Mosaic religion became alloyed with a pagan religion.

Accordingly, the only time pantheist ancient Egypt ever came closer to accepting monotheism as a state religion was at the time of the glorious Eighteenth Dynasty under the leadership

---

[4]PG p. 605.
[5]Ibid. P. 606.

of which Egypt first became a world power. About the year 1375 B.C., a young Pharaoh by the name Amenophis IV (who later changed his name to Ikhnaton) came to the throne and introduced a strict monotheistic religion, a belief in the sun god Aten. There had, however, already been tendencies towards monotheism long before Amenophis, which could partly be recognised in the attempt of the priesthood of the sun temple at On (Heliopolis) to attribute moral qualities to their deities in addition to their material qualities. For example, Ma'at, the goddess of truth, order, and justice, was the daughter of the sun god Re'.

As Egypt started to take a prominence in world politics and the rule of its Pharaoh extended beyond its borders (to Nubia, Palestine, and Syria), it was natural to extend the significance of its deities to other nations as well. Similar to ancient Greece and Rome, this also means that Egypt became accessible to foreign influences and deities. Since some of the royal wives were Asiatic princesses, it is possible that some of them (in particular those from Syria) brought with them monotheism into Egypt:

> Political conditions in Egypt had about that time begun to exert a lasting influence on Egyptian religion. Through the victorious sword of the great conqueror Thothmes III, Egypt had become a world power. Nubia in the south, Palestine, Syria and a part of Mesopotamia in the north had been added to the Empire. This imperialism was reflected in religion as Universality and Monotheism. Since Pharaoh's solicitude now extended beyond Egypt to Nubia and Syria, Deity itself had to give up its national limitation and the new God of the Egyptians had to become like Pharaoh the unique and unlimited sovereign of the world known to the Egyptians. Besides, it was natural that as the frontiers extended Egypt should become accessible to foreign influences; some of the

king's wives were Asiatic princesses, and possibly even direct encouragement of monotheism had penetrated from Syria.[6]

So, during the reign of Amenophis IV, the doctrine of a local deity was transformed into a doctrine of universal god and then into a doctrine of strict monotheism. Then the king, with ruthless intolerance, forced his subjects to accept monotheism and throughout his kingdom closed temples, prohibited divine service, and confiscated the properties of temples. Indeed, his zeal had gone so far that he fastidiously had ancient monuments examined and the mention of the word 'gods' in plural form obliterated from them. But Amenophis IV execution was not received without stiff oppositions by the priesthood as well as by the people. Even though less is known about his death, shortly thereafter, however, his religion was completely abandoned and everything he had undone was re-established. When after a decade of political unrest a firm regime was restored, Egypt returned to its historic pantheism once again.

Freund maintains that Moses lived during the reign of Amenophis or shortly thereafter and had accepted the sun god Aten. This same Moses was either a governor of Goshen or an influential aristocrat or a chief priest with a family of devoted Egyptian priests of his own, who later would become the Levites of Ancient Israel. When Moses saw that the religion of his master was abandoned by the Egyptians, he decided to abandon Egypt altogether. Being ambitious, he also saw the possibility of establishing his own kingdom with the Israelites, who at the time were dwelling in his city. Soon a deal was struck between them. In his part, Moses promised to lead them out of Egypt into a land of their own and, in their part, the Israelites promised to accept his monotheistic religion and

---

[6]SFMOS p. 36.

abide by it. It was further agreed that the Levites, the priestly family to which Moses potentially belonged, would assume the office of priesthood to mediate between the god Aten and the Israelites. Meanwhile, a golden opportunity presented itself when after the death of Ikhnaton a power gap was created in Egypt aiding the safe exit of Moses and the Israelites:

> ...if we place Moses in Ikhnaton's period and associate him with that Pharaoh, then the enigma is resolved and a possible motive presents itself, answering all our questions. Let us assume that Moses was a noble and distinguished man: perhaps indeed a member of the royal house, as the myth has it. He must have been conscious of his great abilities, ambitious and energetic; perhaps he saw himself in a dim future as the leader of his people, the governor of the Empire. In close contact with Pharaoh he was a convinced adherent of the new religion, whose basic principles he fully understood and had made his own. With the king's death and the subsequent reaction he saw all his hopes and prospects destroyed. If he was not to recant the convictions so dear to him then Egypt had no more to give him; he had lost his native country. In this hour of need he found an unusual solution. The dreamer Ikhnaton had estranged himself from his people, had let his world empire crumble. Moses active nature conceived the plan of founding a new empire, of finding a new people, to whom he could give the religion that Egypt disdained. It was, as we perceive, a heroic attempt to struggle against his fate, to find compensation in two directions for the losses he had suffered through Ikhnaton's catastrophe. Perhaps he was at the time governor of that border province (Goshen) in which perhaps already in "the Hyksos period" certain Semitic tribes had settled. These he chose to be his new people. A historic decision. He established relations with

them, placed himself at their head and directed the Exodus "by strength of hand." In full contradistinction to the biblical tradition we may suppose this Exodus to have passed off peacefully and without pursuit. The authority of Moses made it possible, and there was then no central power that could have prevented it.[7]

In order to substantiate his claim about Moses, Freud refers to the incompatibility of personalities between the biblical Moses in Egypt and the biblical Moses in Median. Accordingly, whereas the Egyptian Moses is a choleric, impatient, and irascible leader, the Midianite Moses is by contrast longsuffering, compassionate, and a peacemaker. Secondly, the Egyptian Moses is an educated and cultured aristocrat while the Midianite Moses is an illiterate shepherd. Thirdly, the Egyptian Moses is frequently confronted by his violent and murderous followers who find themselves at odds with highly spiritualised monotheistic religion whereas the followers of Moses the Midianite are content with primitive, tangible, and pragmatic laws, statutes, and rules. Freud further asserts that similar incompatibilities can be discovered in the God of Moses the Egyptian and the God of Moses the Midianite. The God of Moses the Egyptian is exalted, dispassionate, and disinterested while the God of Moses the Midianite is an angry, uncanny, and bloodthirsty demon who went about by night and shunned the light of day.

The reason for these incompatibilities, Freud explains, is that after the Exodus and before the conquest of Canaan, the Jews brutally murdered the original Moses, abandoned his religion, and wandered in the wilderness in search of a settlement until they finally arrived at Midian. In Midian they met their kindred tribe whose ancestors had not migrated to Egypt some two hundred years before and discovered that they, too, had been

---

[7]Ibid. pp. 46-48.

introduced to a new religion by a Midianite shepherd, to whom the Mountain (volcano) God Yahweh was revealed, but the Shepherd had long been dead. The two tribes recognised the strength of unity and decided to join forces and to conquer Canaan and to make that land their own. From this union emerged anew a religion containing aspects of the religions of both tribes. However, due to the superiority in education and culture of the migrants from Egypt, the religion of Moses the Egyptian dominated:

> With those who had been in Egypt the memory of the Exodus and of the figure of Moses was still so strong and vivid that it insisted on being incorporated into any account of their early history. There might have been among them grandsons of persons who themselves had known Moses, and some of them still felt themselves to be Egyptians and bore Egyptian names. They had good reasons, however, for "repressing" the memory of the fate that had befallen their leader and lawgiver. For the other component of the tribe the leading motive was to glorify the new God and deny his foreignness. Both parties were equally concerned to deny that there had been an earlier religion and especially what it contained [namely, the murder of Moses]. This is how the first compromise came about, which probably was soon codified in writing; the people from Egypt had brought with them the art of writing and the fondness for writing history. A long time was to elapse, however, before historians came to develop an ideal of objective truth. At first they shaped their accounts according to their needs and tendencies of the moment, with an easy conscience, as if they had not yet understood what falsification signified.[8]

---

[8]Ibid. pp. 110-111.

Freud refers to additional "historical incidents" to substantiate his claim. Firstly, according to the Bible, Moses was slow in speech and that his brother Aaron was assigned by God to be his spokesman in all his dealings with the Israelites. In psychoanalysis terms, he maintains, this amounts to admitting that Moses did not speak Hebrew in the beginning because he was not a Hebrew. Secondly, the division of the Kingdom of Israel into two kingdoms during the reign of King Rehoboam indicates that there had been at least three distinct peoples during the Exodus. The Levites (to whom Joshua did not apportion any land after the Israelites conquered Canaan) must have been ancestrally the closest people to Moses and, therefore, Egyptian by origin, like Moses himself. It must have been due to their devotion to Moses and their shared devotion to monotheism that this group was entrusted in all matters concerning the service of the God of Moses:

> Among the greatest riddles of Jewish prehistoric times is that concerning the antecedents of the Levites. They are said to have been derived from one of the twelve tribes of Israel, the tribe of Levi, but no tradition has ever ventured to pronounce on where that tribe originally dwelt or what portion of the conquered country of Canaan had been allotted to it. They occupied the most important priestly positions, but yet they were distinguished from the priests. A Levite is not necessarily a priest; it is not the name of a caste. Our supposition about the person of Moses suggests an explanation. It is not credible that a great gentleman like the Egyptian Moses approached a people [i.e., the Jewish people residing in Goshen] strange to him without an escort. He must have brought his retinue with him, his nearest adherents, his scribes, his servants. These were the original Levites. Tradition maintains that Moses was a Levite. This seems a transparent distortion of the actual

state of affairs: the Levites were Moses people. This solution is supported by what I mentioned in my previous essay: that in later times we find Egyptian names only among the Levites. We may suppose that a fair number of these Moses people escaped the fate that overtook him and his religion. They increased in the following generations and fused with the people among whom they lived, but they remained faithful to their master, honoured his memory and retained the tradition of his teaching. At the time of the union with the followers of Yahweh they formed an influential minority, culturally superior to the rest.[9]

The people of the southern kingdom must have been predominantly the Levites (Egyptians) whereas the people in the north must have been the Jewish people whose ancestors during the Exodus time and again rebelled against Moses and eventually murdered him.[i] Freud alleges that a similar dissolution took place in Germany following Luther's reformation, because at the time the Germans were composed of two distinct peoples, the Roman Germania which remained faithful to the Catholic Church and the independent Germania which rejected Catholicism.

Meanwhile, how could the Levites, a minority and which had lost its prominent leader, finally prevail to establish its religion and to win the singular devotion of an otherwise stubborn and rebellious people for many centuries? This is characteristic mass psychology at work, Freud explains, and is reminiscent of the hostile rejection with which some scientific discoveries were first met. For example, Freud explains, the Darwinian doctrine of evolution was first vehemently rejected and the ensuing decades witnessed violent debates between its advocates and opponents. Then a generation passed and the doctrine was

---

[9]Ibid. pp. 62-63.

recognised as mankind's significant step towards the truth. Furthermore, Freud attributes the devotion of the Jewish people to their religion and the richness of their biblical literature and poetry to the psychology of trauma and compulsion. Traumatic experiences in the early stages of development leave in a child's memory inerasable impressions to which the child time and again returns, he maintains. In the same way, traumatic experiences in the early stages of a great culture or civilisation leave in the psyche of the masses strong and lasting nostalgia to which they return again and again. People with artistic dispositions provide an outlet to this strong emotion in their epic poetries, paintings, and sculptures. Indeed, as the distance between the traumatic events and the time of creation increases, the compulsion to return to the past, if only in the imagination, increases as well.

The condition we have specified for the origin of folk-epics are as follows: there exists a period of early history that immediately afterwards is regarded as eventful, significant, grandiose and perhaps always heroic; yet it happened so long ago and belonged to times so remote that later generations receive intelligence of it only as an obscure and incomplete tradition. Surprise has been expressed that the epic as a literary form should have disappeared in later times. The explanation may be that the conditions for the production of epics no longer exist. The old material has been used up and so far as later events are concerned history has taken the place of tradition. The bravest heroic deeds of our days are no longer able to inspire an epic; Alexander the Great himself had grounds for his complaint that he would have no Homer to celebrate his life. Remote times have a great attraction, sometimes mysteriously so, for the imagination. As often as mankind is dissatisfied with its present—and that happens often enough—it harks back to the past and hopes at last to win belief in the never-forgotten dream of a Golden Age. Probably man still stands under the magic spell of his childhood, which a not-unbiased memory presents to him as a time of unalloyed bliss. Incomplete and dim memories of the past, which we call tradition, are a great incentive to the artist, for he is free to fill in the gaps in the memories according to the behest of his imagination and to form after his own purpose the image of the time he has undertaken to reproduce. One might almost say that the more shadowy tradition has become the more meet is it for the poet's use. The value tradition has for poetry, therefore, need not surprise us, and the analogy we have found of the dependence of epic poetry on precise conditions will make us more inclined to accept the strange suggestion that with the Jews it was the tradition of Moses which turned the Yahweh worship in the direction of the old Mosaic religion.[10]

Freud claims that the rich explosions of Greek mythologies and Homeric epics must have followed a period of outward splendour and highly developed culture, which then ended in great and sudden catastrophe. Freud further enumerated similar revivals in folk-epics among the Germans, Indians, and Finns after their culture underwent unexpected catastrophe. Similarly, for the Israelites, the Exodus from Egypt under the leadership of Moses and the receiving of the Mosaic religion were unique and profound experiences. They were, unfortunately, inseparably linked to the tragic end of their great leader. But the Israelites brought with them from Egypt the art of writing through which they could externalise their horror and disbelief at what had happened and their undying wish to atone for their sin. In the beginning, they shaped their stories

---

[10]Ibid. pp. 114-116.

according to their intellectual infancy and the demand of the time, but as their literary skill matured, they also learned to appreciate the recording of objective history, which is why the latter accounts, such as I and II Samuel and I and II Kings should be taken as authentic historical accounts, according to Freud.

Freud's attempt to reconstruct the Pentateuch had been sharply criticised from the very beginning by historian as well as Jewish and Christian theologians. As Peter Gay, Freud's biographer, remarks, the book "is a curious production, more conjectural than *Totem and Taboo*, more untidy than *Inhibition, Symptoms and Anxiety*, more offensive than *The Future of an Illusion*."[11] Freud himself was acutely aware of the profound deficiency of the book and its lack of adequate historical facts to substantiate the outrageous claims he made within it. At one instance Freud even wished to produce it in the form of a novel, but felt it uncalled for. Moreover, he was aware of the lack of novelty in the claims. Already several decades before him eminent historians, sociologists, and theologians had questioned the historicity and the true identity of Moses, such as Eduard Meyer, who claimed that Moses was a legend, and Max Weber who claimed that Moses was an Egyptian.[12] As we have already seen, the theologian Sellin, too, had already questioned the authenticity of the account pertaining to the death of Moses, claiming that Moses had most likely been murdered by the Israelites themselves in the wilderness.

So, it is important to ask why Freud wrote *Moses and Monotheism* in the first place? One may attribute the absurdity of the claims he makes in the book to the infirmity of old age, but this will not do justice to the book. Freud himself was hopeful of finding an answer concerning the identity of the Jews and their

---

[11]PG p. 604.
[12]Ibid. 606-607.

place in the world. Indeed, in relation to the question of Jewish identity, Freud concludes, "the Jew is the creation of the man Moses."[13] As to their place in the world, Freud addresses this question by examining a theme familiar to some of his other works. A closer examination of the underlying theme of *Moses and Monotheism* reveals that it is essentially similar to the underlying themes of *Totem and Taboo*, *Dostoevsky and Parricide*, and *Civilisation and Its Discontents*, works Freud produced when his intellectual virility was effervescent. In all of them, Freud grapples in depth with murder and the enduring consequence of the guilt it produces. As all human beings are bound together by a common, unconscious, and abiding sense of guilt as a consequence of the murder of the primeval father, committed by their ancestors, in *Totem and Taboo*, so the Jews also suffer from the additional and unconscious sense of guilt as a consequence of the murder of Moses, committed by their ancestors. Furthermore, in *Civilisation and Its Discontents*, Freud seems to allude that the emergence of the cultural superego potentially abstracts the existence of an unconscious and abiding sense of guilt arising from the death of Jesus Christ.

Supplementary to this, Freud had a complex attitude towards the person of Moses. In *Moses and Monotheism* he sharply criticises monotheism in general and Judaism and Christianity in particular as intolerant religions, hostile to diversity, social understanding, and progress. By contrast he celebrates the open-mindedness of Egyptian, Greek, and Roman pantheisms. No doubt in this regard Freud considered Moses intolerant and found him partly responsible for some of the vices he discovered in Judaism and Christianity. But Freud's fascination with Moses much outweighed his recognition of flaws in the great man. For example, it took Freud more than a decade and several travels to Rome to study and analyse the Moses of

---

[13]Ibid. 605.

Michelangelo. He admired Moses for virtually calling to life a sovereign and enduring nation from nothing and proudly identified himself as a Jew. Furthermore, inasmuch as the biblical Moses felt to have been called to liberate the Israelites from slavery and bondage, Freud, too, felt to have been called to liberate humanity from the slavery of unconscious ambivalence and neurosis. Indeed, on a number of occasions Freud acknowledged only three distinct and seminal scientific revolutions in human history, carried out by Copernicus, Darwin, and himself. "Copernicus has established that the earth is not the centre of the universe; Darwin had invited mankind into the animal kingdom; now he, Freud, was teaching the world that the ego is largely the servant of unconscious and uncontrollable forces in the mind."[14] Consequently, one can interpret *Moses and Monotheism* as Freud's identification of the fierce opposition Moses encountered from his own people during the Exodus with the fierce opposition some of his ideas and theories encountered from the scientific community as well as the general public.

Perhaps, Freud, who has taught us to examine the merit of a literary work from three different psychological dimensions, namely, the oedipal complex of the character, the author, and the readers, was also grappling with his own book and trying to come to terms with (1) his own lifelong and deeply felt guilt as a Jew living in a predominantly Christian and hostile nation, (2) as a Jew who nevertheless was an outspoken atheist, and (3) as a person of marked sensitivity to ethics but who nevertheless rejected and in some situations acted contrary to the teaching of Jesus. No matter how one evaluates *Moses and Monotheism*, it is impossible to underestimate how much Freud relied on the Bible to study the personality and character of Moses and the Jewish nation he brought to existence.

---

[14] PG p. 449; 580.

Dostoevsky

Most of Dostoevsky's characters, regardless of their religious views, are well versed in the Bible. "I have been interpreting [the Apocalypse] for the last fifteen years,"[15] avows Lebedev in *The Idiot*, a man who is otherwise portrayed as untrustworthy in many other things of life. The atheist Ivan Karamazov in his *poem in prose* (The Grand Inquisitor) makes extensive reference to the Gospels and the Book of Revelation and is well educated in church history. Indeed, none of Dostoevsky's characters question the divine message of the Bible; instead, having adequately understood it, some of them choose to disagree with God and his concept of freedom.

Dostoevsky himself regarded the Bible as his spiritual compass. "What a book the Bible is," declares Father Zossima with elation in *The Brothers Karamazov*, his eyes full of tears. "What a miracle, what strength is given with it to man. It is like a mould cast of the world and man and human nature, everything is there, and a law for everything for all the ages. And what mysteries are solved and revealed... I only speak from rapture, and forgive my tears, for I love the Bible."[16]

Dostoevsky was about the same age as Father Zossima when he wrote *The Brothers Karamazov,* his last and most profound book. Like Zossima, he, too, was frail and sickly, suffering from a chronic illness, and "was almost dying of weakness and disease".[17] Inasmuch as Zossima carries the burden of the future of his monastery and the Russian Orthodox Church, Dostoevsky, too, felt he had been called to carry the spiritual burden of his country, particularly, the spiritual burden of its young generation. Russia was at a crossroads at the time,

---

[15] FDIDI p. 185.
[16] FDBRO p. 264.
[17] Ibid. 21.

dreadfully pulled apart by strange and untried ideological forces, which would forever change the fate of that country and its people as well as the fate of many countries and peoples around the world; the meaning and value of human freedom, and the concept of individuality.[ii] So, in a sense, Zossima is giving expression to Dostoevsky's most cherished ideas about the Bible and its significance both for the individual and for society when he makes his farewell address to his selected listeners in his small chamber.

In fact six years prior to his death, in a letter he wrote to his wife, Dostoevsky had expressed in similar words his deep affection for the Book of Job: "I am reading Job and it puts me into a state of painful ecstasy; I leave off reading and I walk about the room almost crying... This book, dear Anna, it's strange; it was the first to impress me in my life. I was still practically an infant."[18]

Dostoevsky found in Job a fellow sufferer who endures inexorable pain and unashamedly expresses his horror, confusion, and helplessness at what he perceives as divine injustice. Almost all Dostoevsky's major characters share and resonate Job's lamentation. "Suffering is part and parcel of extensive intelligence and a feeling heart. A man who is really great, it seems to me, must suffer considerably," observes Raskolnikov in *Crime and Punishment*.[19]

Dostoevsky's characters portray suffering in different ways. In Raskolnikov, Ivan Karamazov, and the *Underground Man*, suffering is mainly expressed as mental anguish and deeply felt disappointment with the fate of creation; in Dmitri Karamazov, Sonia Semyonovna, and Nastasya Filippovna suffering is expressed as emotional agony, as deeply felt shame of a reprehensible past life which keeps on interfering with the

---

[18]JF p. 704.
[19]FDCRI p. 184.

present life; in Marya Timofyevna, it is both physical and emotional affliction; in Prince Myshkin and Kirillov, suffering is felt as a physical affliction and as an immense spiritual burden; in Ippolit Terentyev, suffering manifests itself in a tangle of physical, emotional, and spiritual torments.

In terms of the psychological manifestations of suffering, one can identify at least three similarities between Job and Dostoevsky's characters. To begin with, suffering for most of Dostoevsky's characters (and most likely for Dostoevsky himself as well) is not only a daytime experience nor does it exist solely in the conscious mind. The night, too, brings no relief, for they are haunted by bad dreams and menacing nightmares. "When I think my bed comforts me and my couch will ease my complaint," laments Job in the Bible, "even then you frighten me with dreams and terrify me with vision." (Job 7:13-14). In *Crime and Punishment* Raskolnikov is disturbed multiple times by distressing dreams and nightmares which are so vivid and detailed even the reader is forced into believing they are real; in *The Devils*, the lame and heartbroken Marya Timofyevna spends much of the day alone in a dark, dirty, and cold room, sitting on a shabby couch and telling fortunes; what remains of the night, after her drunken and violent brother has returned home to assault and terrify her with his uncontrollable rage, is filled with menacing dreams. We shall never know how many of the dreadful stories she tells of her stay at a nunnery are actually true (she is a virgin and could not have a baby). In *The Idiot*, foreboding dreams haunt the saintly prince and the rebellious Ippolit alike. In *The Brothers Karamazov* Dostoevsky spends an entire chapter to relate Ivan's intriguing encounter with the Devil, which happens to be at the boundary of wakefulness and sleeping.

"In a morbid condition of the brain," Dostoevsky tells us in *Crime and Punishment* (published in 1866), "dreams often have a singular actuality, vividness, and extraordinary semblance of reality. At times monstrous images are created, but the setting and the whole picture are so truth-like and filled with details so delicate, so unexpectedly, but so artistically consistent, that the dreamer, were he an artist like Pushkin or Turgenev even, could never have invented them in the waking state. Such sick dreams always remain long in the memory and make a powerful impression on the overwrought and deranged nervous system."[20] Fourteen years later, in *The Brothers Karamazov* (published in 1880, shortly before his death), the Devil uses a similar expression to torment Ivan: "Listen, in dreams and especially in nightmares, from indigestion or anything, a man sees sometimes such artistic visions, such complex and real actuality, such events, even a whole world of events, woven into such a plot, with such unexpected details from the most exalted matters to the last button on a cuff, as I swear Leo Tolstoy has never invented. Yet such dreams are sometimes seen not by writers, but by the most ordinary people, officials, journalists, priests. ... The subject is a complete enigma."[21]

The consumptive Ippolit in *The Idiot* recounts one of these "sick" dreams ("one of a kind that I have hundreds of just now") in its monstrous detail. In the dream, the suffering patient helplessly but acutely witnesses in its minute detail the deathly battle (and final defeat) of a faithful dog against a venomous and overpowering monster which has scuttled into the unfamiliar room where the patient is resting.[22]

One of the saddest consequences of suffering is the sense of abiding guilt and insufficiency it produces in the mind of the sufferer. "If I say, 'I will forget my complaint, I will change my expression, and smile,' I still dread all my sufferings, for I know you will not hold me innocent. Since I am already found guilty, why should I struggle in vain?

---

[20] FDCRI p. 44.
[21] FDBRO p. 594.
[22] FDIDI pp. 357-358.

Even if I washed myself with soap and my hands with cleansing powder, you would plunge me into a slime pit so that even my clothes would detest me," confesses Job (Job 9: 27-31). Considering his extraordinary capacity for suffering and repentance, Freud, perhaps accurately, diagnosed Dostoevsky as a sinner and as a masochist[iii]. In his literary world, too, we find some of Dostoevsky's best characters struggling with the same sense of insufficiency as Job. Prince Myshkin, besides suffering from frequent and stupefying epileptic seizures (like Dostoevsky himself), takes upon himself the immense psychological and emotional burden of those living around him and yet he is indwelt by a steadfast sense of inadequacy and self-reproach. Similarly, suffering has tempered Alexei Karamazov and made him selfless, compassionate, generous, patient, and uncommonly cheerful; he is nevertheless keenly aware of his sinful nature and is afraid of becoming more sinful. One day while listening to the candid confession of his wild brother Dmitri, Alexei finds himself suddenly blushing.

"I wasn't blushing at what you were saying or at what you've done," he is quick to reassure his brother. "I blushed because I am the same as you are."

"You? Come, that's going a little too far!"

"No, it's not too far," said Alexei warmly (obviously the idea was not a new one). "The ladder's the same. I'm at the bottom step, and you're above, somewhere about the thirteenth. That's how I see it. But it's all the same. Absolutely the same in kind. Anyone on the bottom step is bound to go up to the top one."

"Then one ought not to step on at all."

"Anyone who can help it had better not."

"But can you?"

"I think not."[23]

---

[23] FDBRO 95-96.

The outspokenly rebellious characters of Dostoevsky who struggle with the problem of being are reminiscent of Job in their bold and well-articulated objections against what they perceive as divine indifference and injustice. The *Rebellion* chapter in *The Brothers Karamazov* is essentially a retelling, both in tone and content, of Job 24. Interestingly, however, inasmuch as the rebels seem to disagree with God and reject his arrangement of life on earth, there is, at the same time, a deep craving for God. The difference between them is that Job is keenly aware of his craving and makes frequent reference to it, whilst Dostoevsky's rebels are not conscious of their longing for God. Job is convinced that his intolerable suffering has something to do with God's anger, for he perceives it an expression of his undesirable closeness. If not God in his close watchfulness making him suffer who else then can it be? So Job begs to be left alone. "Am I the sea or the monster of the deep that you put me under guard?" (Job 7:12); "What is man that you make so much of him, that you give him so much attention, that you examine him every morning and test him every moment? Will you never look away from me, or let me alone even for an instant?" (Job 7: 17-19); "If only there were someone to arbitrate between us, to lay his hands between us both, someone to remove God's rod from me, so that his terror would not frighten me no more. Then I would speak up without fear of him, but as it now stands with me, I cannot." (Job 9:33-35); "Are not my few days almost over? Turn away from me so that I can have a moment's joy." (Job 10:20); "Man born of a woman is of few days and full of trouble. He springs up like a flower and withers away; like a fleeting shadow, he does not endure. Do you fix your eyes on such a one? Will you bring him for judgement before you?" (Job 14:1-3); "Man's days are determined; you have decreed the number of his months and have set limits he cannot exceed. So look away from him and let him alone, till he has put in his time like a hired man." (Job 14:5-6); "If only you would hide me in the grave and conceal me till your anger has passed! If only you would set me a time and then remember me!" (Job 14: 13); "God assails me and tears me in his anger and gnashes his teeth at me; my opponent fastens on me his piercing eyes." (Job 16:9).

But the sufferer does not merely perceive the nearness of God and his pointed rapier; he feels at the same time God's remoteness and the absence of his forgiving and reviving voice. "Why do you hide your face and consider me your enemy?" (Job 13:24); "If only I knew where to find him; if only I could go to his dwelling. I would state my case before him and fill my mouth with arguments... but if I go to the east, he is not there; if I go to the west, I do not find him. When he is at work in the north, I do not see him; when he turns to the south, I catch no glimpse of him." (Job 23:3-4, 8-9).

Likewise, the elderly Zossima correctly interprets Ivan's rebelliousness as despair that is born out of a 'Job complex'. Ivan is obsessed with the suffering of creation because he misses God in his own life, because the real question, Zossima tells him, whether or not Ivan should admit God into his heart, is not yet answered and has become his greatest grief, "for it clamours for an answer."[24] If this question cannot be answered in the affirmative, "it will never be decided in the negative. You know that that is the peculiarity of your heart, and all its suffering is due to it. But thank the Creator who has given you a lofty heart capable of such suffering; of thinking and seeking higher things, for our dwelling is in the heavens."[25]

Kirillov, too, struggles with the same question, but unlike Ivan, he gets an occasional glimpse of the divine mind, from which he recoils in terror in the same way the Israelites at the foot of

---

[24]Ibid. p. 59.
[25] Ibid. pp. 59-60.

Mount Sinai trembled with fear and begged to be spared of the sight, because it was unendurable to behold:

> There are seconds—they come five or six at a time—when you suddenly feel the presence of the eternal harmony in all its fullness. It is nothing earthly. I don't mean that it is heavenly, but a man in his earthly semblance can't endure it. He has to undergo a physical change or die. This feeling is clear and unmistakable. It is as though you suddenly apprehended all nature and suddenly said: "Yes, it's true—it's good." God, when He created the world, said at the end of each day of creation, "Yes, it's true, it's good." It is not rapture, but just gladness. You forgive anything because there is nothing to forgive. Nor do you really love anything—oh, it is much higher than love. What is so terrifying about it is that it is so terribly clear and such gladness. If it went on for more than five seconds, the soul could not endure it and must perish. In those five seconds I live through a lifetime, and I am ready to give my life for them, for it's worth it. To be able to endure it for ten seconds, you would have to undergo a physical change.[26]

For Dostoevsky the greatest character in the Bible is, however, not Job, but Christ, in whom he finds the ideal "man" having matchless beauty, unequalled by any character, in all literary creation. Therefore, for Dostoevsky, a rejection of the Bible is no less than a rejection of Christ, for the meaning and purpose of Christ's existence is explained there. One of the qualities of Christ he frequently refers to and portrays through his characters, either in its authentic form or by creating stark contrasts to it, is self-abnegation. Unlike Freud, who insists that human basic instinctual needs have to be gratified for them to

---

[26]FDDEV pp. 586-587.

be happy and normal, Dostoevsky maintains that human beings have to learn to control their instincts and even to forfeit their gratification, for otherwise they interfere with their freedom to love and undermine their capacity to establish meaningful relationships with God as well as with other fellow human beings. Those of Dostoevsky's characters who unquestionably yield to their basic instinctual needs rarely discover happiness and spend their whole life "without finding their true selves in themselves."[27]

All Dostoevsky's great books are experimentations with the impact of ideas contradicting the biblical ideal, Christ. In *Crime and Punishment*, the university dropout and impoverished Raskolnikov believes that geniuses like himself and Napoleon can overstep the law and commit murder when they consider the cause to be justified. He carefully lays out a plot to kill and rob a greedy and loveless pawnbroker, whose money he aims to spend for a good cause. Besides, he reasons, the world will be rid of a shameless leech and a vermin. Raskolnikov carries out his plan to the end and kills and robs the pawnbroker but unexpected events unfold compelling him to murder her sister as well, against whom he holds no complaints. He extricates himself from the crime scene unobserved but finds himself in agonising moral and emotional turmoil from which he cannot free himself.

In *The Devils*, Nicholas Stavrogin portrays a young, intelligent, and rich aristocrat who possesses an extraordinary physical strength. He seems to be "a paragon of beauty" [iv] and yet at the same time there is "something hideous about him."[28] He effortlessly wins the attention and admiration of the people surrounding him, because he is indifferent to both attention and admiration. He is incapable of distinguishing between good

---

[27] FDBRO p. 22.
[28] FDDEV p. 57.

and evil, regarding these notions as mere prejudices. For example, he cannot distinguish the difference in beauty "between some voluptuous and brutish act and any heroic exploit, even the sacrifice of life for the good of humanity"[29] and finds equal enjoyment in both extremes. The only force that carries him through life is a feeble curiosity within him that every once in a while motivates him to experiment with ideas, during which time life seems to be "infinite". Often his experiments involve an assault on established moral values such as mercy, compassion, and the respect for human dignity. Thus he publicly drags an old man of high social standing by the nose, openly kisses a married woman at her own wedding ceremony; and mercilessly bites the ear of a respected governor. Stavrogin's most outrageous experiment concerns a poor, crippled, and beggarly young woman whom he encourages to fall in love with him with the objective of finding out what will become of her ("You have purposely chosen one of the most wretched human beings ...a cripple, a woman deemed to suffer disgrace and blows all her life, knowing, too, that this poor woman was dying of comic love for you, and you're trying to spoof her on purpose just to find what would come of it."[30]).
He carries out his plan earnestly and detachedly and the poor woman falls in love with Stavrogin to a desperate depth. To bring the lurid game to its obnoxious climax he secretly marries her, but before she hardly composes herself to barely comprehend what is happening in her life, he leaves Russia for Switzerland, alone. In Switzerland, he will neither see nor communicate with her for four and a half years. As to what actually happens following her abandonment, we know only a fraction of it (if at all). She tells of having been confined to a nunnery against her will and having lost a child (we learn later

---

[29]Ibid. p. 260.
[30]Ibid. p. 196.

that she is still a virgin). The unfortunate girl populates her life with fantasy when existence becomes intolerable for her. Like many of Dostoevsky's victims, she too, takes the blame upon herself and unceasingly questions where things went wrong:

> I suppose I must have done something very wrong to him," she suddenly added, as though speaking to herself. "Only I don't know what it is. Oh, the consciousness of that will haunt me all my life. Always—always—all these five years—day and night—I was afraid that I'd done something wrong to him. I've prayed and prayed, thinking all the time how greatly I've wronged him. And now it turns out to be only too true.[31]

But after those dreadful and lonely years the two finally meet in a small village where she discovers for the first time her true position and his quintessential nature. She understands clearly that he has never been and cannot be in love with her, that he is a commonplace mortal, and that she, very regrettably, mistook "the owl in him for a falcon all along"...

> ...it cannot be that a falcon has become an owl. ... Only mine is a bright falcon and a prince, and you're an owl, and a shopman! Mine will bow down to God if it pleases him, and won't if it doesn't. ... Oh heavens! That alone kept me happy for those five years that my falcon was living somewhere beyond the mountains, soaring, gazing at the sun...[32]

For Nicholas Stavrogin, to whom there is no distinction between right and wrong and good and evil, the insight, courage and rejection of the young woman is an entirely new experience, but one which comes too late and which cannot

---
[31]Ibid. p. 280.
[32]Ibid. 283-284.

redeem him. "I am still capable," he confesses towards the end of his life, "as I always was, of desiring to do something good, and of feeling pleasure from it; at the same time I desire evil and feel pleasure from that too. But both feelings are always too petty, and are never very strong. My desires are too weak; they are not enough to guide me... I know I ought to kill myself, to brush myself off the earth like a nasty insect; but I am afraid of suicide, for I am afraid of showing greatness of soul. I know that it will be another sham again—the last deception in an endless series of deceptions. What good is there in deceiving oneself, simply to play at greatness of soul? Indignation and shame I can never feel, therefore not despair."[33] Nicholas Stavrogin commits suicide in the end.

Similarly, Ivan Karamazov makes a clean break with Christ's notion of freedom in *The Brothers Karamazov*. In his "Poetry", Ivan introduces his younger brother Alyosha to the Grand Inquisitor, one of the most significant characters of the book. He is a ninety year old, majestic, and fervent cardinal overseeing the burning of "the enemies of the Holy Roman Catholic Church"[34] during the Spanish Inquisition. One day, after he put to fire more than hundred "heretics" in the presence of "the king, the court, the knights, the cardinals, the most charming ladies of the court, and the whole population of Seville"[35], Christ comes to the distraught city, quietly and unobserved, but everybody on the streets of Seville recognises him and begins to surround and silently follow him. He does not utter a word but looks at his people with infinite compassion and a soft, sympathetic smile.

On his way to the famous cathedral, he heals some of the ill people as in the days of his ministry on earth 1500 years ago. He even raises a little child from the dead right in front of the

---

[33]Ibid. 666.
[34]FDBRO p. 225.
[35]Ibid.

cathedral, at which point in time the cardinal meets him and, like all the others, immediately recognises him. But the cardinal is neither surprised nor pleased. Indeed, he is indignant and furious. The sudden appearance of Christ, the cardinal alleges, is an interference with the authority of the church, an infringement of human freedom, and in contradiction with the attitude Christ himself exhibited in the wilderness when the "dreaded spirit" tempted him to do miracles in order to win followers, and Christ refused. The cardinal orders his guards to lay hands on the stranger and put him in a vaulted prison. "And such is his power, so completely are the people cowed into submission and trembling obedience to him, that the crowd immediately makes way for the guards, and in the midst of deathlike silence they lay hands on Him and lead him away."[36] That evening the cardinal visits the prisoner to express his mind freely. The core meaning of life may rest in the concept of freedom, he owns, but freedom is intolerable for the majority of human beings, because it necessarily entails uncertainty and suffering and deprives the basis to safe and secured human existence. Besides, freedom inflames man's innate rebelliousness and his desire to destroy boundaries, contradicting with the divine call for obedience and submission. So, the cardinal has enticed the multitude (in the Name of Christ) to relinquish their God-given freedom in favour of bread, a secure life, and a parish. He has also permitted them to sin and to find pleasure in their wickedness ("Oh, we shall allow them even sin, they are weak and helpless, and they will love us like children because we allow them to sin. We shall tell them that every sin will be expiated, if it is done with our permission, that we allow them to sin because we love them, and the punishment for these sins we take upon ourselves."[37]).

---

[36]Ibid. p. 226.
[37]Ibid. p. 235.

A handful of them, the "heretics", have rejected the cardinal's proposal in favour of the heavenly bread which Christ promises in his Gospels and which the believers accept by faith, the Cardinal admits, "Thou didst promise them the bread of Heaven, but, I repeat again, can it compare with earthly bread in the eyes of the weak, ever sinful and ignoble race of man? And if for the sake of the bread of Heaven thousands shall follow Thee, what is to become of the millions and tens of thousands of millions of creatures who will not have the strength to forego the earthly bread for the sake of the heavenly? Or dost Thou care only for the tens of thousands of the great and strong, while the millions, numerous as the sands of the sea, who are weak but love Thee, must exist only for the sake of the great and strong?"[38]

Like Stavrogin's, Ivan's idea comes to a bitter reality check when he realises that he consciously and wilfully paves the way for the murder of his own father when he decides to depart for Moscow leaving the old man alone and defenceless. "Away with the past," he tells himself once he is on the train. "I've done with the old world forever, and may I have no news, no echo, from it. To a new life, new places, and no looking back!" But instead of freedom and relief, he finds himself being oppressed by gloom and his heart aching in anguish. He sinks into melancholic meditation throughout the drive and towards daybreak, when the train approaches Moscow, he suddenly interrupts his meditation and pronounces a judgment upon himself: "I am a scoundrel," he whispered to himself.[39]

This realisation eventually brings Ivan to the understanding that one may wilfully give up freedom for slavery but one may never be able to wilfully trade knowledge of good and evil for

---

[38]Ibid. p. 229.
[39]Ibid. p. 254.

ignorance, and the consequence of wilful slavery is a perpetual mental agony.

Einstein

Spinoza's bold and comprehensive evaluation of the claims of the Bible and the conclusions he drew afterwards provided the foundation for the beliefs, not only of Einstein but also of Tolstoy and Freud, about the Bible. This is not to suggest that they agreed with Spinoza on every issue. Einstein, in particular, made his agreements and disagreements with Spinoza known both directly and indirectly. For example, Spinoza regards the knowledge that can be derived from the Bible as elementary knowledge in comparison to the knowledge that can be derived through rational and inferential reasoning. Einstein, on the other hand, regards biblical and rational knowledge as belonging to two different regimes, and a comparison of the two sources as, therefore, meaningless. Spinoza maintains that one can attain knowledge of God without the Bible (through rational endeavour alone) whilst Einstein maintains that rational knowledge alone is insufficient. Spinoza values a piece of scientific discovery as more precious than any spiritual revelation, including the Ten Commandments. Einstein, on the contrary, values spiritual revelation more precious to human existence and aspiration than any scientific discovery, including his own.

> Humanity has every reason to place the proclaimers of high moral standards and values above the discoverers of objective truth. What humanity owes to personalities like … Moses and Jesus ranks for me higher than all the achievements of the inquiring constructive mind.[40]

Furthermore, unlike Spinoza, who claims that human beings can achieve true blessedness without the Bible, Einstein identifies in the Bible "super-personal" values and lofty goals which can enrich human life with meaning and purpose:

---

[40] AEHUM p. 70.

The highest principles for our aspirations and judgments are given to us in the Jewish-Christian religious tradition. It is a very high goal which, with our weak powers, we can reach only very inadequately, but which gives a sure foundation to our aspirations and valuations. If one were to take that goal out of its religious form and look merely at its purely human side, one might state it perhaps thus: free and responsible development of the individual, so that he may place his powers freely and gladly in the service of all mankind.[41]

Elsewhere Einstein borrows an expression from the New Testament to restate human beings' highest destiny in life, which is to serve rather than to rule or to impose oneself in any way upon others.

In agreement with Spinoza, however, Einstein rejects the claims of the Bible as regards supernatural intervention, life after death, and divine reward and retribution. Instead, Einstein regards the Bible as a collection of partially reliable historical books in which the gradual evolution of religion can be partly traced. This evolution, according to Einstein, began with a religion of fear (based on divine reward and retribution) to develop into being a moral religion. Some of the books in the Bible, such as the Psalms of David and the Major and Minor Prophets, Einstein maintains, convey what he calls a cosmic religious feeling, human beings' noblest and highest form of religious experience. Einstein characterises this experience by its ability to stipulate the perception and genuine appreciation of the richness and complexity of creation and the marvellous beauty and order with which it is endowed, independent of its immediate and material advantages to human existence.

Einstein is at the same time forthcoming in his emphasis on the Bible's in-exclusivity as a means of experiencing a cosmic

---

[41]AEIDE p. 43.

religious feeling. Indeed, some of the great personalities he refers to and who experienced cosmic religious feeling in the past (Spinoza being one of them) were not biblical figures or religious in the usual sense of the word. Moreover, Einstein does not hesitate to remark that the biblical super-personal values can make sense only insofar as they can be freed from their "superstitious" husk: "If one purges the Judaism of the Prophets and Christianity, as Jesus Christ taught it, of all subsequent additions, especially those of the priests, one is left with a teaching which is capable of curing all the social ills of humanity."[42]

The additions Einstein refers to here have been closely scrutinised by Spinoza in his Theological-Political Treatise (*Tractatus Theologico-Politikus*)[43], and it is helpful to closely examine them. Spinoza, in his great tendency to cleanly and distinctly sort and organise concepts, so as to precisely examine their essence and their causal relationship with one another, classifies all objects of legitimate human desire into three categories, namely, knowledge, virtue, and a secure and healthy life. According to Spinoza, human desire, regardless of the way in which it is manifested, is quintessentially selfish, and its primary goal is to perpetuate life. Human beings desire knowledge because it invests them with power to reign over nature as well as their fellow human beings. They desire virtue to bridle their passions and to overcome fear stemming from the uncertainty of life. In the absence of virtue, human happiness depends on external causes, which cannot be wholly known, controlled, appeased, or influenced; as a result, human peace inevitably fluctuates and remains unpredictable ("When the mind is in a state of doubt, the slightest impulse can easily steer it in any direction, and all the more readily when it is

---

[42] Ibid. pp. 184-185.
[43] BSCOM pp. 383-583.

hovering between hope and fear, though it may be confident, pompous and proud enough at other times."[44]). Human beings desire a secure and healthy life because existence would otherwise be painful and unpleasant to them.

As human beings acquire more knowledge, their ability to comprehend causal relations and to use this knowledge for their own advantage, increases. Spinoza calls the widening of the intellect's horizon by accumulating and synthesising knowledge a process of perfection (perfection being related to completeness). However, this process can be continuously frustrated by passions, which interfere with and distract human beings from intellectual occupations. Spinoza asserts that passions produce illusory perceptions in the mind with regard to its own state of being as well as the world outside. In the same way that electrons surrounding an atom can be excited by an external energy (such as by a beam of light) to leave their orbit for a higher orbit or to give up energy in order to descend into a lower orbit, human passions, too, produce in the mind the impression that it is experiencing transitions to a higher or a lower state of perfection, Spinoza maintains. For example, when human beings experience joy, their mind perceives this condition as a transition into a higher state of perfection. When, on the other hand, they experience sadness, their mind perceives it as a transition into a lower state of perfection. Some passions, such as love and hatred, hope and despair, produce more complex perceptions. Love and hatred, for instance, are essentially joy and sadness, respectively, but the mind not only perceives them as transitions into a higher or a lower state of perfection, but it is also aware of the external objects which are the cause of transition. Not all passions can be correctly and distinctly perceived or interpreted by the mind.

---

[44]BSCOM p. 388.

Some of them are perceived partially and some of them erroneously.

Since the passions themselves are excited by external factors or causes, insufficient knowledge of these causes and their relationship with the realm of ideas (the mind) inevitably leads to inaccurate perception of one's own state of mind and the state of the real world, thereby leading to frequent emotional fluctuation. As long as passions are free, ungoverned by the intellect and through rational understanding of causal relations, Spinoza explains, man is their prisoner. Thus, virtue is the endeavour to restrain and moderate passions and to liberate the intellect from their influence or oppression. In this sense alone Spinoza considers human beings as free beings. The only way human beings can cultivate virtue, according to Spinoza, is by pursuing knowledge; precisely speaking, by understanding the nature of primary causes, which are the attributes of God, and the sources of all other causes.

Spinoza classifies the means by which human beings acquire knowledge into three classes, based on the level of perfection their intellect has attained. These are experience, reasoning, and intuition. The acquisition of knowledge through experience follows the realisation of the relationship between a cause and its effect after an instance of this relationship occurred (but not before). Spinoza refers to this type of knowledge as knowledge assumed by example. The experience may directly relate to the persons themselves who witness the interplay of a cause and its effect, and, in consequence, add knowledge, or it may relate to others who record and pass their story for others to learn. In either case, Spinoza grades this type of knowledge as elementary knowledge. It is the easiest form of knowledge to acquire and, therefore, the shallowest and the form of knowledge most likely to be subjective, incomplete, and ephemeral. It is also the type of knowledge that can be acquired by the masses. Spinoza maintains that the knowledge that can be found in the Bible is chiefly of an experiential nature:

> Therefore, since the whole of Scripture was revealed in the first place for an entire nation, and eventually for all mankind, its contents had to be adapted particularly to the understanding of the common people, and it had to appeal only to experience. Let us explain more clearly. The teachings of Scripture that are concerned only with philosophic matters can be summed up as follows: that there is a God or Being who made all things and who directs and sustains the world with supreme wisdom; that he takes the utmost care of men, that is, those of them who live moral and righteous lives; and that he severely punishes the others and cuts them off from the good. Now Scripture establishes this simply by appealing to experience, that is, by its historical narratives; it does not provide any definitions of the terms it employs, but its language and reasoning is adapted to the understanding of the common people. And although experience can give no clear knowledge of these matters, and cannot teach what God is and in what way he sustains and directs all things and cares for men, it can still teach and enlighten men as far as suffices to impress on their minds obedience and devotion *(Theological-Political Treatise)*.[45]

Rational knowledge, which is the second in the rank, according to Spinoza's classification, can be acquired by comprehending causal relationships a priori; no instance needs to occur. The mind draws conclusions from firmly established general truths and a few axioms, through a long chain of logical and orderly arguments. This process, Spinoza warns, requires great caution, acuteness, and self-restraints. Rational knowledge enables the mind to filter the interference or the influence of the passions

---

[45]Ibid. p. 441.

as well as existential fear, so that it can perceive objective truths as they are, in their entirety (one is neither desperate nor complacent of how things are arranged in the objective universe).

The highest form of knowledge, according to Spinoza's ranking, is the one that comes naturally, through intuition. It is the comprehension of ideas, which are neither contained in nor deducible from general truths and axioms, in their natural form. At this stage, the mind simply perceives primary causes vividly, distinctly, and completely. According to Spinoza, Jesus Christ is the only person who had been endowed with this gift.

> ... a man who can by pure intuition comprehend ideas which are neither contained in nor deducible from the foundations of our natural knowledge, must necessarily possess a mind far superior to those of his fellow men, nor do I believe that any have been so endowed save Christ. To Him the ordinances of God leading men to salvation were revealed directly without words or visions ... and it may be said that the wisdom of God (that means, wisdom more than human) took upon itself in Christ human nature, and that Christ was the way of salvation (*Theological-Political Treatise*).[46]

Spinoza maintains that intuition and reasoning can lead to the knowledge and love of God, but knowledge by experience does not lead to this end. So, Spinoza concludes, the Bible (the Old Testament) does not contribute to the knowledge and love of God. In fact, it leads to confusion, Spinoza argues, for God appears in the Bible as spontaneous, unpredictable, and contradicting the natural laws he himself ordained.

Spinoza conclusively states that the aids to acquire the knowledge of God and to cultivate virtue should come from within the human mind alone. No external revelation,

---

[46]BSCOM p. 398.

aspiration, miracle, or prophecy, including the Bible, is necessary. God has innately enabled human beings and put the desire and the sense of duty in them to seek the knowledge of God and to love him:

> Since, then, the human mind contains the nature of God within itself in concept, and partakes thereof, and is thereby enabled to form certain basic ideas that explain natural phenomena and inculcate morality, we are justified in asserting that the nature of mind …is the primary cause of divine revelation. For … all that we clearly and distinctly understand is dictated to us by the idea and nature of God—not indeed in words, but in a far superior way and one that agrees excellently with the nature of mind… (*Theological-Political Treatise*).[47]

Spinoza limits the scope and usefulness of the Bible, particularly, the Old Testament, to providing the basis for a secure and healthy societal life. The Old Testament, he explains, is a story about the Jewish people, why and how the nation of Israel comes to existence, thrived as a sovereign nation for a long time, and eventually disintegrated. From the Bible one can learn, as it were, imperfectly, how the goal of a secure and healthy life may be achieved. Inasmuch as human beings are social beings, their social surroundings affect them. Natural and human forces (misfortunes) affect the wise as much as the unwise, the virtuous as well as the wicked, the strong as well as the weak. Thus, human beings' endeavour to protect themselves from harm necessarily involves the assistance of others, requiring the organisation of people in communities, and the occupation of a strip of territory with well-defined borders, which they can claim as their own land in which to live and thrive, and a set of laws, which all citizens

---

[47]BSCOM p. 395.

subject themselves to, so that internal peace and harmony can be maintained.ᵛ

Likewise, Moses brought out the Israelites from Egypt and promised them a strip of territory and a sovereign nation; he gave them a set of fixed laws which should be observed by all members, irrespective of their spiritual, intellectual, and social standing; he persuaded the Israelites to relinquish part of their individual freedom in favour of a commonwealth and to concentrate all the defence force into one body, which is the social body. Moses could have not persuaded the Israelites to commit themselves to his idea of one nation, one people, and one religion, Spinoza alleges, without ascribing his vision and his laws to a one God, to divine revelation, and to the direct order and involvement of God, and to divine reward and retribution. Consequently, Moses (and later all the prophets, Jesus, and the Apostles) used expressions and terminology the people would easily comprehend, remember, and submit to.ᵛⁱ As for Moses, the Israelites were stubborn and rebellious so that he time and again needed the illusion of miracles and wonders to persuade and win over the Israelites: "The fact is that when Moses realised the character and the obstinate spirit of his nation, he saw clearly that they could not accomplish their undertaking without mighty miracles and the special external help of God, and must assuredly perish without such help; and so he besought this special external help of God so that it should be evident that God willed them to be saved."[48]

In truth, Spinoza alleges, those were not really miracles and wonders what the Israelites experienced in the wilderness or afterwards. Even though the Israelites in their simple-mindedness believed that extraordinary things happened in their behalf due to a direct divine intervention, the biblical stories of miracles can and must be understood either as

---

[48] Ibid. p. 422.

imaginary or symbolic expressions. Spinoza refers to several miracles in the Bible that can have rational explanations. Some of them are found in the Book of Exodus where Moses confronts Pharaoh and tells him to let the Israelites leave Egypt. The biblical account states that when Pharaoh refuses to heed to Moses' demand, God afflicts the Egyptians with ten plagues. In one of these plagues, for example, God brings a dense swarm of locusts over Egypt and covers the entire land with them.

> ... an east wind blow across the land all that day and all that night. By morning the wind had brought the locusts; they invaded all Egypt and settled down in every area of the country in great numbers. Never before had there been such a plague of locusts, nor will there ever be again. They covered all the ground until it was black. They devoured all that was left after the hail—everything growing in the fields and the fruit on the trees. Nothing green remained on tree or plant in all the land of Egypt.
> (Exodus 10:13-15, NIVUK)

When later Pharaoh regrets his decision and consents to release the Israelites, God brings a strong west wind, which catches up and carries the locusts into the Red Sea. In reality, Spinoza explains, the east wind, the locusts, and the west wind, were, all, natural phenomena, which worked favourably to the Israelites, but both the Israelites and the Egyptians perceived them as signs of divine judgement for the mistreatment of the Israelites. Similarly, the Egyptian troop which pursued the Israelites, with the intention of forcefully bringing them back to Egypt, might indeed have perished in the Red Sea, Spinoza explains, but not because God miraculously divided the sea or ordered the waters to return to their original place after they divided, but simply because a sudden strong wind blew once the Egyptian troop started crossing the sea, raising strong waves, which prevailed over the troop and drowned it. But the Israelites, as it were, collectively perceived the occasion as divine judgement and deliverance, and, indeed, it can be perceived as such, but not in the way the Israelites understood, Spinoza alleges.

Spinoza in like manner attempts to rationally explain many of the miracle stories of the Bible. He also remarks that some of the miracles required preconditions, which can provide some hints as to what actually happened. For example, during his confrontation with Pharaoh, Moses scattered ashes before the Egyptians were infected with blains and Aaron struck the dust of the earth for the gnats to emerge. Elsewhere Elisha bent over the dead boy to revive him; and Jesus performed preparatory acts before he healed the man born blind ("After saying this, [Jesus] spit on the ground, made some mud with the saliva, and put it on the man's eyes. 'Go,' he told him, 'wash in the Pool of Siloam'" (John 9:7-7, NIV)).

Other miracles, such as God's visitation of Adam and Eve in paradise, God's descent on Mount Sinai and the mountain smoking, and the rapture of Elijah by chariots of fire, should be understood symbolically rather than literally, Spinoza maintains. Still others—such as the disobedience of Adam and the story of Job—should be understood as allegories.

Since Spinoza accepts the Exodus of the Israelites out of Egypt, he does not explain how so many events could have occurred naturally and sequentially, in precise order, to facilitate the peaceful exit of so many unarmed Israelites. He also does not explain how Jesus could have performed so many other miracles without any preparation or preconditions.

There were no prophecies either nor divine revelations as the Bible claims, Spinoza maintains. They were the vivid imaginations of peculiar and exceptionally gifted people. The prophets were individuals who dedicated their whole life to specific missions, to which they felt called. Some of these missions concerned the continuation of the nation of Israel as a sovereign nation and the security and well-being of its people.

The prophets accurately realised that moral decline, corruption, injustice, and poverty would bring disintegration and ruin to the nation as well as to the surrounding nations. So, they warned of these ills in the name of God, for otherwise their message would have carried no authority. In essence, Spinoza claims, the messages the prophets brought were ordinary messages, promises and retribution, the promises being the most desirable things the people craved for and the retribution being the threats they chiefly dreaded.

Spinoza refers to the tone and content of the messages of the prophets and how they betray the temperament, worldview, experience, culture, and education of the prophets to support his argument that those messages were of human origin. He also remarks that the prophets themselves often sought for divine confirmation in form of tangible and extraordinary signs, because they were doubtful of the origin of their message—whether they were product of their own imagination or messages they directly received from God. Spinoza lists several examples where prophecies and divine revelations were accompanied by signs. In fact, Spinoza argues, Moses himself, acknowledging and anticipating the difficulty of distinguishing divine revelations from pure human fantasy, specifies conditions by which the authenticity of prophecies should be examined, and these conditions should entail tangible and extraordinary signs. But most importantly, biblical prophecies, Spinoza adds, did not make the prophets themselves any wiser or holier or more knowledgeable of God than they were before. Spinoza claims that the relevance of the Old Testament ended with the disintegration of the Jewish nation. He acknowledges the moral significance of the New Testament, particularly, the teaching of Jesu., He, nevertheless, adds that the moral instructions of the New Testament, too, can be acquired without the Bible. Spinoza borrows expression from one of the

Epistles of the Apostle Paul, to summarise the central message of the New Testament:

> But the fruit of the Spirit is love, joy, peace, patience, kindness, goodness, faithfulness, gentleness and self-control. Against such things there is no law. (Galatians 5: 22-23. NIV.)

If human beings seek and attain these attributes outside or without the help of the Bible, Spinoza positively concludes, then it should be all right; they have achieved the moral ideal set by the Bible.

For Spinoza, it is a matter of complete indifference to determine whether the Bible is indeed the Word of God. He sees no reason why God shouldn't communicate directly with the human mind, choosing a direct way as opposed to the fixed and unchangeable laws that govern the infinite chains of causes and effects through which God normally reveals his essence (in adherence to the eternal laws of nature). But even then there is no way that God would contradict himself, Spinoza maintains. The laws of nature by which God establishes and sustains the universe are perfect, having infinite scope. Consequently, if God communicates with human beings, whatever the channel he may choose, he does so without contravening the laws of nature. Spinoza maintains that natural phenomena which can be clearly and definitely understood are better conceived of as the work and revelation of God, because they reveal, as far as their essence and perfection extend, the essence of God in a predictable manner. In contrast, the miracles as narrated in the Bible, fail to explain the essence of God, since they do not have natural causes or are contrary to natural laws. In either case, instead of producing a belief in God, they lead to confusion and doubt, because they suggest randomness and disorder and unpredictability in the nature of God.

Spinoza's arguments have two serious implications. Firstly, to the same extent that we understand nature and natural laws—

gravity and electromagnetism included—we also understand the essence of God and how to love him. Therefore, a piece of scientific discovery is more precious than the revelation at Mount Sinai or the Ten Commandments. This is consistent with Spinoza's pantheism. Since God and his creation are causally and intimately interlinked (it is not absolutely clear where God's essence stops and nature begins), the knowledge of one inevitably leads to the knowledge of the other. Secondly, since the natural laws are immutable and there is no free will in creation as well as in God, every claim in the Bible that contradicts the laws of nature is logically inconsistent with and contradicts the nature of God.

Einstein agrees with Spinoza that the prophets and biblical editors incorporated their anthropomorphic concept of God into the Bible. But Einstein does not accept Spinoza's assertion that the knowledge of God can be adequately acquired by rational or scientific inquiry alone. He regards scientific knowledge and biblical knowledge as belonging to different realms, each providing vital insights about God that cannot be provided by the other. The first one mainly addresses questions pertaining to the universe and its construction (what is) whereas the second addresses questions pertaining to the purpose of life (what should be). Einstein is very clear that the application of scientific methodology demonstrates nothing else beyond the relationship between and the conditioning of facts by one another. He is equally clear that knowledge of "what is" does not open the door directly to "what should be".

According to Einstein, even the clearest and most complete knowledge of what is may not be adequate to determine what the goal of human aspirations should be. He further admits that even if science were one day to discover the ultimate goal of human existence, it may still fail to convince human beings to pursue and achieve this goal. ("The knowledge of truth as such is wonderful, but it is so little capable of acting as a guide that it cannot prove even the justification and the value of the aspiration towards that very knowledge of truth."[49]) So, for Einstein it is imperative to complement scientific knowledge to make existence worth living.

Einstein may reject the supernatural claims of the Bible but he acknowledges its ethical claims. In doing so, however, he anticipates a legitimate question. If the Bible does not have divine authority, as it claims, whence does it get its authority to command human beings as to how to lead their lives? The authority of the Bible, Einstein argues, cannot be stated or justified merely by human reasoning; its existence can be recognised visibly in healthy societies, positively acting upon the conduct and aspiration and judgement of its members; it is there as something living, without it being necessary to find a justification for its relevance, asserting itself simply and clearly through the medium of powerful personalities.[50] One of these personalities to whom Einstein refers is Jesus Christ. Einstein describes Jesus as luminous and enthralling. No one can read the Gospels without feeling his actual presence, he confesses. "His personality pulsates in every word. No myth is filled with such life."[51] But Einstein remarks that knowledge of "what should be" can also be found outside the Bible.

---

[49] AEIDE p. 42.
[50] Ibid. pp. 42-43.
[51] WI p. 386.

Tolstoy

In the preface to *The Gospel in Brief*, Tolstoy compares his engagement with the Bible to that of someone who desperately searches the contents of a sack full of refuse. After a long, tedious, and exasperating labour the person discovers some infinitely precious pearls in it. He does not hesitate to call the sack by its name but understands and even admires those who preserved the pearls inside it. In the same way, he explains, the Bible contains precious truth which is unfortunately mixed up with numerous lifeless traditions and superstitions. "The source of Christian teaching is the Gospels, and in them I found the explanation of the spirit which guides the life of all who really live. But together with this source of the pure water of life I found, wrongfully united with it, mud and slime which had hidden its purity from me: by the side of and bound up with the lofty Christian teaching I found a Hebrew and a Church teaching alien to it."[52]

Tolstoy maintains that the Bible is the product of thousands of brains and had been edited, enlarged, and commented upon for many centuries as a result of which it is now full of inconsistencies and misinterpretations. Among those who allegedly introduced these faults are the apostles of Jesus and the early church fathers. Tolstoy accuses the Apostles of trying to harmonise the teaching of Jesus with Hebraism (the Old Testament) even though the two are quintessentially incompatible; and in doing so, they unrightly added into the Gospels doctrines, which undermine and obscure the core meaning of the teaching of their Master. Moreover, Tolstoy alleges, they carried out the task of harmonising in the name of the Holy Spirit, so that for many centuries it had been impossible to question, challenge, and correct their claims.

---

[52]LTGOS p. 5.

According to Tolstoy, this tradition had further been carried out by the early church fathers up until the late fourth century, so much so that it finally became impossible to distinguish the original teaching of Jesus from all the rest.

Tolstoy argues that if one were to reject the claim that the Bible was inspired by the Holy Spirit and scrutinises its claims based merely on their reasonableness to the rational mind and their harmony with the loftiest human aspirations, it would be possible to re-establish the original teaching of Jesus and discard all the rest. Consequently, in *The Gospel in Brief*, Tolstoy endeavours towards this end. In the preface of the same book Tolstoy explains that after he completed the book, he discovered to his great surprise and delight that the essential structure of his "harmonised" gospel perfectly aligns with the Lord's Prayer, a prayer Jesus taught to his disciples. Hence, Tolstoy divides his book into six chapters, each chapter containing a pair of leading predicates, which are causally related to one another. According to Tolstoy, these predicates correspond with the verses of the Lord's Prayer as follows[53]:

1. God is the infinite source of life. Human beings are uniquely related to God because they are his spiritual offspring (according to Tolstoy, this predicate corresponds to: "Our father" in the Lord's Prayer).
   Therefore the service human beings can offer God is primarily of spiritual nature ("Who art in heaven").
2. Since God is the origin of human life, human life is sacred ("Hallowed be Thy name").
   This implies that the ultimate purpose of human life entails serving fellow human beings. This is the will of God ("Thy kingdom come").
3. The spiritual bread of human life comes from the doing of God's will ("Thy will be done, as it is in heaven").

---

[53]Ibid. p. 2

Therefore human happiness does not depend on the gratification of one's own will ("on earth").
4. The temporal life (the life subject to time) should serve to enrich the true life ("Give us ... our daily bread").
The true life itself, however, is independent of time; it is lived in the present ("this day").
5. Time gives an illusion of the true life; time past and time future conceal the true essence of the present life ("And forgive us our debt, as we also have forgiven our debtors").
Therefore, human beings should strive to destroy the illusion arising from the influence of the past and the future ("And lead us not into temptation").
6. The true life manifests itself in loving all human beings, independent of time ("And leads us not into temptation").
Therefore, love is the glue which unites the individual's life both with God and with fellow human beings ("For Thine is the kingdom and the power and the glory").

Tolstoy alleges that biblical passages, which are neither compatible with nor contribute to amplifying the truth in these predicates can be removed from the Bible without endangering its authority or undermining its significance. Tolstoy moreover alleges that the twelve predicates can serve as the basis to extract the original meaning and intentions of some of the passages, which "were deliberately modified" by latter biblical editors. In the subsequent sections, we shall review his gospel from different angles.

(i) Identity

Tolstoy alleges that one of the primary reasons as to why some grievous errors were introduced into the New Testament is due to a fundamental misunderstanding of the identity of Jesus.

Whereas the four Gospels claim that Jesus frequently used expressions such as "the Son of Man" and "the Son of God" to indicate his divine origin, Jesus, Tolstoy argues, never intended them to be taken literally. Tolstoy explains that Jesus on many occasions also tells his disciples that they are God's children and that God is their father. Indeed the Lord's Prayer begins by acknowledging God as the heavenly and sovereign father of all human beings. Therefore, when Jesus claims to be the Son of God, Tolstoy concludes, he is alluding to God as being the spiritual father of the entire human race. Tolstoy likewise asserts that when Jesus refers to himself as being the Christ, he uses the word to convey a spiritual concept rather than to refer to a particular person who should literally deliver mankind from sin and damnation. "Christ is that same Lord, our Ruler, whom we know in ourselves as our life. Christ is that consciousness which is within us."[54]

Thus Tolstoy's gospel begins by claiming that Jesus was an illegitimate son who was adopted into the family of a God-fearing Joseph who did not wish to humiliate Mary, the mother of Jesus. The child was exceptionally gifted and early on exhibited an extraordinary disposition towards spiritual matters. Even at the age of twelve, Jesus conversed with Jewish priests and teachers of the Mosaic Law in the Temple in Jerusalem, fascinating them with his questions and answers. When Jesus was about thirty years old, the preaching of John the Baptist, by whom he was also baptised, fascinated him and induced him to separate his life for God. After his baptism Jesus withdrew into the wilderness to fast, meditate, and pray, and there, after having fasted for forty days, he suffered from excruciating hunger, fatigue, hallucinations, and loneliness, as a result of which he was tempted by his own carnal desire to carry out things which were contrary to his ideals and character. But

---

[54]Ibid. P. 54.

Jesus overcame the temptation by choosing not to gratify physical needs and by fixing his attention on spiritual matters. Thus Tolstoy interprets the temptation of Jesus in the wilderness by the devil. Tolstoy leaves out the passages relating the miraculous conception of John the Baptist, the genealogy of Jesus, the escape into Egypt and the massacre of all the boys under the age of two in Bethlehem by the soldiers of Herod the Great in their indiscriminate attempt to destroy the future King. Other passages referring to the divine nature of Jesus but which cannot be removed from the Bible without affecting the central theme of the Gospels, Tolstoy attempts to reinterpret and to give them "rational" meaning.

(ii)   Mission

According to the four Gospels of the New Testament, Jesus had a specific mission to accomplish on earth, which is the redemption of mankind from sin and damnation through his death and resurrection. All four Gospels allege that this mission had been known to and told by the ancient prophets long before Jesus was born. Indeed, according to the Gospels, not only his mission, but also his birth, ministry, death, and resurrection were foretold by the prophets. Since Tolstoy strongly rejects the notion of sin and damnation, he rejects these claims and either rejects altogether or modifies those passages in the Gospels which allude to these claims. But in doing so, the difference between the Jesus of the Bible and the Jesus of Tolstoy becomes distinct. Whereas the Jesus of the Bible claims that human destiny depends up on a relationship with him ("I told you that you would die in your sins; if you do not believe that I am [the Christ], you will indeed die in your sins (John 8:24; NIV)."), the Jesus of Tolstoy does not make such claims ("He who does not accept my teaching is accused, not by my teaching but by the understanding which is in himself. It is that which accuses him. I do not speak of myself, but say what my Father—the living spirit within me—suggests to me"[55]). Likewise, the Jesus of the Bible teaches "as one who had authority, and not as their scribes (Matthew 7:29; NIV)", whereas the Jesus of Tolstoy offers non-binding insights about life and God ("I point out to you only the direction to life"[56]).

(iii) Ministry

In the fourth chapter of the Gospel according to Matthew, the writer summarises the ministry of Jesus as follows: "Jesus went throughout Galilee, teaching in their synagogues, proclaiming the good news of the kingdom, and healing every disease and illness among the people. News about him spread all over Syria, and people brought to him all who were ill with various diseases, those suffering severe pain, the demon-possessed, those having seizures, and the paralysed; and he healed them. Large crowds from Galilee, the Decapolis, Jerusalem, Judea and the region across the Jordan followed him (Matthew 4: 23-25; NIV)."

All four Gospels, in complete agreement with this summary, give specific and detailed accounts of the multiple miracles Jesus performed during his earthly ministry. There are 20 accounts of miracles in Matthew, 18 in Mark, 21 in Luke, and 8 in John. Tolstoy's gospel, however, excludes all of these save a handful of them. He neither denies nor accepts the truthfulness of the miracle stories but argues that however one takes them, they bring to the teaching of Jesus neither contradiction nor confirmation of its truth. He maintains that the miracles are powerless to prove the divinity of Jesus to a person who does not believe in miracles and a person who is ready to recognise, appreciate, and accept the truth revealed in his teaching does not need to believe in his divinity.

---

[55] Ibid. p. 58.
[56] Ibid. p. 61.

One of the miracle stories Tolstoy includes in his gospel deals with the healing of an impotent man in a place called Bethesda. This story Tolstoy includes as it is told in the Gospel of John (John 4: 46-54) in its entirety. The others, however, Tolstoy modifies, so that they can be rationally explained. The first story relates the miraculous multiplication of five loaves of breads and two fishes to feed more than five thousand Galileans. All four Gospels (this is the only miracle in the Bible which is reported by all the evangelists) maintain that one day Jesus spends the whole day with a multitude of followers, teaching. Towards the evening, his disciples approach and request Jesus to dismiss the people as it is getting late, the place is remote, and the people do not have food to eat, whereupon Jesus requests his disciples to call upon the people to sit down on the grass; he takes five loaves of bread and two fishes from his disciples and miraculously multiplies them to feed the people.

Tolstoy insists that this miracle should not be taken literally. According to Tolstoy, there had been no miracle as such, except in the morality of the lesson Jesus wishes to teach his followers. What "actually happened" was that when Jesus realised that some of his followers were poor and without food whereas the rich selfishly kept plenty of food for themselves, he persuaded his disciples to give up their own food to the poor. Feeling themselves to be reproached in the face of this act of generosity, the rich also shared their food with the rest and as a result all ate and were satisfied and the disciples gathered twelve baskets of rest food.

The other story, which is originally told in the ninth chapter of the Gospel according to John, relates the healing of a man who is born blind. Unlike the previous miracle story, the rational explanation Tolstoy attempts to give to this story does not appear to be convincing. In order to highlight the contrast, I have included here both accounts, first the original account according to John, followed by Tolstoy's account:

As [Jesus] went along, he saw a man blind from birth. His disciples asked him, "Rabbi, who sinned, this man or his parents, that he was born blind?"

"Neither this man nor his parents sinned," said Jesus, "but this happened so that the works of God might be displayed in him. As long as it is day, we must do the works of him who sent me. Night is coming, when no one can work. While I am in the world, I am the light of the world."

After saying this, he spat on the ground, made some mud with the saliva, and put it on the man's eyes. "Go," he told him, "wash in the Pool of Siloam". (This word means 'Sent'). So the man went and washed, and came home seeing.

His neighbours and those who had formerly seen him begging asked, "Isn't this the same man who used to sit and beg?" Some claimed that he was.

Others said, "No, he only looks like him."

But he himself insisted, "I am the man."

"How then were your eyes opened?" they asked.

He replied, "The man they call Jesus made some mud and put it on my eyes. He told me to go to Siloam and wash. So I went and washed, and then I could see."

"Where is this man?" they asked him.

"I don't know," he said.

They brought to the Pharisees the man who had been blind. Now the day on which Jesus had made the mud and opened the man's eyes was a Sabbath. Therefore the Pharisees also asked him how he had received his sight. "He put mud on my eyes," the man replied, "and I washed, and now I see."

Some of the Pharisees said, "This man is not from God, for he does not keep the Sabbath."

But others asked, "How can a sinner perform such signs?" So they were divided.

Then they turned again to the blind man, "What have you to say about him? It was your eyes he opened."

The man replied, "He is a prophet."

They still did not believe that he had been blind and had received his sight until they sent for the man's parents. "Is this your son?" they asked. "Is this the one you say was born blind? How is it that now he can see?"

"We know he is our son," the parents answered, "and we know he was born blind. But how he can see now, or who opened his eyes, we don't know. Ask him. He is of age; he will speak for himself." His parents said this because they were afraid of the Jewish leaders, who already had decided that anyone who acknowledged that Jesus was the Messiah would be put out of the synagogue. That was why his parents said, "He is of age; ask him."

A second time they summoned the man who had been blind. "Give glory to God by telling the truth," they said. 'We know this man is a sinner."

He replied, "Whether he is a sinner or not, I don't know. One thing I do know. I was blind but now I see!"

Then they asked him, "What did he do to you? How did he open your eyes?"

He answered, "I have told you already and you did not listen. Why do you want to hear it again? Do you want to become his disciples too?"

Then they hurled insults at him and said, "You are this fellow's disciple! We are disciples of Moses! We know that God spoke to Moses, but as for this fellow, we don't even know where he comes from."

The man answered, "Now that is remarkable! You don't know where he comes from, yet he opened my eyes. We know that God does not listen to sinners. He listens to the godly person who does his will. Nobody has ever heard of opening the eyes of a man born blind. If this man were not from God, he could do nothing."
To this they replied, "You were steeped in sin at birth; how dare you lecture us!" And they threw him out.

Tolstoy maintains that this miracle, too, should be taken figuratively, for "what must have actually happened" was that Jesus gave a fresh spiritual insight to an otherwise uneducated and unmotivated man as a result of which the man's perspective of life was instantly and completely transformed:

And on the road, Jesus saw a man who had no understanding from the time of his birth. And his pupils asked him, "Who is at fault that this man is without understanding since his birth, he, or his parents for not having taught him?"
And Jesus replied, "Neither his parents nor he are at fault. It is God's doing, that there may be light where there was darkness. If I have a teaching, it is the light of the world"
And Jesus explained to the ignorant man that he was a son of God in the spirit, and on receiving this teaching the ignorant man was conscious of light.
Those who had known him previously did not recognize him. Though resembling what he had been, he had now become another man.
But he said, "I am he, and Jesus has shown me that I am a son of God, and the light has reached me, so that now I see what I used not to see."

This man was taken to the Orthodox teachers; and it was on a Saturday. The Orthodox asked him how he had come to understand what he had not seen before.

He said, "I do not know how; I only know that now I understand everything."

They said, "You do not understand in a godly way, for Jesus did this on a Saturday, and besides, a layman cannot enlighten people."

And they began to dispute, and asked of the man who had been enlightened, "What do you think of Jesus?"

He said, "I think he is a prophet."

But the Jews did not believe that he had been ignorant and was now enlightened, so they called his parents and asked them, "Is this your son, who has been ignorant since his birth? How is it he has now become enlightened?"

His parents said, "We know that he is our son and that he was ignorant from his birth, but how he has become enlightened we do not know. He is of age, you should ask him."

The Orthodox called the man a second time, and said, "Pray to our God, the real God. The man who enlightened you is a layman, and is not sent by God. We are sure of that."

And the man who had been enlightened said, "Whether he is from God or not I do not know. But I know that I used not to see the light and that I see it now."

The Orthodox again asked, "What did he do to you when he enlightened you?"

He replied, "I have told you already, but you do not believe. If you wish to be his pupils I will tell you again."

They began to revile him and said, "You are his pupil, but we are the pupils of Moses. God Himself spoke to Moses, but we do not even know whence this man is."

And the man answered, "It is strange that he has enlightened me and yet you do not know whence he is. God does not hear sinners but hears those who honour Him and do His will. It can never be that one who is not from God could enlighten an ignorant man. If he were not from God he could do nothing."
The Orthodox were angry at this, and said, "You are altogether sunk in delusions and yet you want to teach us." And they drove him away.[57]

One recurring subject in the four Gospels is the bitter disagreements and disputes between Jesus and the spiritual leaders. The latter are often indignant of Jesus, because he, among other things, does certain things which are "forbidden" to do on the Sabbath day, a day the Jewish hold as a sacred and resting day. Since they cannot reconcile his "breaking" of one of the Ten Commandments with the miracles he performs on Sabbath, they are forced to think that he performs the miracles with the help of an evil spirit. So, they call him demon-possessed. On his part, Jesus is furious of their intention to kill him on account of their disagreement on the interpretation of the scriptures and calls them the children of the devil. Even though Tolstoy rejects the miracle stories and the casting out of demons, the conflict between Jesus and the spiritual leaders strikes him as very authentic and typical, for it starkly mirrors his own experience with the leaders of the contemporary Russian Orthodox Church.

During a typical heated argument, the spiritual leaders accuse Jesus of casting out demons by the power of Beelzebul, which they believe is the Prince of Demons. Jesus challenges the accusation by telling them a parable: "Every kingdom divided against itself will be ruined, and every city or household divided

---

[57]Ibid. pp. 42-43.

against itself will not stand. If Satan drives out Satan, he is divided against himself. How then can his kingdom stand? And if I drive out demons by Beelzebul, by whom do your people drive them out? So then, they will be your judges (Mathew 12:25-27; NIV)". Tolstoy includes this parable in his gospel with a slight modification. He states that the spiritual leaders' reference to Beelzebub merely indicates their superstition, but the reference Jesus makes of demons should be understood in the context of his teaching, according to which, Tolstoy alleges, Jesus is alluding to his casting out of bad or evil thoughts from the human mind through the power of the truth contained in his teaching: "You say that I drive out evil by evil. But no power destroys itself. If it destroyed itself it would cease to exist. You try to drive out evil by threats, executions, and murders, but evil still exists precisely because it cannot fight against itself. I do not drive out evil by evil as you try to. I drive out evil by calling on men to fulfil the will of the Father's spirit which gives life to all men."[58]

(iv) Teaching

For over a quarter of a century Tolstoy repeatedly remarked that the teaching of Jesus was the most essential element of the Bible and maintained that no information about his identity and ministry is required in order to understand and apply his teaching. Indeed, the teaching of Jesus takes a considerable portion of *The Gospel in Brief*.

Since Tolstoy maintains that inasmuch as Pythagoras and Newton were endowed by nature with unique scientific comprehension, Jesus, too, was endowed by nature with unique spiritual comprehension, he rejects from the New Testament claims that Jesus obtained his teaching by special revelation from God. Subsequently, when Jesus claims that he is "the way,

---

[58]Ibid. p. 32.

the truth, and the life (John 14:1; NIV)", the power of this claim, according to Tolstoy, rests not in the person of Jesus but in the truth he reveals, in the same way the power of the Inertial Laws rests not in the person of Newton but in the truth he revealed. A typical pattern Tolstoy follows throughout his gospel to "correct" the claims of the four Gospels can be illustrated by taking an example from the Gospel of John (John 15) where Jesus explains to his disciples with a parable the importance of remaining in him in order for them to flourish spiritually:

> I am the true vine, and my Father is the gardener. He cuts off every branch in me that bears no fruit, while every branch that does bear fruit he prunes so that it will be even more fruitful. You are already clean because of the word I have spoken to you. Remain in me, as I also remain in you. No branch can bear fruit by itself; it must remain in the vine. Neither can you bear fruit unless you remain in me. I am the vine; you are the branches. If you remain in me and I in you, you will bear much fruit; apart from me you can do nothing. If you do not remain in me, you are like a branch that is thrown away and withers; such branches are picked up, thrown into the fire and burned. (John 15:1-6; NIV)

Tolstoy rewrites this passage in his gospel as follows (notice the emphasis on the teaching rather than the person of Jesus):

> My teaching is a tree of life. The Father is He who tends the tree. He prunes and cherishes those branches on which there is fruit, that they may yield more. Hold to my teaching of life and you will have more life. As a shoot lives not of itself but by being part of the tree, so you should live by my teaching. My teaching is the tree, you are the shoots. He who lives by my teaching of life will bring forth much fruit, for without my teaching there is

no life. He who does not live by my teaching withers and perishes, just as dead branches are cut off and burnt.[59]

Tolstoy claims that the central message of the teaching of Jesus is contained intact in the *Sermon on the Mount*, which he summarises as follows[60]:
1. Do not be angry, but live in peace with all human beings.
2. Do not indulge yourself in sexual gratification.
3. Do not promise anything on oath to anyone.
4. Do not resist evil, do not judge and do not go to law.
5. Make no distinction based on national identity; instead love foreigners as your own people.

Tolstoy explains that the truth as well as the power of these commandments can visibly be demonstrated in children: "They are better than anyone, for they live according to the will of the Father: they are indeed in the kingdom of heaven. Instead of sending them away you should learn from them, for to live in the Father's will you must live as children do. They do not abuse people, do not bear ill-will, do not lust, do not bind themselves by oaths, do not resist evil, do not go to law with anyone, acknowledge no difference between their own and other nations; and so they are better than grown-up people and are in the kingdom of heaven. If you do not become as children and refrain from all the snares of the flesh, you will not be in the kingdom of heaven."[61]

Towards the end of his life (the last two decades) the *Sermon on the Mount* became Tolstoy's exclusive preoccupation. Almost all the books and articles he wrote during this period were intended to defend and to explain the significance of the *Sermon on the Mount* to deal with social and political challenges. In his private life he tried his best to lead a life which was harmonious

---

[59]Ibid. p. 62.
[60]Ibid. p. 24.
[61]Ibid. pp. 49-50.

with the *Sermon on the Mount*. He disowned much of his property and shared it with the poor; he disowned the copyrights to all of his books, considering it sinful to make profit out of a natural endowment he freely received. He refused to be served by others and to be identified with the aristocracy, the rich, and the privileged. Instead, he lived among peasants and the working class and joyfully shared in their physical toil, social challenges, and suffering. Like the prophet Jeremiah, who foresaw the destruction of Jerusalem and its Temple and was deeply distressed by the complacency of its kings and the royal households, Tolstoy, too, vividly foresaw the eventual destruction of the Russian Empire and all of Europe (and accurately foretold their fate), because their social, political, and cultural ideals were fundamentally opposed to the *Sermon on the Mount*. Whereas the latter calls for charity, meekness, peace-making, and non-resistance to evil, the former promote national pride, patriotism, and the limitless accumulation and the misuse of defence forces to advance national interests. The rich, the educated, and the strong minority mercilessly and shamelessly exploited the poor, the uneducated, and the weak majority. But Tolstoy saw that patience was running out amongst the majority, because its existence had grievously been challenged. Similar to John the Baptist, who bravely and publicly confronted the ruthless King of his time, Tolstoy, too, openly condemned the extravagant and parasitic existence of the Russian and European aristocracy and implored them to return to Christian charity. But Tolstoy was equally severe in his criticism of the humanists, the socialists, and the communists who were bent to destroy Christian virtues and replace them with their own false hopes and false gods.

Even though Tolstoy alleges that the teaching of Jesus is incompatible with the Old Testament ("Hebraism"), on numerous occasions in his gospel as well as in the original Gospels, Jesus refers to the Old Testament to back up his claims and to explain and confirm the authority of his teaching. In many of his latter books, Tolstoy himself extensively quoted from the Old Testaments to explain the uniqueness and indispensability of the *Sermon on the Mount*. Nevertheless, except in very few places, he leaves out of his gospel the prophetic verses the original Gospel writers quoted from the Old Testament to explain the messianic ministry of Jesus.

(v) Death and resurrection

In the four Gospels, Jesus frequently foretells his death and resurrection. In Tolstoy's gospel, Jesus frequently foretells his death but the resurrection prophecies are consistently edited, for Tolstoy rejected the resurrection claim and maintains that the resurrection prophecies must not be taken literally. A typical example of how Tolstoy understands the resurrection prophecies can be illustrated by taking a passage from the sixteenth chapter of the Gospel according to John:

> Very truly I tell you, you will weep and mourn while the world rejoices. You will grieve, but your grief will turn to joy. A woman giving birth to a child has pain because her time has come; but when her baby is born she forgets the anguish because of her joy that a child is born into the world. So with you: now is your time of grief, but I will see you again and you will rejoice, and no one will take away your joy (John 16:20-22; NIV).

With this parable Jesus appears to be preparing his disciples to his death on the cross and his subsequent resurrection and the joy his disciples would experience. Tolstoy, however, maintains that the original text must have referred to the joy the disciples would eventually achieve after his death by internalising his teaching and by becoming like him.

> You know how it is in the world: some are sad and grieved while others rejoice. You too will grieve, but your sorrow will be turned into joy. A woman in labour

suffers torment, but when it is over she does not remember the suffering, for joy that she has brought a child into the world. So you will grieve, and will then suddenly realize my presence: the spirit of truth will enter into you and your grief will be turned into joy.[62]

(vi) Afterlife

Tolstoy believed in the continuation of life after death. Indeed, he was deeply persuaded that the true life is the afterlife whereas the earthly life is only a preparation for it. Consequently, he reproduces in his gospel the passages in the four Gospels where Jesus teaches his disciples about the afterlife by and large intact.

(vii) Civil Disobedience

Tolstoy was a confirmed pacifist and a conscientious objector of existing social institutions such as the church, the military, the finance and taxation systems, the government, and national boundaries. He alleges that the rich, the strong, and the educated put these institutions in place in order to oppress and exploit the poor, the weak, and the uneducated immeasurably. At least in one place Tolstoy modifies a biblical passage where Jesus seems to accept the existing social institution. This concerns a parable where Jesus tells of a certain Master who intends to set out on a long journey. Before his departure, the master distributes to his servants money for them to invest and make profits until he returns. Upon his return the master settles account with his servants. One of these servants, who has not invested the money given to him for fear of bankruptcy and has buried it in the ground, comes forward and gives the money back to the master: "Sir, here is your [money]; I have kept it laid away in a piece of cloth. I was afraid of you, because you are a

---

[62]Ibid. p. 63.

hard man. You take out what you did not put in and reap what you did not sow. (Luck 19:20-21; NIV)" Whereupon the master replies: "I will judge you by your own words, you wicked servant! You knew, did you, that I am a hard man, taking out what I did not put in, and reaping what I did not sow? Why then didn't you put my money on deposit, so that when I came back, I could have collected it with interest?" (Luke 19:22-23; NIV)."

Tolstoy, who considered the banking system as dishonest and corrupt and depositing money for interest as sinful, refuses to include this parable as it is, so he makes correction to the master's reply:

> And the master said to him: Foolish servant! I will judge you by your own words. You say that from fear of me you hid the money in the earth and did not make use of it. If you knew that I am severe and take from where I have not put, then why did you not do as I bade you? If you had used my money the estate would have been added to and you would have fulfilled what I bade you. But now you have not done what the money was given you for, and so you must not have it.[63]

Tolstoy closes his autobiography (*Confession*) by sharing a dream he once had during his struggle with a belief in God. The dream not only suggests a divine revelation but also a divine intervention, claims Tolstoy himself was highly sceptical of when it comes to judging the divine authority of the Bible based on its claim of divine revelation. According to the dream, every rational effort Tolstoy was exerting to make sense of the worth of human life proved to be baseless and futile and inched him towards a desperate, frightful, and destructive end. But when he gave up relying on his own wisdom and trusted God,

---

[63]Ibid. p. 29.

he realised that the desperate descent he had been taking towards perdition suddenly stopped and his life appeared to have found a firm foundation. Moreover, for the first time he heard a heavenly voice reminding him to look upward and to continue trusting. I have reproduced it here in its entirety in order to contrast it with his interpretation style of the Gospels and the Bible in general:

> The other day, as I was looking over this printed portion and returning to the thoughts and feelings that went through me when I was experiencing all this, I had a dream. This dream expressed for me in a condensed form everything I lived through and wrote about; therefore I think that for those who have understood me, a description of the dream will refresh, clarify, and gather into one piece what has been discussed at length in these pages. Here is the dream: I see that I am lying in bed. Feeling neither good nor bad, I am lying on my back. But I begin to wonder whether it is a good thing for me to be lying there; and it seems to me that there is something wrong with my legs; whether they are too short or uneven, I do not know, but there is something awkward about them. As I start to move my legs, I begin to wonder how and on what I am lying, something that up till now had not entered my mind. Looking about my bed, I see that I am lying on some cords woven together and attached to the sides of the bed. My heels are resting on one of the cords and my lower legs on another in an uncomfortable way. Somehow I know that these cords can be shifted. Moving one leg, I push away the furthest cord. It seems to me that it will be more comfortable that way. But I have pushed it too far away; I try to catch it, but this movement causes another cord to slip out from under my legs, leaving them hanging down. I rearrange my whole body, quite certain I will be settled now; but

this movement causes still other cords to shift and slip out from under me, and I see that the whole situation is getting worse: the whole lower part of my body is sinking and hanging down, and my feet are not touching the ground. I am supported only along the upper part of my back, and for some reason I begin to feel not only uncomfortable but also terrified. Only now do I ask myself what had not yet occurred to me: where am I and what am I lying on? I begin to look around, and the first place I look is down toward where my body is dangling, in the direction where I feel I must soon fall. I look below, and I cannot believe my eyes. I am resting on a height such as I could never have imagined, a height altogether unlike that of the highest tower or mountain.

I cannot even tell whether I can see anything down below in the bottomless depths of the abyss over which I am hanging and into which I am drawn. My heart stops, and I am overcome with horror. It is horrible to look down there. I feel that if I look down, I will immediately slip from the last cord and perish. I do not look, yet not looking is worse, for now I am thinking about what will happen to me as soon as the last cord breaks. I feel that I am losing the last ounce of my strength from sheer terror and that my back is slowly sinking lower and lower. Another instant and I shall breakaway. And then a thought occurs to me: this cannot be real. It is just a dream. I will wake up. I try to wake up, but I cannot. "What am I to do, what am I to do?" I ask myself, looking up. Above me there is also an abyss. I gaze into this abyss of sky and try to forget about the one below, and I actually do forget. The infinity below repels and horrifies me; the infinity above attracts me and gives me strength. Thus I am hanging over the abyss suspended by the last of the cords that have not yet slipped out from

under me. I know I am hanging there, but I am only looking upward, and my terror passes. As it happens in a dream, a voice is saying, "Mark this, this is it!" I gaze deeper and deeper into the infinity above me, and I seem to grow calm. I recall everything that has happened, and I remember how it all came about: how I moved my 1egs, how I was dangling there, the horror that came over me, and how I was saved from the horror by looking up. And I ask myself, "Well, am I still hanging here?" And as soon as I glance around, I feel with my whole body a support that is holding me up. I can see that I am no longer dangling or falling but am firmly supported. I ask myself how I am being supported; I touch myself, look around, and see that there is a single cord underneath the centre of my body, that when I look up I am lying on it firmly balanced, and that it alone has supported me all along. As it happens in a dream, the mechanism by which I am supported seems quite natural, understandable, and beyond doubt, in spite of the fact that when I am awake the mechanism is completely incomprehensible. In my sleep I am even astonished that I had not understood this before. It seems that there is a pillar beside me and that there is no doubt of the solidity of the pillar, even though it has nothing to stand on. The cord is somehow very cleverly yet very simply attached to the pillar, leading out from it, and if you place the middle of your body on the cord and look up, there cannot even be a question of falling. All this was clear to me, and I was glad and at peace. Then it is as if someone is saying to me, "See that you remember."
And I awoke.[64]

---

[64]LTCON pp. 88-90.

[i] It is this dissolution the theologian Sellin refers to in his book *Mose und seine Bedeutung für die israelitisch-jüdische Religionsgeschichte* (1922). In the first chapter of the Book of Hosea, God declares that he shall disown the people of the northern kingdom for their idolatry, and vows to uproot them from their land. But he also declares that after their punishment, he will accept them and replant them in their land. It was in this context Hosea declares: "The people of Judah and the People of Israel will be reunited, and they will appoint one leader and will come up out of the land, for great will be the day of [replantation] (Hosea 1:11, NIV)". Similarly, in the twelfth chapter of the Book of Hosea, God lists the iniquities of Ephraim (one of the strongest tribes of the northern kingdom), including bloodshed: "The Lord used a prophet to bring Israel up from Egypt, by a prophet he cared for him. But Ephraim has aroused his bitter anger; his Lord will leave on him the guilt of his bloodshed and will repay him for his contempt" (Hosea 12:13-14, NIV). The first passage refers to a future event, while the second to a past event. In both passages, Moses is not mentioned. The second passage clearly refers to a murder committed by Ephraim but does not specify where and when. Indeed, it does not seem to allude to a single person. Freud insists, however, that both passages are indirect and involuntary admissions to what actually the Israelites did to Moses.

[ii] The public prosecutor in *The Brothers Karamazov* compares contemporary Russia with a troika blindly galloping to a distant and unknown destination: "Our fatal troika dashes on in her headlong flight perhaps to destruction and in all Russia for long past men have stretched out imploring hands and called a halt to its furious reckless course. And if other nations stand aside from that troika that may be, not from respect,… but simply from horror. From horror, perhaps from disgust. And well it is that they stand aside, but maybe they will cease one day to do so and will form a firm wall confronting the hurrying apparition and will check the frenzied rush of our

lawlessness, for the sake of their own safety, enlightenment and civilisation (FDBRO p. 670)."

[iii] Almost all Dostoevsky's biographers (including Joseph Frank) agree with Freud that Dostoevsky suffered from a consuming sense of guilt which manifested itself in a pathological shyness. "All the people who had any prolonged personal contact with Dostoevsky remark on the secretiveness and evasiveness of his personality; he was not someone who opened himself easily or willingly to others. There is scarcely a memoir about him that does not comment on this lack of expansiveness, and one suspects that this elusiveness may well have developed from the need to dissimulate as a means of copping with his father's capriciousness and severity. ... as Freud noted, Dostoevsky internalised as a child a highly developed sense of guilt. (JF p. 21)."

[iv] This is an allusion to Hamlet's reference to man.

[v] Freud, in *Civilisation and Its Discontents* builds on this idea to reason about the emergence of collective superego.

[vi] Tolstoy argues likewise in The Kingdom of God is Within You to reject the divine origin of the Bible.

Summary

In this book I have surveyed the beliefs of Dostoevsky, Tolstoy, Freud, and Einstein on the origin and the purpose of human life. In this chapter I will give a compact summary of each part of the book by highlighting the essential ideas.

The Significance of God

Except for Freud, all the others maintained that God is the source of human life, but Freud denied the existence of God and attributed human existence to chance. On the role God plays in everyday human life, however, the three theists were not of the same mind. Dostoevsky accepted the biblical account that God is actively interested in human decision and action and intervenes through acts of grace, counselling, and chastisement to influence the essence and purpose of human existence. Tolstoy agreed with Dostoevsky, but rejected the notion that God can intervene in human existence in extraordinary ways such as through miracles and prophecies. Instead, he believed that God has endowed human beings with the necessary mental faculties to discover and do his will. Tolstoy and Einstein believed that in the same way scientific truths could be revealed to exceptionally gifted and dedicated individuals, spiritual truths can be revealed to exceptionally gifted and dedicated individuals, of which Moses and Jesus Christ are typical examples. Einstein, however, rejected the notion that God is interested in human decision and action as well as in human existence in general. He insisted that attributes such as will, interest, and purpose are not divine qualities but human impressions, and applying them to God does not make sense. In agreement with Baruch de Spinoza, Einstein believed in causal determinism wherein an infinite chain of causes and effects determine human behaviour. Consequently, according to Einstein, human beings cannot be responsible for their actions inasmuch as a corporal object cannot be responsible for the motion it undergoes. Freud rejected the idea of an impersonal or disinterested God and believed that God does not exist and is the creation of human fantasy.

Dostoevsky referred to the exceptional qualities and authenticity of biblical stories and characters to substantiate his belief in God, maintaining on numerous occasions that human fantasy has never been able to conceive of characters such as Job and Jesus. He further argued that the Bible should be trusted in its claims. Similarly, Tolstoy referred to the exceptional spiritual insights revealed in the teaching of Jesus and accepted some of the biblical claims about God and human existence. Einstein, on the other hand, cited three reasons for accepting Spinoza's theory of an impersonal God and a deterministic universe. Accordingly, first, the complexity, orderliness, and beauty revealed in the construction of the universe strongly suggest the existence of an underlying plan in the creation of the universe. Secondly, the fundamental laws governing the universe are accessible to human comprehension, suggesting that it is the Creator's will to reveal his plan to human beings. Third, there is no objective and reproducible evidence to suggest that God intervenes in any extraordinary way in the operation of the universe on behalf of human beings; instead, God seems to have perfect (complete) laws in place to let Nature run its course undisturbed.

Freud referred to the strong similarity between the attributes accorded to the God of the Bible and the image of a father in the mind of his children to argue that God must be the creation of human beings' worst fears and anxieties. Furthermore, Freud referred to some formative psychological phases in the development of a child to explain the coming into existence of an omnipotent, omniscient, and omnipresent God.

Accordingly, an infant initially does not distinguish between itself and the external world, and believes that the two are one and the same entity. But gradually and through the painful process of deprivation, the child realises that not everything that exists is accessible to its pleasure-seeking instincts and this realisation creates in the child a profound desire to be reunited with the universe (in its mother womb the child must have felt a sense of perfect unity). Freud maintained that this unconscious desire must be the prime reason why human beings find comfort in religion, because religion gives the illusion of unification with God, the "creator of the universe". Having thus explained how the desire for religion comes into existence, Freud explained the contents of religion (God, angels, devils, hell, sin, guilt, condemnation, redemption, afterlife, etc.) as the result of two psychic externalisation processes, namely, projection and displacement.

Dostoevsky, who was intimately acquainted with and wrote extensively about suffering, realised the intellectual difficulty of believing in a loving God who, nevertheless, permits suffering into his creation. To give voice to this timeless dilemma, Dostoevsky populates his novels with rebellious characters who question divine justice. But the idea which strengthened his own faith in God and which recurred in Dostoevsky's famous books is that love and freedom would have not been possible without admitting freewill and suffering into creation.

A careful examination of Tolstoy's books and his autobiography reveals that Tolstoy sought perfection throughout his life in himself as well as in others. One can say that his yearning for perfection made him a sharp and unsympathetic critic of almost all kinds of professionals, both domestic and foreign: philosophers, writers, emperors, military generals, statesmen, bishops, medical doctors, diplomats, pedagogues, and so on. Indeed, his anarchistic tendency towards the end of his life, his indiscriminate rejection of established institutions such as churches and states, altogether, and his passionate appeal for a different world order established on the ideas of social justice and none-violence, are certificates of his deep yearning for perfection in all aspects of life. Tolstoy was equally critical towards himself and the people who were very close and dear to him, including his wife. He finally discovered perfection in Jesus Christ and in the *Sermon on the Mount* and held on to them wholeheartedly to the end. Tolstoy's singular attention to perfection also makes him reject the concept of grace and the forgiveness of and the redemption from sin, arguing that such concepts make human beings irresponsible for their actions and hinder them from discovering their full potential to please God.

There is a strong correspondence between Freud's conception of guilt and Christianity's conception of sin. Christians believe that a woman (Eve) persuaded the primal father to disobey God and through one act of disobedience all the descendants of this man became sinners. Freud believed that on account of women, the sons of the primal father killed their father, became conscious of their guilt, experience a strong desire to atone for their guilt but despite their attempt they could not get rid of their guilt; instead, they transmitted their guilt to all their descendants, which is why all their descendants exhibit a strong affinity with religion. Similarly, according to Christianity, all human beings are the descendants of one man, Adam. Freud likewise believed that all human beings are the descendants of one man, the primal father.

If one accepts Darwin's description of the primal father (Freud did accept) that he must have been selfish and violent, then it is plausible to assume that all males of his generation, including the brothers of the primal father, must have been equally selfish and violent, in which case entering into a fight with one another and killing and seeing others kill a fellow human being should have been ubiquitous phenomena and should not have come as a traumatic and haunting experience to the sons of the primal father who eventually "killed" and "ate" their father and "share amongst themselves the females he selfishly possessed". Why should then the sons and their descendants experience a lasting sense of guilt, which they neither overcame nor atoned for completely, and whence came their and their descendants' capacity to indefinitely endure such a sense of guilt?

Einstein subscribed to Spinoza's assertions that both physical objects and thoughts are subject to strict causal determinism and that nothing exists by accident or as a consequence of freewill. Indeed, Einstein made causal determinism the foundation of his religion as well as his scientific research. The basic premises he made when he set out with the task of describing the relationship between the curvature of spacetime, on the one hand, and the energy and momentum of matter and radiation, on the other, in his General Relativity Theory, presuppose strict causal determinism. This would enable him to correctly predict the behaviour of light inside a gravitation field. Nevertheless, despite his commitment to causal determinism, Einstein paradoxically accommodates the concept of love and freedom. Accordingly, an appreciation of truth and the love and pursuit of knowledge invoke in human beings a "cosmic religious feeling" which can be manifested in an appreciation of the beauty of creation and a love for God. Moreover Einstein was sceptical of Spinoza's idea of God as a singular, self-sustaining substance having both matter and thoughts as his attributes. His image of God makes a separation between God and his creation whereas Spinoza's conception seems to suggest that the two are inseparable.

But quantum physics, to the emergence of which Einstein made a seminal contribution, puts Einstein's commitment to causal determinism to a formidable test claiming the existence of certain pairs of physical phenomena (such as the momentum and velocity and the energy and lifetime of a subatomic particle) which cannot be determined simultaneously with definiteness, regardless of the sophistication of the mechanism with which these phenomena are observed. This claim is mathematically supported and has gathered the support of a plethora of repeatable and reproducible experiments; Einstein nevertheless regarded quantum physics as an incomplete science, referring to some of the inexplicable conclusions to which it inevitably leads, such as the potential of subatomic particles having memory and travelling at a speed faster than the speed of light.

The Purpose of Human Life

As regards the purpose of human life, the philosophy of my subjects is better understood by first considering the social and political contexts surrounding their personal and professional lives. After the publication of his first book at the age of twenty-four, Dostoevsky was admitted into the most coveted literary circle in St. Petersburg the treasured members of which consisted of much-acclaimed literary figures such as Vissarion Grigoryevich Belinsky, Alexander Herzen, Ivan Turgenev, Mikhail Bakunin, and Nikolay Nekrasov. This circle had for some time been debating the relevance of religion in contemporary Russia and its compatibility with different forms of socialism, the prevailing social and political ideology of the time amongst the Russian intelligentsia. The overwhelming majority regarded religion and a belief in God not only as impotent in setting human beings free from enduring oppression and abject poverty but also as a spiritual opium which was effectively used by the oppressors against the oppressed, to subdue and rule them. Socialism, on the contrary, they construed, would elevate human dignity with its emphasis on satisfying human needs through the free access and distribution of wealth and on placing human destiny exclusively in the hands of each and every individual rather than in the hands of a divine or fate or an emperor anointed by a divine. The young Dostoevsky was of different opinion. At its best, he argued, socialism may be able to feed and protect individuals but in exchange requires of them the sacrifice of their freedom, however small or insignificant the portion of freedom they are asked to forego may appear. And this demand will make them inevitably unhappy, for the very essence of their life finds meaning in the completeness of their freedom. Even though they may be flayed alive, obtain no work, starve to death, and their freedom amounts to nothing, Dostoevsky maintained, still they would prefer to retain their freedom in its entirety. Likewise, Dostoevsky defended faith in God by arguing that human beings do not merely wish to exist but they wish to have a reason for their existence and only through a belief in God can their existence find a steadfast reason.

Tolstoy lived at the time the predominant Russian population was living in veritable serfdom and abject poverty whilst the privileged few, the aristocracy, were leading what he regarded as a false, parasitic, and shameless life. Tolstoy would make these social-ills, particularly, self-deception, the subject of his lifetime literary occupation. Referring to his own experience, Tolstoy maintained that leading an aimless life tempts one to regard life in general as meaningless. Thus, according to Tolstoy, the question of whether or not human life has any meaning or a definite purpose sets as a prerequisite for the habitual appreciation of and the obedience to truth. Furthermore, whereas this capacity appears to be innate and most vivid in children, Tolstoy maintained, it tends to get weaker as one grows old. Hence, the cultivation of this essential capacity calls for conscious decision, endeavour, and enduring discipline, in the same way as any other pursuit of physical and mental perfections require these qualities. A closer look into the life of Tolstoy during his struggle to discover the truth about life and after his "discovery" of meaning in the *Sermon on the Mount* reveals the singular devotion with which Tolstoy pursued his goal, the intensity of the personal, familial, social, and political conflicts into which it brought him, and the sacrifice he paid to attain it.

Freud and Einstein lived at a time when Jews were persecuted in Germany and Austria and in fact across in Europe, albeit to variable degrees. As the persecution was often made in the name of religion, both of them regarded religion (Christianity) to a certain extent responsible for fostering prejudice against Judaism and for ostracising Jews[i]. In addition, in his professional life as a psychoanalyst, Freud frequently witnessed that most of his neurotic patients were predominantly Catholic by confession and suffered from arrested sexual developments or from sexual repressions[ii]. These two factors might have influenced Freud's identification of the instinct of aggression and the sexual instinct as the two fundamental human instincts on which human happiness rests. Freud challenges the existence of absolute good and absolute evil and an innate capacity in human beings to differentiate between good and evil alleging that in the psychic realm what human beings regard as good is the gratification of the two instincts and as evil the deprivation of the two instincts. Moreover, Freud asserted that the sense of guilt in human beings does not emerge as a result of the consciousness of having committed something wrong or having done harm to others, but instead as a result of fear of punishment or fear of the loss of love (i.e., fear of punishment for an action committed in the past and loss of love in the future).

Einstein's philosophy of life is firmly grounded upon Spinoza's causal determinism but exhibits aspects that are inherited from Dostoevsky's notion of freewill and Tolstoy's perfectionism. The apparent contradiction between causal determinism and freewill may be detected in his personal and professional life.

Until the Second World War Einstein subscribed to Tolstoy's passive non-resistance and expressed his great admiration of Mahatma Gandhi. Nevertheless, he abandoned passive resistance altogether when the Nazis' persecution of the Jews intensified and the Second World War broke out. He had made an active contribution towards the development of the atomic bomb which was planned in order to bring about the defeat of Nazi Germany, but was very much perturbed when he learned that it had been used against Japan. After the war was over, Einstein actively and strongly opposed the rearmament of Germany and yet privately Einstein accepted that Hitler acted in accordance with causal determinism and was persuaded that he could have acted in no other way. He reconciled these odds by borrowing a statement from Schopenhauer that human beings are free to do what they will but cannot choose what they will.

The Significance of the Bible

In their endeavour to establish their philosophy of the purpose of human life, my subjects closely examined the claims of the Bible and passed their verdicts. Freud turned to the Bible towards the end of his life in order to investigate the real cause for the long-standing persecution of Jews in Europe. As a writer and literary critic, Dostoevsky examined the quality of the stories and characters of the Bible and frequently referred to them as a source of inspiration for his own stories and to make sense of his own suffering. Tolstoy disregarded many of the miracle accounts and the prophecies, instead establishing his non-violent social and political theories essentially upon the *Sermon on the Mount*. Likewise, Einstein rejected the biblical accounts pertaining to God's intercourse with humanity, but acknowledged the poetry and moral qualities of the Psalms and the Prophets and the unique ethical merits conveyed in the teaching of Jesus. Whilst accepting Spinoza's assertion that the biblical depiction of God is anthropomorphic, Einstein, nevertheless, disagreed with Spinoza on the type of knowledge that can be obtained from the Bible. Spinoza asserts that the type of knowledge the Bible can give is elementary and experiential and does not lead to the knowledge and love of God and valued rational and inferential knowledge more than experiential knowledge. Einstein, on the other hand, viewed the ethical values revealed in the Bible as being more precious than any scientific discovery.

Indeed, Tolstoy and Freud went further than investigating the claims of the Bible and attempted to rewrite portions of the Bible—Tolstoy the Gospels and Freud the Pentateuch—claiming that biblical writers, editors, the Apostles, and the Church Fathers deliberately distorted them for "tendentious" reasons. In doing so, Tolstoy either removed from or rationalised the miracle and wonder stories in the four Gospels in order to make the teaching of Jesus "comprehensible" to the rational mind. His basic premises for doing so were that Jesus did not possess an extraordinary power as the Gospels claim and, hence, the miracles and wonders were either latter additions or wrongly perceived or interpreted. Similarly, Freud rejected miracle and wonder accounts from the first five books of the Torah and contested the authenticity of the story about Moses, strongly assuming that Moses was an Egyptian by birth, was converted to a monotheistic religion later in life by an Egyptian Pharaoh, introduced monotheism to the Israelite migrants who were at the time living in the northern part of Egypt, led this same people peacefully out of Egypt to establish his own kingdom after the death of the Pharaoh and the abolishing of monotheism in Egypt by a succeeding Pharaoh, and was finally murdered by the very same Israelites in the wilderness of Qadesh-Barnea.

Freud relied on several "evidences" which he "discovered" within the Bible itself to establish his entire theory about Moses, the Exodus, and the origin of monotheism. One of the most significant of these is the disintegration of the ancient Kingdom of Israel (1 Kings 12), which Freud takes as a reliable historical account. According to this account, after having persisted as a single nation for over 370 years, the Kingdom of Israel disintegrated into two kingdoms around 930 B.C. Whereas the Bible maintains that the Israelites were composed of twelve tribes stemming from the twelve sons of a single father, Jacob, Freud asserts that the population must have consisted of two distinct peoples who were different in identity as well as in culture: civilised Egyptians and barbaric Israelites. According to Freud, both people followed Moses out of Egypt during the Exodus of the Israelites. Even though Freud rejects the miracle and wonder accounts in the Pentateuch, he nevertheless accepts the biblical claims about the Exodus of the Israelites out of Egypt and the eventual conquest of Canaan. According to Freud, the Egyptians, who were the minority and to whom also Moses belonged, occupied the southern part of the ancient Kingdom whilst the Israelites, who were the majority, occupied the northern part of the Kingdom. During the Exodus, the Egyptians remained faithful to Moses and to his religion but the Israelites found his highly abstract and elevated monotheism intolerable and, therefore, long before the two people conquered and settled in Canaan, murdered Moses in Qadesh-Barnea and diluted his religion to a less abstract and less elevated Judaism by introducing restrictive laws, sacrificial rites, and worship rituals. Freud maintains that it must have been this great dichotomy of culture between the two peoples which must have eventually led to the disintegration of the ancient Israel into two kingdoms.

Both Tolstoy and Freud had access to the best research materials and to the council of biblical, historical, anthropological, and archaeological authorities during the writing of their books and both of them had taken several years of preparation and careful research to produce their accounts. But they also relied on speculations, "reasonable assumptions", and "expert interpretations". Consequently, their accounts suffer from frequent inconsistencies, implausibility, and contradictions both with respect to the body of text they produced as a whole and the widely accepted scholarship on the subjects.

For instance, according to the ninth chapter of the Gospel of John, Jesus heals a blind man in Jerusalem. The spiritual leaders are incensed because this incident takes place on a Sabbath day and a bitter dispute concerning the identity of Jesus ensues between them and the blind man and his family. During the dispute the spiritual leaders even question the true identity of the man in question suspecting mere resemblance between him and the blind man. But both the man and his parents insist that he is indeed the man who was blind but who can now see. Tolstoy maintains that the healing to which the original Gospel referred is a spiritual rather than a physical blindness. This would, however, raise some questions. Firstly, if indeed Jesus gave the person a spiritual insight, then the incident is hardly worth disputing since the Torah does not prohibit teaching on a Sabbath day. Therefore, the entire chapter does not make sense if the cause of the dispute is contested. Secondly, assuming that the original Gospel referred to the sudden transformation of the spiritual comprehension of a person who had difficulty of comprehending spiritual matters all his life (if, indeed, the spiritual leaders questioned the true identity of the person, the transformation must have been remarkable), should that not be regarded as a miracle? In which case, Tolstoy should have rejected the inclusion of the entire chapter from his book given his rejection of miracles. Thirdly, how can the sudden and extraordinary transformation of the spiritual comprehension of a person be perceived in a short time? Similarly, Freud maintained that the Israelites left Egypt peacefully but did not explain how more than a million people could be suddenly converted to a new religion and agree in unison to leave their country of settlement for more than four centuries for an uncertain future and an uncertain destination trusting a leader who was not their own and whom they hardly know? Neither did he explain how the Egyptians, who might have held the Israelites as their slaves, freely agreed to let them leave peacefully with all their belongings, which they acquired in Egypt. Besides, Freud does not provide an answer as to how a great multitude of migrants survived living in a wilderness for many decades.

From the works of Tolstoy and Freud two conclusions may be made. Firstly, the works clearly demonstrate the difficulty associated with editing the Bible in order to obtain a historically accurate, rationally comprehensible, and textually consistent version. Secondly, both Freud and Tolstoy began their works with heavy-handed criticism of biblical writers and editors for allegedly carrying out their job with tendentious motive and bias, yet their own versions are not free of these faults.

In conclusion, if one were to summarise the central philosophy of life of each of my subjects with a single word for each, one might use *freedom* for Dostoevsky, *perfection* for Tolstoy, *externalisation* for Freud, and *determinism* for Einstein.

---

[i] During the Second World War, Einstein would regret the unexamined prejudice he once held towards the Catholic Church. In an article which appeared in *Time* magazine on September 23, 1940, Einstein expresses his great admiration of the bravery of the Catholic Church in opposing Hitler's persecution of the Jews singlehandedly: "Being a lover of freedom, when the revolution came in Germany, I looked to the universities to defend it, knowing that they had always boasted of their devotion to the cause of

truth; but no, the universities immediately were silenced. Then, I looked to the great editors of the newspapers, whose flaming editorials in days gone by had proclaimed their love of freedom; but they like the universities were silenced in a few short weeks… Only the Church stood squarely across the path of Hitler's campaign for suppressing truth. I never had any special interest in the Church before, but now I feel a great affection and admiration because the Church alone had had the courage and intellectual truth and moral freedom. I am forced to confess that what I had once despised I now praise unreservedly." After the war, in a personal letter to a friend, Einstein once again confirmed his admiration: "Only the Catholic Church protested against the Hitlerian onslaught on liberty. Up till then I had not been interested in the Church, but today I feel a great admiration for the Church, which alone has had the courage to struggle for spiritual truth and moral liberty. (*The Catholic World Report*, Band 8, Ignatius Press, 1998, p. 62)."

[ii] When assessing the life style of contemporary Viennese middle class young women, Peter Gay refers to Stefan Zweig's autobiography, where the Austrian writer relates how the young women were assiduously protected by the "polite society" from all "contaminants", and kept "in a completely sterilised atmosphere" by way of censoring their reading, supervising their outings, and diverting them from erotic thoughts with lessons in piano, drawing, and foreign languages. These young women were carefully and groomed to become "foolish and untaught, well-bred and unsuspecting, inquisitive and shy, uncertain and impractical"; they were "predetermined by this unworldly education to be shaped and led in marriage by their husbands without a will of their own". Furthermore, in reference to a claim made by the famous neurologist and psychiatrist Paul Julius Möbius that women in general exhibit psychological feeble mindedness, Freud, too, conceded that indeed such "intellectual atrophy" might be evident among women, for they were "prevented from occupying their minds with what interested them most, which is, sexuality". (Gay, pp. 511-512).

Biographical Reference

JF	Frank, J., 2009. *Dostoevsky: A writer in his time*. Princeton University Press.
AM	Maude, A., 2008. *The Life of Tolstoy*. Wordsworth Literary Lives.
PG	Gay, P., 1998. *Freud: A life for our time*. WW Norton & Company.
WI	Isaacson, W., 2008. *Einstein: His life and universe*. Simon & Schuster.

Content Reference

Dostoevsky

FDIDI	Dostoyevsky, F. 2003. *The idiot*. Courier Corporation.
FDNOT	Dostoevsky, F. 2014. *Notes from the Underground*. Broadview Press.
FDCRI	Dostoyevsky, F. 2014. *Crime and punishment*. Penguin UK.
FDBRO	Dostoyevsky, F. 2005. *The Brothers Karamazov*. Courier Corporation.
FDDEV	Dostoyevsky, F., 1971. *The Devils*. Penguin.
SFDOS	Freud, S (Strachey, J.E.). 1964. The standard edition of the complete psychological works of Sigmund Freud.
Pisma	Dostoevsky, F. *Pisma*, (edited and annotated by A.S. Dolinin), 4 vols. (Moscow, 1928-1959)

Tolstoy

LTCOS	Tolstoy, L., 2009. *The Kreutzer Sonata and Other Stories*. Oxford World's Classics.
LTWAR	Tolstoy, L., 1993. *War and peace*. Wordsworth Classics.
LTANN	Tolstoy, L., 2003. *Anna Karenina*. Penguin Classics.
LTDEA	Tolstoy, L., 2010. *The death of Ivan Ilyich and other stories*. Random House.
LTMAS	Tolstoy, L. 2005. *Master and Man and other stories*. Penguin UK, 2005.
LTKIN	Tolstoy, L. 2007. *The Kingdom of God is Within You*. Cosimo Classics.
LTKIN2	Tolstoy, L. 2005. *The kingdom of God is within you*. Barnes & Noble Books.
LTCON	Tolstoy, L., 1983. Confession. W. W Norton & Company.
LTGOS	Tolstoy, L., 2012. *The Gospel in brief*. Andrews UK Limited.
SMLAN	Massie, S., 1983. *Land of the Firebird: The beauty of Old Russia*, Simon & Schuster.
LTRAI	Tolstoy, L. 1982. The Raid and Other Stories. Oxford World's Classics.

Freud

SFDOS	Freud, S., 1928. Dostoevsky and parricide. *The Brothers Karamazov and the Critics*, pp.41-55.
SFCIV	Freud, S., 2002. *Civilization and its discontents*. Penguin Books.
SFESS	Freud, S., 1905. Three essays on the theory of sexuality. *Se*, 7, pp.125-243.
SFTOT	Freud, S. 1950. *Totem and taboo: Some points of agreement between the mental lives of savages and neurotics*. WW Norton & Company.
SFFEM	Freud, S., 1932. Female sexuality. *The International Journal of Psycho-Analysis*, *13*, p.281.
SFFUT	Freud, S., 1928. The Future of an Illusion, trans. J. Strachey (1927).
SFMOS	Freud, S. 2001. *Moses and Monotheism: An Outline of Psycho-analysis; and Other Works: (1937-1939)*. Vintage.
LFESS	Feuerbach, L., 1841. The Essence of Christianity (trans. George Eliot & intro. Karl Barth).
PRPHI	Pojman, L., and Rea, M., 2008. *Philosophy of Religion, An Anthology* (5th ed.). Thomson Learning Inc.

Einstein

ACSTO	Chekhov, A. 2000. *Stories*. Bantam books.
AEREL	Einstein, A., 1948. Religion and Science: Irreconcilable? *The Christian Register*, *127*, p.19.
APSUB	Pais, A., 1982. *Subtle is the Lord: The Science and the Life of Albert Einstein: The Science and the Life of Albert Einstein*. Oxford University Press, USA.
BSCOM	de Spinoza, B. and Shirley, S., 2002. Complete Works. *Mineola: Hackett Publishing Company, Inc.*
AEIDE	Einstein, A., 1954. Ideas and Opinions, translated by Sonja Bargmann. *New York: Crown*.
MJEIN	Jammer, M., 2011. *Einstein and religion: physics and theology*. Princeton University Press.
MPWES	Planck, M., 1944. *Das Wesen der Materie* (The Nature of Matter), speech at Florence. Italy (1944) (from Archiv zur Geschichte der Max-Planck-Gesellschaft, Abt. Va, Rep. 11 Planck, Nr. 1797).
TF	Ferris, T., 1988. *Coming of Age in the Milky Way*, New York, Morrow.
GSV	Viereck, G. S. 1930. *Glimpses of the Great*. Duckworth.
EPR	Einstein, A., Podolsky, B. and Rosen, N. 1935. Can quantum-mechanical description of physical reality be considered complete? *Physical review*, *47*(10), p.777.
AEHUM	Einstein, A., 2013. *Albert Einstein, The Human Side: Glimpses from his archives*. Princeton University Press.
SHTIM	Hawking, S., 2011. *A Brief History of Time*. Bantam Book.
NNEIN	Nathan, O. and Norden, H. (Ed). 1960. *Einstein on Peace*. Schocken Books.

Index

Aeolus 49
Afterlife 24, *41*, 76, 68, 248, 258
Afterlife 248
Aim-inhibited 105
Alexander the Great 196
Amenophis 189, 190
Amunhatep 182
Andrew, Prince 157, 158, 159, 160, 161, 163, 162, 171
Anna Karenina 12, 18, 77, 82, 148, 155, 157, 163, 166, 167, 271
Apocalypse 201
Apostles 224, *231*, 265
aristocracy 16, *84*, 86, 155, 246, 262
Atheism 13
Augustine, St. 143
Baruch de Spinoza 22, 256
Beelzebul 242
Belinsky 261
Benjamin 183
Bezukhov 77, 157
Bible 12, 19, 22, 62, 66, 67, 71, 89, 68, 98, 144, 179, 180, 181, 182, 183, 185, 186, 187, 194, 200, 201, 202, 203, 208, 216, 217, 221, 222, 223, 225, 226, 227, 228, 229, 230, *231*, *232*, 233, 235, 237, 243, 249, 224, 257, 264, 265, 266, 268
Bolkonsky 157
Boson 54, 55, 58
Boson W+ 54, 58
Brekhunov 172
Buddha 84
Canaan 182, 183, 184, 185, 186, 188, 192, 194, 266
Caucasus 15, 78
Chekhov 120
Christ 23, *41*, 61, 62, 64, 66, 69, 70, 72, 76, 78, *87*, *112*, 144, 179, 181, 199, 208, 209, 212, 213, 218, 222, 230, 234, 235, 256, 259
Christian 13, 14, 18, 62, 87, 88, 133, 155, 198, 200, 217, *231*, 246, 273
Church Orthodox 78
Civilisation and Its Discontents 13, 20, 100, 103, 170, 199, 224
Complex 11, 17, *28*, 30, *34*, *37*, 39, *43*, 57, 101, *108*,

273

115, 135, 142, 199, 200, 204, 207, 219
Compulsion 11, *123*, 134, 196
Confession 77, 81, 143, 166, 167, 168, 162, 249, 271
Copernicus 22, 200
Cossacks, The 77, 78
Crime and Punishment 60, 61, 75, 133, 202, 203, 209
Crimea 15
Cupiditas 129
Dark Continent 114
David, King 144, 183, 185, 217
de Broglie, Victor 53
Death of Ivan Ilyich *157*, 171
Death of Ivan Ilyich, The 84, 171
Deity 189
Delusion *21*, 25, 101, *110*, 118, 169
Democritus 22, *44*
Devils, The 60, 61, 72, 75, 134, 203, 209, 270
Dickens 64
Displacement 11, 27, *28*, *29*, 30, 32, 38, 31, *108*, 258
Divine 125
Don Quixote 64
Dostoevsky 3, 11, 12, 13, 14, 18, 19, 20, 21, 22, 23, *38*, 39, 60, 61, 62, 63, 64, *65*, 66, 67, 68, 70, 71, 72, 73,

74, 39, 67, 98, 133, 134, 135, 138, 139, 142, 143, 144, 146, 148, 150, 151, 152, 133, 179, 199, 201, 202, 203, 205, 206, 208, 209, 211, 205, 256, 257, 258, 261, 263, 264, 268, 270, 272
Ego 25, 26, 27, 30, 65, 66, 31, *103*, *105*, *108*, *109*, *110*, *112*, 145, 181, 200
Egypt 13, 180, 182, 184, 185, 186, 187, 188, 189, 190, 191, 192, 193, 197, 224, 225, 226, 235, 195, 265, 266, 268
Einstein 3, 11, 13, 14, 17, 18, 19, 21, 22, *43*, *44*, 45, *47*, *48*, *49*, *50*, *51*, 52, *53*, 56, 58, 59, 55, 83, 98, 117, 119, 120, *121*, *122*, *123*, 131, 124, 181, 216, 217, 218, 229, 230, 256, 257, 260, 263, 264, 268, 263, 270, 273
Epicureanism 85
Epilepsy 39, 67, 39
Equivalence principle 51
Erogenous zones 11
Essence of Christianity 41, 272
Ethics 46, *47*, *50*, *123*, 127, 130, 131
Exodus 180, 185, 186, 187,

192, 193, 194, 195, 197, 200, 225, 226, 266
Extension 46, 47, *124*, 127
Externalisation *21*, 24, 27, 29, 30, 38, 40, *42*, 258, 268
Ezra 186
Female Sexuality *114*
Feuerbach 41, *42*, 272
Fixation 11
Foma Fomich 62
Francis of Assisi 22, *44*
Frank, Joseph 60, 71, 39, 143, 205, 270
Freud 3, 11, 12, 13, 14, 17, 18, 19, 20, 21, 22, 24, *25*, 26, 27, *28*, *29*, 30, 31, 32, 33, *34*, *35*, 36, *37*, 38, 39, 40, *42*, *60*, 74, 31, 39, 97, 100, 101, 102, *103*, *104*, *105*, *106*, *107*, *108*, *110*, *111*, *113*, *114*, *115*, 134, 145, 103, 114, 115, 130, 170, 180, 181, 182, 183, 185, 186, 187, 188, 192, 194, 195, 197, 198, 199, 200, 205, 208, 216, 195, 205, 224, 256, 257, 259, 263, 264, 265, 266, 268, 263, 270, 272
Freud, Sigmund 11
Future of an Illusion 13, 198, 272
Gandhi 264
Gauss 11

Gay, Peter 116, 198, 263, 270
Gerasim 171
Gospel in Brief, The *231*, *232*, 243
Gospel of John *69*, 142, 237, 244, 267
Gospels 12, 180, 201, 214, 230, *231*, 234, 235, 236, 237, 242, 244, 246, 247, 248, 250, 265
Guilt 13, 24, 27, 31, 36, 37, 39, 40, *42*, 102, 103, *109*, 133, 141, 148, 149, 150, 170, 181, 199, 200, 204, 195, 205, 258, 259, 260, 263
Hamlet *38*, 40, 209
Heisenberg 17, 54, 55, 57
Heliopolis 189
Herzen 261
Holbein 69
Homer 196
House of the Dead 18
House with the Mezzanine, The *120*
Hume 45, 124
Hyksos 191
Identification 11, 23, 36, 38, *103*, *108*, 130, 132, 200, 263
Idiot, The *60*, 63, *64*, 69, 70, 72, 133, 143, 201, 203, 204
Ikhnaton 189, 191

Illusion 65, 84, 98, 224, 233, 258
Ilyusha 75, 144
Internalisation 103, *108*, *109*, *115*
Ippolit 69, 72, 73, 203, 204
Jacob 67, 67, 182, 183, 266
Jeremiah 67, 68, 246
Jeroboam 183
Jerusalem 183, 234, 236, 246, 267
Jesus 12, 22, 23, 40, 66, 67, 68, 76, 88, 89, 90, *112*, 132, 143, 155, 179, 181, 199, 200, 216, 218, 222, 224, 226, 230, *231*, *232*, 233, 234, 235, 236, 237, 238, 239, 240, 241, 242, 243, 244, 245, 246, 247, 248, 256, 257, 259, 265, 267
Jew 188, 199, 200
Job 67, 68, 68, 179, 202, 203, 205, 206, 207, 208, 226, 257
Joseph 60, 71, 39, 143, 182, 183, 234, 205
Judah 183, 195
Judaism 12, 13, 40, *42*, 181, 199, 218, 263, 266
Kant 45, 124
Karamazov 11, *38*, *60*, 61, 62, 69, 72, 73, 74, 135, 136, 137, 138, 139, 140, 141, 142, 143, 144, 146, 147, 148, 150, 151, 133, 201, 202, 203, 204, 205, 206, 212, 202, 270, 272
 Dmitri 38, *60*, *77*, 135, 136, 137, 139, 140, 141, 142, 146, 147, 148, 150, 151, 202, 205
 Fyodor Pavlovich 60, 135, 138, 144, 151, 133
 Ivan 38, 62, 72, 73, 74, 135, 136, 137, 139, 141, 142, 146, 147, 150, 151, 171, 201, 202, 203, 204, 207, 212, 214, 271
 The Brothers 38, *60*, 74, 75, 135, 137, 212
Karenin 165, 166
Kazan 15
Kepler 44
Kingdom of God is within You, The 87, 153
Kingdom of Israel 183, 187, 194, 266
Kingdom of Israel, the 183
Kirillov 60, 61, 207
Kitty 163, 164, 166
Kuzma Samsonov 139
Lebedev 201
Lebyadkin, Captain 72
Lebyadkina, Marya Timofeevna 75

Levin 77, 82, 148, 163, 164, 166, 169, 170
Levites 180, 190, 194, 195
Libido 11, 30, 31, *107*
Lord's Prayer, The 232, 234
Ma'at 189
Mach 45
Master and Man 172, 271
Maude, Aylmer 15, 154, 270
Mesopotamia 189
Meyer, Eduard 198
Midianite 184, 187, 192, 193
Modes 46
   finite 46
   infinite 46
Moscow 14, 78, 82, 141, 155, 159, 214, 270
Moses 12, 22, *38*, 89, 132, 180, 182, 183, 184, 185, 186, 187, 188, 190, 191, 192, 193, 194, 195, 197, 198, 199, 200, 216, 224, 225, 226, 227, 239, 241, 195, 256, 265, 266, 272
Moses and Monotheism 12, *38*, 186, 187, 188, 198, 199, 200, 272
Myshkin 60, 70, 73, 133, 134, 143, 133, 203, 205
Napoleon 159, 161, 209
Nastasya Filipovna 133
Nature 46, *50*, 126, 273

Nehemiah 186
Nekrasov 261
Nervous system 17, 204
Neurosis 11
Neurotics 24, 30, *34*, 272
Newton 22, 44, *51*, 56, 57, 243
Newtonian physics 17
Nikita 172, 173, 174, 175
Oblonsky 154
Oedipal 11, 17, *34*, 39, *115*
Oedipal complex 115
Oedipus 37, *38*, 40
Oedipus the King 38
Old Man 145, 146
Olenin 77, 78, 80
Orthodox 13, 16, 71, 77, 93, 143, 201, 241, 242
Ottoman Turks 155
Paranoia 11, 101, *110*
Paranoids 24, *34*
Pathology 26
Pentateuch 180, 186, 187, 198, 265, 266
Petersburg 14, 71, 78, 261
Petersburg, St. 71
Petrashevsky 71
Pharaoh 67, 180, 182, 184, 189, 191, 225, 226, 265
Phobia 11
Pickwick 64
Pierre 77, 78, 80, 81, 157, 158, 159, 162, 163, 159, 162, 171
Pithom 182

Planck 55, 55, 273
Planck, Max 55
Pleasure principle 106
primal father 21, 33, 35,
  36, 40, *42*, *104*, *105*, 144,
  114, 259
projection 11, *21*, 27, *28*,
  31, 32, *33*, 40, 258
Promise Land, the 182,
  185
Pushkin 18, 204
Qadesh-Barnea 265, 266
Quantum physics 13, 45,
  260
Rameses 182
Raskolnikov 60, 61, 73,
  133, 133, 202, 203, 209
Re' 189
Reality principle 106
Red Sea 182, 184, 225
Rehoboam, King 183, 187,
  194
Relativity
  General 11, 22, *50*, *51*,
    260
  Special 59
Religion 12, 13, *21*, 24, *25*,
  27, 30, 31, 33, 36, *37*, 40,
  41, *42*, *43*, 44, 62, *77*, 83,
  87, 90, 91, 92, *110*, 118,
  154, 180, 187, 188, 189,
  190, 191, 192, 193, 195,
  197, 217, 224, 258, 259,
  260, 261, 263, 265, 266,
  268, 273

Repression 11
Rogozhin 133, 134
Savage, Thomas 35
Schopenhauer 45, 84, *123*,
  168, 264
Schreber 31, 31
Schrödinger, Ervin 53, 54
Sellin, Ernst 187, 198, 195
Semyonov Square 71
Sermon on the Mount 12, 23,
  76, 93, 99, 180, 245, 247,
  259, 263, 264
Shakespeare 11, *38*
Sin 24, 40, 66, 68, 87, 133,
  139, 142, 143, 144, 145,
  148, 149, 151, 197, 213,
  234, 235, 240, 258, 259
Sinai 182, 184, 185, 186,
  208, 226, 229
Slavs 155, 156
Smerdyakov 61, 74, 135,
  137, 138, 139, 141, 142,
  144, 146, 147, 151
Socrates 84, 162
Soldner 51
Soldner, Johann Georg von
  51
Solomon 84, 158, 183
Sonia 133, 202
Spacetime 11
Spinoza 22, *44*, 45, 46, *47*,
  48, *49*, *50*, 56, 57, 59,
  123, *125*, 127, 128, 129,
  130, 131, 124, 130, 216,
  217, 218, 219, 220, 221,

222, 223, 224, 225, 226,
227, 228, 229, 257, 260,
263, 265, 273
Stag Street 29
Stavrogin 61, 73, 134, 209,
210, 211, 212, 214
Stinking Lizaveta 138, 144
Substance 24, 27, *46*, 97,
102, 170, 260
Syria 186, 189, 236
Taboos 27, *33*, *34*, 37
Ten Commandments 182,
185, 216, 229, 242
Theological-Political Treatise
49, 218, 221, 222, 223
Thothmes 189
Thought 46, *47*, *124*, *125*,
127
Thutmose 182, 186
Tolstoy 3, 11, 12, 13, 14,
15, 16, 18, 19, 21, 23, 76,
77, 78, 80, 81, 82, 83, 84,
85, 86, 87, 88, 89, 90, 91,
92, 93, 83, 99, 148, 149,
153, 154, 156, 157, 166,
170, 159, 162, 162, 171,
179, 180, 181, 204, 216,
231, *232*, 233, 234, 235,
236, 237, 240, 242, 243,
244, 245, 246, 247, 248,
249, 224, 256, 257, 258,
262, 263, 264, 265, 266,
267, 268, 270, 271
Totem *33*, *34*, 36, *37*
Totem and Taboo 12, 33, *37*,
110, 198, 199
Totemism 37
Transference 11
Trinity 88
Turgenev 204, 261
Ulm 14
Uncertainty principle *54*, 55
Uncertainty Principle 17
Vasili Andreevich 172, 173,
174, 175
Verkhovensky
 Peter 134
 Stepan 134
Vienna *29*, 188
 University of 17
Vronsky, Count 156, 163,
164, 165, 166
War and Peace *77*, 78, 80,
81, 82, 157, 162
Wave equation 53
Württemberg 14
Yasnaya Polyana 14, 82
Zossima, Father 60, 61, 73,
144, 201, 202, 207

Made in the USA
Lexington, KY
21 January 2017